TONY **BLACKBURN**
POPTASTIC

My Life In Radio

TONY **BLACKBURN**
POPTASTIC

My Life In Radio

CASSELL
ILLUSTRATED

To my wonderful family; Debbie, Victoria, Simon
and my sister Jackie and in memory of my loving
parents, Pauline and Kenneth, who I miss very much.

First published in Great Britain in 2007 by Cassell Illustrated,
a division of Octopus Publishing Group Limited,
2–4 Heron Quays, London, E14 4JP
www.octopusbooks.co.uk

Text Copyright Tony Blackburn.

Design and Layout © 2007 Octopus Publishing Group Limited
Octopus Publishing Group is a division of Hatchette Livre (UK)

A CIP catalogue record for this book is available
from the British Library.

ISBN: 978-1-84403-600-4

Publishing Director: Iain MacGregor
Project Editor: Laura Price
Creative Director: Geoff Fennell

Printed in Spain

CONTENTS

NOEL EDMONDS

FOREWORD

Some broadcasters entertain – some inform – very few actually inspire.

The moment I first heard Tony Blackburn on the pirate radio ship Caroline, I knew that my future just had to lie in radio.

In the mid 1960's I was at school at Brentwood in Essex and the arrival of pirate radio made a huge impact upon me. Within weeks I could name every station, every DJ and hum most of the jingles. When Tony moved from Caroline to the slicker, more professional sounding Radio London (Big L) it was very big news in the world of one pirate radio "anorak". Along with the legendary Kenny Everett, Tony introduced me to a unique medium in which the words of one, can impact upon the lives of millions. A truly intoxicating concept for a teenage lad from Essex!

In the year I left school, 1967, Tony launched Radio One. As I listened to his first show for Auntie Beeb, I dreamed of emulating his success, but in reality trudged off to explore life as a trainee Primary School teacher.

In today's multi-channel radio environment, it is difficult to appreciate the enormous impact that Radio One had upon so many young lives. The DJs were real stars and Tony Blackburn was the biggest. Every morning his breakfast show reached out to over fifteen million eager listeners. The show carved the shape of the weekly pop chart and Tony became that most peculiar of media inventions – "a household name". Remember this was broadcasting far removed from today's multiple presenter – "zoo radio". Life on the Radio One Breakfast Show was a solitary, sometimes lonely affair. The workload was punishing and the pressure immense. I know – I've been there!

It speaks volumes for the talent and professionalism of Tony Blackburn that he kept it going for over five years. Believe me he was a bloody tough act to follow.

It's fair to say that Tony wasn't best pleased when I took over "his show" and certainly the warm friendship we both now enjoy wasn't evident back then. He simply didn't realise that I was actually no match for his supreme singing talent, his extraordinary footballing skills and of course his prodigious success rate with the ladies. His appalling jokes have of course become legendary and what can one say about Arnold the Dog? (well, probably not too much bearing in mind I inflicted Mr Blobby on the nation!).

The 1990's saw Tony guesting on Noel's House Party where he exhibited one of the essentials of our business – the ability to laugh at one's self. As Crinkly Bottom's hapless village idiot, he endured, with remarkably good grace, terrible scripts. One sketch had him hospitalised after he apparently misunderstood the directions on his new deodorant – "remove top and push up bottom".

Tony's enthusiasm for his work, and total commitment to his listeners are truly infectious. I have never doubted that he is at his happiest wearing a set of headphones, laughing into the microphone and "spinning the platters that matter". As I know only too well, the broadcasting industry is tough. It is extremely difficult to climb to the top and even harder to stay there. Tony has succeeded for decades where so many fail.

Oh, and there is one other rather charming aspect to the man's character. He honestly doesn't realise how well loved and highly regarded he is throughout the industry. The term "legend" is horribly over worked these days, but in Tony's case it is the only appropriate description. Tony, you are to me and your millions of fans a true broadcasting legend.

PS – You are also a jolly decent bloke!

1

ONEDERFUL!

"Good morning everyone! And welcome to the exciting new sound of Radio One."

The launch of Radio One on Saturday, September 30, 1967 is rightly regarded as a landmark in post-war British popular culture. It didn't do my career any harm either.

Opening up the BBC's new flagship pop station at 7am on that thrilling Summer Of Love Saturday morning seemed like the most natural thing in the world to me. I'd been DJ-ing on the pirate ships for over three years, and knew exactly how to win over an audience and keep it. There was absolutely no fear of failure because, like everything else I've tackled in my life, I approached the task with an entirely positive frame of mind. And I wasn't fazed when newspapers said it was the most important day in the BBC's history since the launch of television in the 1930s. I just couldn't wait for Station Controller Robin Scott to finish his impeccably rehearsed, Cape Canaveral style countdown . . .

"Now with the clock tickling slowly up to 7am, it's going to be time to welcome Radio One's first ever show on 247 meters medium wave . . . Ten seconds to go before Radio One . . . stand by for switching . . . 5, 4, 3, Radio Two, Radio One, Go!"

. . . and hand over to me.

"THE MICROPHONE HAS BEEN MY BIGGEST FRIEND IN THE WORLD"

I first hit the airwaves on a hot afternoon in July 1964 when I made my broadcast debut on Radio Caroline, and I'm still on air more than 40 years later with my Classic Gold breakfast show. Mornings are, as I'll explain later, when I'm at my best. I love getting people up in the morning. It's what gets me out of bed and into the DJ's hot seat on time, whether that's 5.15am as it was back in the days of the Radio One breakfast show or 3.30am as it is now. But I'm not fussy. Whether morning, noon or night, it's the prospect of that waiting microphone that I virtually live for. For me, the disc jockey who loves his job, the microphone has been my biggest friend in the world. It loves what I do, never answers back and is much easier to talk to than a real live human being.

To be brutally honest with you – and that's my intention with this book so please read on – while I was delighted to shoulder the responsibility of opening up the station we ceaselessly plugged as 'Radio Onederful', I was glad when I got those first few words out of the way. And, in the first of many secrets you'll find in these pages, I have to tell you that it had all been rehearsed for a press call the previous morning. Unlike a lot of people in the entertainment industry, I hate performing to a script, but unveiling Radio One was one of the few occasions where I had the words jotted down on a piece of paper and repeated them parrot-fashion. The show was being recorded for posterity and I knew that if I fumbled it, the moment would haunt me for the rest of my life.

Happily, the words came out naturally and smoothly, as did the rest of the 90-minute show. And for the next six years, 7am-8.30am (9am from 1968), Monday to Saturday, I was BBC Radio's golden boy with an audience that regularly nudged the 20 million mark. I loved every minute of it – at least, on air. Away from the microphone, life wasn't always so *'funderful'*. As one of the best-known celebrities in Britain, I was constantly in demand – doing star turns at discotheques, opening supermarkets and judging beauty contests, making my own records and hosting my own television show. And, despite my own dreadful insecurities, I seemed to be a magnet for an extraordinary cross-section of women – from desperate housewives to drop-dead gorgeous Playboy Bunnies. I was earning fabulous money – £500 per week went a long way in the late '60s – and had a succession of glamorous girls on my arm but none of that was able to banish the loneliness I often felt in my private life. It was only when I met my second wife Debbie 17 years ago that I truly began to find genuine happiness.

I don't think I'm alone in my profession in suggesting that there's something rather odd about counting a microphone as one's best friend. In fact, some of the best DJs in the business are those that have been wildly extrovert in front of an audience and yet painfully shy, alienated and alone off-air. Kenny Everett springs immediately to mind. Jimmy Young is an extremely shy man, and I've always felt that Johnny Walker is too. Though it's by no means a scientific judgement, in my estimation those who know loneliness are better equipped to understand the needs of a radio audience and therefore make the best DJs.

As if one major character defect isn't enough, there are always other factors at work that can tear any DJ's nerves to shreds. Does the audience like me? Well, if you're good at your job, then of course they will. But even that can count for nothing should a new Programme Controller come along determined to stamp his authority on a radio station – as I've discovered to my cost on a couple of occasions.

After more than four decades on air, I've experienced both the thrills and the hardships that a life in radio can bring. And though I've certainly had more fun at other times in my career, particularly during my 'sex'n'soul' years at Radio London during the '80s, it's those six years spent at the helm of the breakfast show on Radio One with which I'll always be most associated. Those were terrific times, that's for sure, when pop music and – with half the country listening in – Radio One itself provided the heartbeat of the nation. As one of those 'Onederful' jingles had it, it was an era when "More fun . . . more music" was a way of life and not just an empty catchphrase. And, as I'm forever being reminded, it was a time when an endless stream of bad jokes ruled the airwaves.

I'd already earned my 'King Of Corn' reputation long before Radio One poached me from the pirate ships, so the station knew exactly what it was getting. By the time I joined the BBC, I'd amassed a huge collection of jokes, dutifully scrawled into 26 exercise books. And I wasn't shy in sharing them. On that first late September morning, I was quick off the mark with a string of daft one-liners. "I was talking to a tightrope walker the other day," I said, as I smiled into the microphone. (A key trick that puts an all-important laugh into a DJs voice.) "He was saying his future was in the balance." Of course I knew that the jokes were groan-inducingly awful, but the important thing was that within days, everyone was talking about them. Britain was soon divided into pro- and anti-Blackburn factions. I didn't mind at all. I observed the old adage, that there's no such thing as bad publicity.

I'd be forced to fend that off many years later. For now, in the autumn of 1967 as the summer flowers began to wilt, the launch of

Radio One was just the tonic the country needed. These were heady times with The Beatles releasing their Sgt Pepper LP and the arrival of a strange new hippie cult dressed in beads, bells and kaftans. It wasn't for me. *"Bells? Me? I'll stick to Big Ben,"* I told one newspaper in October 1967, and I meant it. I knew it was a passing fad, that the smiles were phony and the music often an ungodly racket. Yet, sentimentality aside, I'd much rather the world tuned in to positive songs that gently advise, *"Be sure to wear some flowers in your hair"*, than suffer some of the hateful nonsense we hear nowadays.

Although the launch of Radio One is forever associated with Flower Power – after all, the song I chose to open my show was The Move's druggy *Flowers In The Rain* – the reality was more grey and cosy than wild and psychedelic. In fact it's a testament to the power of the BBC publicity machine, as much as to the skill of the DJs and producers, that the station was accepted so quickly. In fact those brave souls who had pioneered pop radio in this country, who had risked their time, money and even gambled with their freedom to make the pirate stations work, were the real heroes. After the Marine Offences Bill took effect at midnight on August 14, 1967 some commentators likened it to "legalised murder". After blasting the pirate ships out of the water, [the BBC] have turned out to be the biggest pirates of them all," complained Screaming Lord Sutch, who owned a pirate station before he went all 'Monster Raving Loony'. "They have copied the best ideas from the illegal stations." I have to admit that he was right – although when the Beeb came sniffing round and offered me a contract, there was no way I was going to turn down the opportunity. I knew our pirating days were numbered, and after three years' 'national service' at sea, I was ready to come ashore, make peace with the establishment, and seize the chance to become the best-known DJ in the country.

* * *

"THIS DEAR OLD WOMAN WAS KNITTING A JUMPER..."

I was first approached by the BBC in 1966, while working on the pirate ship Radio London, or *'Big L'* as we all called it. I was at a reception for Decca Records, where they were promoting some artist or other, and this man appeared from behind a pillar and said, "Hi, I'm Teddy Warrick, I'm a BBC radio producer and I'm not supposed to be talking to you." He told me he'd been listening to my breakfast show, and said that, if I wanted it, there was a job for me on BBC Radio. Of course, I was flattered to be asked but I was having such a ball on *Big L*, and the BBC seemed so stuffy and behind the times that I didn't bother to follow it up. What was the point? The future was in the hands of the pirates, who were broadcasting what teenagers wanted to hear. The BBC seemed to have no idea what it meant to be young and have fun.

Everything changed on July 2, 1966, when Harold Wilson's Labour Government published the bill that, little over a year later, closed the loophole that had made pirate radio broadcasting possible. By Christmas, a White Paper on the future of sound broadcasting had recommended the setting up of a new popular music station on BBC Radio, one that would soon replace the old BBC Light Programme – famous for its homely Two-Way Family Favourites and The Billy Cotton Band Show. [The Home and Third Programmes would also go in what was the first major restructuring of BBC Radio since the end of the war.] I had been extremely happy broadcasting from the choppy North Sea waters three miles off the east coast of Britain near the port of Felixstowe, Suffolk. Now, with one eye trained towards furthering my ambition, I knew this was one boat I could ill afford to miss.

It was agent Harold Davison, one of the most powerful men in the entertainment business at the time and certainly one of the most important figures in my life, who fixed it up for me. I will talk about

Harold in more depth later on but for now, it's important to know just one thing. He invited me to his Regent Street office, in Regent House, a building he shared with that other entertainment industry heavyweight Lew (later Lord) Grade, and said, "Sign with me, Tony, and I'll make you the top disc jockey in the country in six months." He was nearly right – he did it in three. Harold was an amazing man, and the best agent anybody could have had.

My new protector understood the implications of the Marine Offences Act, and knew it was crucial that I jump ship early, before the great scramble ashore that happened in the weeks before the Act became law. Although I was in the dark at that stage, I suspect he already knew the BBC had me in mind for the breakfast show when I walked in to Broadcasting House for my first 45-minute Midday Spin slot one Wednesday early in August 1967.

I had anticipated the Beeb's notoriously grey and labyrinthine corridors and officious, tweed-wearing staff. But I hadn't bargained for tightly scripted shows, finger-wagging producers – or the dear old woman who sat in the corner of the basement studio knitting jumpers. When I was on the pirate ships, I'd always joked that behind every radio presenter at the BBC was an old lady knitting. And here she was. Ostensibly, she was there to open up 'the pots', the microphones in lay language, but as soon as that was done, she'd be back to her needles and wool. I swear she knitted a whole sleeve during that first programme. I even remember the colour – purple! Well, it was the summer of psychedelia.

From a professional point of view, I was more perturbed by the presence of a producer in the studio. His name was Peter Jones, a lovely guy, very BBC and with an obsessive interest in tennis. I could cope with that. It was him asking for a script before the programme that really threw me. I'd spent the past three years on air ad-libbing, and here I was being asked to itemize every 'if', 'but' and 'so' before each show. I had absolutely no idea what to write down; that just wasn't how I worked. Peter dug out a script for Alan Freeman's *Pick Of The Pops* chart rundown show, which disappointed me because every "Not 'arf!" and "Greetings, pop-pickers!" was there in double-spaced black-and-white. I adored 'Fluff' as a DJ but this revelation did take away some of the mystique for me. Despite Peter's insistence that we do 'tops and tails', the links between each record, I convinced him to let me do it my way. To please his bosses, we still had to meet an hour before each programme, so he suggested that we sat down for tea and doughnuts instead. Tea, doughnuts and knitting – my unofficial BBC Radio welcome.

That and a man called Mark White. He was one of the executives involved in the transition from the Light Programme to Radio One and the person responsible for giving me the chance to be heard on Midday Spin. One of the first things he asked me was, "Which school did you go to?" "Millfield," I replied, silently thanking my father whose wish it was that I attended one of the top fee-paying schools in the country. A public school background counted for a lot at the BBC back then. I clearly remember wearing a suit for the interview, and referring to Mark as "Sir", both of which would have earned me a ribbing on the pirate ships. Despite the strong whiff of old school tie snobbery, I quickly took to life at Broadcasting House, and the strange array of people who lurked within its famous walls. The BBC was, I soon discovered, a haven for old-fashioned British eccentricity. One of my earliest memories of the place was watching this Radio 4 producer talk to things. I'd be waiting for a lift, and he'd be standing there saying, "Hello, I'm looking forward to you arriving," as he pressed the button. When the lift turned up, he'd continue, "Hello, Mr Lift, are you going to take me to the sixth floor?" When he got to the sixth floor, he'd walk into the restaurant, and start up again. "Ah, where's Mr Tray? Oooh, Weetabix! I love you, don't I. Can I have you this morning? Where's Milk? Hello, how are you?" And he'd go on like this. I also noticed that he'd tend to eat his breakfast as he queued for the till, proof again that a little eccentricity goes a long way at the BBC.

It was as if all the barmiest characters in the Civil Service had been shunted off into this strange, rounded edifice called Broadcasting House – driven more mad still by its eight floors and 800 doors, its warren of studios and mile of corridors. But there was nothing barmy about the latest project to emanate from within its impossibly thick walls. For several years, the pirate stations had been having it all their own way. Stations such as Caroline and London, with their younger, hipper DJs and incredibly exciting radio jingles caught the era's swinging mood, whereas Billy Cotton and Sam Costa over at the Beeb meant nothing to Carnaby Street kids. Now, having launched BBC-2 and colour television broadcasting earlier that summer, Radio One was the Corporation's attempt to spruce up the radio airwaves.

Radio One had been a long time coming. Although the authorities hotly disputed claims that the pirates were regularly reaching 10 million or more listeners, it was clear to everyone concerned that the Beatles-inspired pop music explosion of 1963 and 1964 had caught the Light Programme on the hop. When the pipe-smoking Harold Wilson became Prime Minister in 1964, he'd made a point of actively courting The Beatles in a fairly shameless attempt to portray Labour as the modernising political party after 13 years of Conservative rule. But the white heat of the technological revolution certainly didn't warm to the pirates, whom Labour actively pursued for three years before pulling the plug and sinking the lot of them. Years later, I met Tony Benn who was Postmaster-General at the time and the man charged with pursuing the pirates. Like me, he loves his gadgets and I warmed to him. But when I put it to him that the pirates were nowhere near as lawless or threatening as his party had led the public to believe, I swear I saw a little twinkle in his eye. I think he secretly admired our attempt to push the boat out a bit, so to speak. Several months before the anti-pirate legislation was pushed through Parliament, Wilson shunted him to a different cabinet post. Perhaps that twinkle helps explain why.

In fact, the whole point of the pirate ships wasn't to bring about Radio One or change within the BBC at all. It was an attempt to bring the exciting sound of commercial radio, a given in America, to Britain. And that didn't happen – at least, not until October 1973, when the BBC's 50-year monopoly came to an end with the launch of two independent stations, LBC and Capital. Radio One was the antithesis of commercial radio. It was a monopoly, just as the old Light Programme had been, except that now it began to look, sound and sometimes even behave like a pirate radio station. At least, if you didn't listen too closely.

I was sad to leave behind all those pioneers who had changed the face of British radio during the mid-'60s – Allan Crawford and Ronan O'Rahilly at Radio Caroline and Philip Birch at Radio London spring to mind. But passing my audition at Midday Spin and being handed First Prize – the Breakfast Show – meant I didn't cry too many tears. From the moment I heard the news, my entire life began to revolve around Radio One, and I loved every fabulous minute of it.

"BREAKFAST SHOWS ARE A BIT SPECIAL ..."

I knew the Breakfast Show was the cream of the crop for any radio station. Forty years later, it's still the big one and I'm still doing it – albeit no longer on Radio One. In theory, it's by far the most stressful show, too, because it's the one upon which radio stations build their schedules and stake their reputations. If the Breakfast Show fails then it's likely that the rest of the station will suffer. But any failing broadcasters will have been fired long before that happens – as Radio One's Mark & Lard, who lasted for just eight months in 1997, will remember only too painfully.

All the big boys have done time in the Breakfast slot – Wogan, DLT, Edmonds, Evans. I'd put Radio One's current wake-up boy Chris Moyles right up alongside them. I know some people find him rude and abrasive but I think he's done a marvelous job in the face of so much competition. I had the privilege of seeing him in action after he invited me on his show when I came out of the Jungle late in 2002. Back in autumn 1967, when I started broadcasting for Radio One, my main competitor – besides the *Today* programme on Radio 4 aimed squarely then and now at the chattering classes – was Paul Hollingdale over on Radio 2. What do you mean you've never heard of him...?

I've been doing breakfast shows for most of my years as a broadcaster and I've always found it a bit special. Not everyone likes doing them but for me, there's just something about getting people up in the mornings. I always visualise the same scenario. The alarm rings, mum and dad rouse themselves, and they're making breakfast with you. The children get out of bed and gather round the breakfast table. Then they're on the school run. I love the idea of getting everyone safely to work. And then it's, "Goodbye, and I'll see you again tomorrow morning!"

The breakfast show has all the right ingredients. I get a particular kick out of all the time checks and travel news. I know it might sound ridiculous but I'm actually very proud of inventing the persistent time check. Don't laugh. I was the first person in this country to give out time checks after every record, and it's something I still enjoy doing. The BBC only used to give one out every 10 minutes or so and I just didn't think that was good enough. When I was doing breakfasts at Caroline, I thought, "People are getting out of bed and rushing around. They need to know exactly what the time is." One day, the Programme Controller at Caroline took me aside. "Do you know you're giving out time checks the whole time?" "Yes, of course," I replied. "On a breakfast show, it's exactly what people need."

When the time comes, and I'm not expecting it just yet, all I want engraved on my tombstone are just five words:

I GAVE YOU TIME CHECKS

You think I'm joking, don't you...

I was well aware that, as host of the new Radio One breakfast show, I was key to the success or failure of the new station. It didn't bother me in the slightest. I knew that I was more than capable of hosting a show that could create headlines and that – unlike many people in my profession – I was able to get up in the mornings and make the arrival of a new day sound like a party. Celebrity shindigs and schmoozing didn't interest me. I was in the business because I loved radio and I wanted to entertain as large a slice of the British public as possible. I had no interest in being part of some pampered super-elite, most of whom have no idea what the public want because they're too busy congratulating each other over complimentary cocaine, champagne and canapés.

Time checks weren't the only thing that the BBC inherited from the pirates. There's a famous photograph of the first intake of Radio One DJs, taken on the steps of All Souls Church next to Broadcasting House, and almost half of us learned our trade on pirate radio. The stuffy bods in management at BBC Radio knew pirate radio DJs had stolen a march on them and I admired their decision to swallow their collective pride and take a lesson or two from those who knew best. They took the biggest names, the fabulous jingles – and those all-important time checks. I'd say that a lot of that was down to Johnny Beerling, the man who had the unenviable task of producing my breakfast show. I say unenviable only because I regard producers as irrelevant at best and, more often than not, a downright nuisance.

But I discovered that they do make incredibly good tea-boys and it wasn't too long before I had Johnny making me my morning cuppa.

Instead of resting on his laurels and saying, "Oh, the BBC do it much better," Beerling knew damn well where the flair originated and decided to simply copy the format. That really was the secret to Radio One's early success. I'd also credit Robin Scott, who was Controller of both Radios One and Two, and Senior Producer Derek Chinnery. They knew that the Light Programme's attempts at pop broadcasting had been stodgy and half-hearted, and they were big enough to tell us, "You teach us how to do it because you're better at doing pop radio."

"JIMMY YOUNG WAS FORCED TO SING HIS OLD HITS TO PLEASE THE NEEDLE TIME NAZIS."

Unfortunately, unlike the pirates, the BBC DJs had to work around an antiquated practice known in the industry as Needle Time. In essence, Needle Time restricted the number of hours that BBC Radio could transmit recorded music, that is, music on discs. In 1967, this was something like 50 hours per week, and the practice severely hampered the efforts of those forward-thinking souls within the corporation who believed in the idea of a continuous pop music station.

Needle Time was there to protect the working musician. In practice, though, it was a total nightmare and threatened to keep British radio in the Dark Ages. At the pirate stations we'd spin pop records from something like six in the morning to eight o'clock at night. But in the early days of Radio One, Needle Time severely cramped our style. Giving up an inordinate amount of precious air-time to the handful of live musicians who benefited from the arrangement did give rise to some frankly bizarre musical soundclashes. You might get The Northern Dance Orchestra playing live versions of The Rolling Stones' *Jumpin' Jack Flash*, or The Jimi Hendrix Experience's *Purple Haze*. Ridiculous, though I'm sure a lot of people would pay good money to hear those nutty tapes now.

Luckily, because the breakfast show was a priority, the powers that be declared that I needn't be restrained by such an archaic practice. Others weren't so fortunate – although I don't think Jimmy Young minded interrupting his mid-morning show by bursting into a few live songs of his own in order to please the Needle Time Nazis! And, yes, in case any of you need reminding, Jimmy Young – and his famous recipes – was part of Radio One's initial set-up. His was one of several shows that were shared by Radios One and Two, again as a way of conserving that precious Needle Time. Actually, Jimmy was a lovely man, tremendously shy, but I'm sure he, like many listeners, wondered just why he was crooning his old '50s hits on what was meant to be the nation's newest, coolest station.

That honour, in my book, will always go to Radio London. *Big L*, as everyone called it, was the prototype on which Radio One was based. But because it operated on what I like to call piratical lines, it didn't suffer from the same restrictive practices which threatened to strangle the Beeb's initiative. I blame the Musicians' Union for holding radio back in this country. Its rulebook-waving tendency was incredibly short sighted. There's no doubt that *Big L* was the best radio station this country's ever had – and I'll explain why later on.

The MU weren't the only culprits. I still find it slightly annoying that the Performing Rights Society collects money on behalf of musicians whenever their record is played. That's like Woolworth's paying for the privilege of putting a company's product in their shop window. It doesn't make any sense to me at all. And the royalty bill for an organisation as large at the BBC is absolutely astronomical. If it hadn't been illegal to do so, I would have happily paid someone to play my records on air!

Money certainly wouldn't have been any object. During my final days on the pirates, I was making around £50 per week. Now, in autumn 1967, I was making nearly ten times that amount. I had a fashionable bachelor-pad flat at 5 Ovington Square, Knightsbridge. Each morning, I'd get into my little red MGB sports car and make the eight-minute drive to Broadcasting House in Portland Place, just off Oxford Circus. It was glamorous – but hard work. I'd arrive at 6am, where I'd be met by producer Johnny Beerling. Over tea and biscuits, we'd discuss the contents of the show and, shortly before 7am, I'd lower myself into the Continuity Studio One swivel chair, check the sound balance with the engineer and for the next 90 minutes I'd have the time of my life.

I often tell people that I've made a career out of talking nonsense to a microphone for a few hours every morning. They always laugh, but I'm serious. I love entertaining and cheering people up. I've never been one of those DJs who bores listeners with details about who plays what on each record. Most people aren't interested in whether Fred Bloggs is on drums and Fred Flintstone plays bass and neither am I. Now that doesn't mean I don't like music, as some critics have tried to claim over the years. I've always been a massive soul music enthusiast, for example, but I don't go on about it. I simply enjoy creating an entertaining radio show, full of fun, jingles, useful morning information like those regular time checks – and, of course, a couple of dozen wonderful records. That's the format I developed on pirate radio, perfected at Radio One, and still use today.

It was a formula that seemed to hit the jackpot in autumn 1967 when the first reviews of the Beeb's new radio station hit the news-stands. "Blackburn is the sort of classless, snappy-thinking hipster who may zip our pop radio up to American and European standards," wrote James Pettigrew in the *Sunday Mirror*. Outside Broadcasting House, a fan known only as Sally cooed: "That man Tony . . . that voice. It's a real knockout." I don't think she was a BBC plant! Even the sniffier broadsheet critics, such as Hunter Davies at *The Sunday Times*, were moved to give a guarded thumbs-up on the basis that me and my new colleagues had succeeded in blending "hysteria with mateyness".

During those earliest weeks at Radio One, only Emperor Rosko, the hip-talking son of Hollywood producer Joe Pasternak, came anywhere near me in terms of press coverage. But while I went straight for mainstream appeal, he preferred to baffle listeners with a string of barely comprehensible sentences, most of which included the words *"Mummios"* and *"Daddios"*. After he signed off from his first show at 12.30pm on that first *'Onederful'* Saturday, the newsreader that followed him couldn't resist an amusing, "And now the news – in English". Well, that was the story that circulated at the time.

My style was upbeat and positive, too, but I never wanted to baffle my audience. In fact, I wanted them to hear every last syllable of nonsense that spilled from my lips! Another critic who was, like so many, wary of the increasing Americanisation of the airwaves wrote approvingly of my delivery: "His accent is uncompromisingly English," he conceded with barely concealed hint surprise. I didn't mind that at all. I had no desire to shock or upset or alienate people. I was happy to please Middle England – and the Upper and Lower strata too. While some of my colleagues would arrive at the studio dressed in multicoloured trousers and bearskin coats, often sporting some strangely sculpted facial hair, I was happy to turn up to work in a suit and tie. That's probably why I usually found myself on the top table when it came to swanky BBC meetings and parties. At 24, I was the youngest DJ at the station, and its cheery pin-up boy. I had, quipped my old Radio London colleague Kenny Everett, *"The most photographed smile in the business."* I was the DJ who the Corporation could trust – for the moment, at least.

Despite my clean-cut image and determination to please, there were always some listeners who managed to find something to complain about. Fifteen minutes into my first Radio One breakfast show, I threw in a bit of my characteristic *'Funderful!'* banter, by suggesting that my new nationwide audience partake in what I described as a "bedroom twisting session". It was my way of injecting a bit of fun into the early morning. "Come on, up you get! Even you, granny!" I pleaded. "Now take a nice big breath, open the window and tell everybody that 'Radio One is wonderful!'" Then it was straight into Diana Ross & The Supremes' latest hit, "a fabulous number called Reflections", after which I probably told one of my daft one-liners – "A hole has appeared in the road at Piccadilly. The police are looking into it . . ." and then had my sound effects dog Arnold give one of his customary barks. After all that excitement, a message came through to the studio. There's been a complaint. Someone's called to say that it's not right for a DJ to encourage children to shout out of open windows! All in a day's work . . .

My riposte to anyone who doesn't like my programme has always been the same: turn it off. On that particular morning, I made light of the trickle of calls that came in from disgruntled Light Programme listeners who complained that they didn't like "that kind of music". "If you can't stand my voice, Breakfast Special is on 1500 metres," I joked on air. "Why not switch over? Try it – and I'll smash your transistors in!"

Very few turned off. As the *Sunday Mirror* boldly proclaimed the following morning, **"ONEDERFUL? IT WAS JUST FANTASTIC."** There were technical gremlins, with some areas, including the Hampshire/Dorset border where my parents lived, picking up more *"mush"* than music. But within two weeks of the station's launch, the BBC had put on an extra two million listeners, and my *'rise and shine'* voice was already well on the way to being the most recognised in the country.

2

CHILDHOOD

When I joined the BBC in summer 1967, one of the first DJs I met was Pete Murray. A veteran both of Radio Luxembourg and the Light Programme, and probably the earliest professional influence on my career, Pete was a lovely man and I admired him very much. He was one of the best broadcasters of his generation, with a witty presentation style that always found room for a dreadful gag or two. He kindly showed me round Broadcasting House and told me the dos and don'ts of working for the Beeb. I should have listened to him more carefully because one of the big no-no's was politics, which was something I found myself unable to keep silent upon when the country began to fall to pieces in the 1970s. Pete, too, failed to heed his own advice. He was a Conservative, and when his political affiliations began to reach the ear of the public, the BBC decided it was time for him to go. Several years after his departure, I once again fell out of favour with the BBC hierarchy and suffered a similar fate. Nowadays, of course, they wouldn't turn a hair. Speaking out about politics, religion, or – most sacred of all – the

Royal Family might even earn you a promotion. Getting nabbed taking cocaine almost certainly will. The old adage *'bringing the network into disrepute'* now roughly translates as bringing the network some gratefully received publicity. But it's not the BBC's fault. It's the way of the modern media.

Radio, and the wider world it serves, was a far less cynical place when I first tuned in to Pete Murray as a teenage schoolboy at Millfield. He presented *Housewives' Choice* for the Light Programme, but it was his regular shows for Radio Luxembourg that really captivated me. Unlike the Light Programme, where millions tuned in to *Workers' Playtime* and countless comedy series, Luxembourg was the hip alternative that dared to play contemporary popular music. That was where I first developed my love of American black music, where songs such as The Drifters' *Here Comes My Baby* and Jackie Wilson's *Reet Petite* would sweeten up the airwaves.

In more recent years, I associated Pete Murray with a perma-tan, tennis at Wimbledon and always forgetting the punchlines to his insufferably long jokes (sorry, Pete!). However, in the late '50s, when I used to smuggle my radio into the dorm at school and listen to him under the bedcovers, he was the epitome of everything I aspired to be. Suave, smart and amusing, he was the top jock – but he did sometimes get me into trouble. On more than one occasion, I was caught listening to his show during class and had my radio confiscated.

As with many children born during, or just after the Second World War, radio had been my first introduction to the world of entertainment. Because my father had a passion for new technology – which is something I've inherited – our family was the first in our road to have a television. I clearly remember all the neighbours coming round our house to watch the coronation of Queen Elizabeth II on June 2, 1953. But for me, its flickering, black and white images were nowhere near as powerful as tuning in to fantastic weekly sci-fi series such as *Journey Into Space* on the Light Programme (with its wonderful sound effects), or *Dan Dare – Pilot Of The Future* on Luxembourg. The flickering light that mattered most to me was that emanating from those carrot-coloured valves inside the big Roberts radio that I kept in my room at home.

Home was a large bungalow in Lilliput, a gloriously unspoilt part of Poole on the south coast of England. If there's something a little make-believe about its name, then that's entirely appropriate, for Lilliput, now rated as the fourth most expensive place in the world for property, is at least as charming and idyllic as its name suggests. At least it was back in the immediate post-war years when I was growing up there. Today, it's become a haven for footballers and yacht-owning executives, which probably explains why I've noticed more than a few rather ugly properties going up in the area in recent years. But the natural beauty of the place has barely changed. I've been going back there, pretty much on a weekly basis, ever since I left home in 1964. And to this day, I quite often park the car up on Evening Hill and look across the magnificent harbour view towards Brownsea Island, or else zip down to Sandbanks and sit and watch the passenger ferry take the naughty naturists across to the nudist beach at Studland. Once in a while, the beach hits the local headlines but I've never once seen anyone naked over there – and God knows I've searched! For me, Lilliput and the surrounding area just oozes happy, uncomplicated childhood memories.

"HIS FAMILY ALWAYS SEEMED SO DEADLY SERIOUS AND DEPRESSING."

My father Kenneth was lovely man, a GP who would be up at all hours of the night to supervise his bed-ridden patients. He worked enormously hard; there was no such thing as 'off-duty' in his book.

Even today, sixty years after he first opened his practice, people still speak fondly of the man they called Dr Blackburn.

My father's family came from Halifax, where they owned a wool mill, but mum and I were never particularly close to them. His mother was always known as Mutti, despite the fact that she didn't have a German bone in her body!

Unfortunately, that was probably the only genuinely amusing thing I remember about that side of the family. They always seemed so deadly serious and depressing. One of my father's sisters, miserable Auntie Joan, lived nearby in a flat that looked right across the harbour. But she was forever complaining about the terrible view and telling us that she was about to commit suicide. As it happened, she lived to a ripe old age, but I could never relax in her company because she was an absolute nervous wreck. She got married once and it lasted all of three weeks. My father's side of the family was a bit barmy.

I was much closer to my mother Pauline's relatives, who were more easy going. Her father, Howard Stone, was the Managing Director of Twinlock, a Beckenham-based firm that manufactured loose-leaf binders. Quite why I always called him Bogar has never been satisfactorily explained to me. I'm pretty sure it had nothing to do with Humphrey over in Hollywood.

By the time I was about eight years old, Bogar and his wife Queenie were living in a house in Croydon, where we'd often go and stay. That's where I first heard my voice played back to me on a tape recorder. I fell in love right away! The machine belonged to Uncle Nick, my mother's youngest brother, whom I adored. He was responsible for arousing my interest in recorded sound, though his recommendations fell of deaf ears when it came to his beloved classical music. I think he pushed it too much because, to this day, I still can't stand orchestras. I'm a popular music man, through and through, and I'm proud of it.

Years later, when I was at Radio One, I used to visit Uncle Nick in his Knightsbridge flat. We used to go out to lunch regularly, always to Italian restaurants, a habit I still keep to this day. He was a bit of a ladies' man, and I think I picked up a few old tricks there, too. I remember him having two girlfriends on the go at the same time, one theatrical and the other matronly, an arrangement that both knew about but neither seemed to mind. I don't know whether it had anything to do with his complicated love life but Uncle Nick always seemed to suffer from poor eyesight and constant neck problems. Eventually, on a flight to New England, he collapsed and died while drinking a glass of wine. I like to think that he simply exhausted himself by enjoying life too much.

My father was the consummate family man who cared for little else except his work, his home life and his hobbies. He wasn't particularly social. In fact, I can hardly remember any visitors to the house let alone something as rowdy as a dinner party and, in that respect, I'm not unlike him. But, strange as it may seem, I think I inherited my showbiz side from him. That's because, in their own way, doctors are performers. I mean, surgeons and doctors are obliged to develop a dark humour because they're confronted with the awful side of life on a daily basis. All that blood and death. They'd go round the twist without it.

As my father worked long hours and my mother had given up her nursing job shortly before I was born, I saw much more of mum in my youth. She was a young mother, just 19 when she had me, which meant that by the time I hit my teens we were good friends as much as anything else. That's why I was a problem teenager – I had nothing to rebel against! I often wonder whether that had an adverse effect on me later on in life. I'm glad, though, because I always had a trouble-free relationship with my mother. Even after I left home I'd call her each day without fail, often three or four times. Sometimes I'd even ring her up during my programme and ask,

"Is the show sounding all right?" I can't recall her ever saying that it was anything less than wonderful!

We were tremendously close so the loss was all the more devastating when she died, in October 2006, after a two-year battle with cancer. That was brought home to me yet again the other day while I was looking through the pile of scrapbooks she'd kept detailing my public life. Every newspaper and magazine cutting had been neatly taped to the page, and dutifully dated, but what broke me up was the handwritten inscription on the first page: "My darling Tony". Losing my mother has made me more aware of my own mortality and it makes me sad to think that, already at 64, I'm certainly not going to be around to see my 10-year-old daughter Victoria celebrate her 64th birthday.

"LILLIPUT WAS AN AFFLUENT AND FAMOUSLY PINE-SCENTED PART OF THE COUNTRY."

My parents first met while they both worked at Croydon Hospital in 1940. It was wartime, they were both tending to victims of the Blitz, but in spite of all that my father still managed to woo Nurse Pauline with promises of coffee at Wilson's Café and afternoon teas in the country at Godstone, a bus ride out of Croydon. They married in 1942, then moved to Guildford just long enough for me to pop along in the early hours of January 29, 1943. I gave my first broadcast at around two in the morning at the Mount Alvernia Nursing Home.

I remember very little of my life before the family settled in Poole. But my mother and I apparently spent a fair bit of time at her parents' holiday home in the beautiful village of Ferring, near Worthing, on the Sussex coast while my father was away in the Merchant Navy doing duty as a ship's surgeon. It was a lovely house, with the garden backing on to the seafront, and we spent many delightful holidays there over the years. The one moment I clearly remember was seeing my baby sister Jackie for the first time, laid out on the dining-room table like some prize exhibit!

That was 1946 when I was three years old. Soon afterwards, we moved further west along the coast. My father, who loved cars and driving, had stumbled upon the Bournemouth and Poole area on an excursion. And that's where he wanted his new family to grow up. I'm very glad that he did.

Bringing up their young children in this affluent and famously pine-scented part of the country obviously helped make things easier for our parents. But the Blackburn household had its own particular difficulties to face because Jackie was born unable to walk. It took me some time to accept this when I was young. I'd come up with all these fanciful ideas about teaching her to walk with sticks but, of course, it was to no avail. Jackie has no muscle in her legs and she's a bit smaller than the average sized person too. My parents did their utmost to make sure she was able to enjoy an active a life as possible.

Of course, that presented us with some practical difficulties but my father rose to the challenge in his own wonderfully obsessive way. He bought a plot of land in Lilliput, recruited a small team of architects and builders and together they designed and built a bungalow with ramps throughout so that Jackie could utilise the facilities like the rest of us. It was an extraordinary achievement and way ahead of its time, I'm sure. Sixty years on, Jackie's still there, enjoying the benefits of our father's vision.

I know that life has often been a terrific struggle for her, but I've not once heard Jackie complain. She's still making the most of her life. In fact, she's far more active than I am. Whenever I call her, she's always on her way to see friends or off to a show or a restaurant. But I must say that watching her go through life without physical abilities the rest of us take for granted has made me a little less patient with people. Celebrities who complain about life in the limelight, for example. I mean, if you don't like it, find another job! If only these people would stop and think how lucky they are.

My father always did his best to make sure that Jackie had as normal an upbringing as possible, though I'm sure he felt frustrated that, as a doctor, there was nothing he could do to get her up and walking. Perhaps it all had something to do with his thirst for perfection. If there was one thing my father was more obsessed about than driving his car, it was making sure that nothing at all rattled when he was at the wheel. If he detected the merest hint of a click or squeak, he'd take it out round the wide, tree-lined roads of Lilliput for hours until he cured the problem. His patients were often similar. One was so obsessed with the idea of getting a crackle-free sound from his gramophone that he'd set up this special fan that blew the dust off the records while the turntable span round. It didn't do him much good. Eventually, he drove himself round the twist.

If my father felt any frustration during our childhood years, he didn't show it. We had a wonderfully happy home, with a wood at the end of the garden and the sea just a short walk away. There was tea on the table when we returned home from school and always enough money for an annual holiday. Having mum at home was the norm in the immediate post-war era, and I still believe it's the best way to bring up children. I know it's not always practical these days, but I'm certainly grateful that our mother was always there for us.

Despite all that, I was more than happy with my own company as a youngster. I'm sure my mother was concerned that I didn't have many close friends but I just didn't need them. To be honest, I found most of my classmates at school rather irritating! So, too, was school itself. I wasn't unhappy at my junior school, Castle Court on Constitution Hill in nearby Parkstone, where I was a day pupil. I simply found it all so dull and uninteresting, so I didn't work very hard. Discipline was strict. Whenever a master or mistress would pass, we had to raise our caps immediately. If you spoke out of turn, the teacher would throw chalk at you or slap you round the head. I got slippered a couple of times, too.

As much as I dislike violence, I don't think being slippered or caned during my schooldays did me much harm. I mean, I didn't have to have psychiatric treatment or go into rehab afterwards! Often I deserved a punishment. It made me think about whether I was doing right or wrong and that's an important lesson in life. My father once rapped me round the ankles for misbehaviour and it left a big impression on me because he'd never done that before. I can't help but think that some children would benefit from a bit more discipline today. That said, I've never smacked either of my own children, Simon or Victoria. I don't think I could. The other day, I gave Victoria a verbal telling off and I felt so guilty afterwards that I ended up apologising to her.

I'm not sure what the answer is. What I do know is that a sense of discipline is important if you want to get on in life. In showbusiness, time is money, and if you turn up late you don't get booked again. I always make sure I'm on time for appointments and do everything as professionally as I can, probably thanks to the few good ground rules I had when I was young.

The best thing about school was playing sport, especially cricket, football and boxing. It got you out of the classroom and I liked the sense of competition too. I didn't do too badly, either, and the family trophy cupboard soon bulged with cups, both for boxing and captaining the cricket team. But none of that persuaded me that school was anything better than something you were forced to do by the government. I learned how to read and write but I don't think I picked up much else of any significance there.

Cubs or Scouts didn't interest me either, though as I prepared for senior school, I did find myself camping on the Isle Of Wight with a Christian organisation called The Crusaders. It was my first time away from home and I absolutely hated it. The only reason I joined was because I'd taken a liking to the badge – a shield bearing a St George's Cross style insignia – and wanted one. I'm not sure it was worth it, though on that trip I learned something that has remained with me ever since.

One evening, I got into a discussion with the camp leader, a vicar if I remember rightly. He told me that he could never marry because he was already betrothed to God. I thought that was preposterous and although I was young it was obvious to me he didn't know what he was talking about. That conversation completely turned me away from religion and nothing has altered my opinion since. If people want to believe this stuff, then good luck to them, but please don't get fanatical about it.

I swore I'd never go camping again. And then, half a century later, the phone rang and it was the people from *I'm A Celebrity, Get Me Out Of Here!* And off to the Australian jungle I went . . .

"EVEN AT FIVE YEARS OF AGE, I FOUND THE IDEA OF KILLING ANIMALS REVOLTING."

Another holiday, this time with my family on a farm in Devon, inspired a second epiphany that inspired another dramatic shift in the Blackburn world view. I was innocently watching this chicken being chased around the farmyard when, in front of my eyes, someone bundled up and took it away. That evening, as dinner was being served, the thought suddenly occurred to me: is this the same chicken I saw running around a few hours ago? "Yes, of course," I was told. I felt sick. It totally put me off my food, and from then on, I decided that I didn't want to eat anything that had a face.

I was only about five years old, but even at that age I found the idea of killing animals so that human beings can eat them personally revolting. It amazes me that we still do it. It's things like that – killing animals, harming children, wars and using religion as an excuse to hate people – which make me realise that I'll never really understand people. It's difficult to have much faith in the human race with all that nonsense going on.

With rationing still very much alive, my request to pass on the chicken was way out of step with the times, when meat was regarded as a mealtime luxury. By the time I was 11 and preparing for senior school, I'd decided that fish too deserved a better life than to end their days prematurely on my dinner plate. My parents respected my decision. In fact, years later, both my mother and sister gave up meat too. My new schoolmasters were, of course, less forgiving. At Castle Court, I would always leave the meat at the side of my plate, and no one seemed to think anything of it. But in autumn 1956, 100 miles away from home and in an austere public school refectory, I was forced to sit at the table until I'd eaten every last slice of meat. "I can't do it, I'm sorry," I pleaded. I sat there, stubbornly for more than an hour before my meantime tormentors finally gave up. That cruel moment aside, I don't remember my vegetarianism putting me in a box marked "different", but I suppose to some extent it must have.

School was Millfield in deepest Somerset. It was one of the top fee-paying establishments in the country. My father put me down to go to Repton, his alma mater, but I failed the entrance exam, which delighted me because I was quite happy living at home. Soon afterwards, Millfield accepted me on a sports scholarship, on the basis of my cricket skills. Years later, I said to my father, "It's a shame you sent me away to boarding school." He had no idea that I hadn't wanted to go. He thought he was doing me a favour, that a public school education gave a child the best start in life, and that's exactly what he wanted for his son. He also sent my sister to a private school. There was absolutely no favouritism involved.

Every cliché about public school life invariably involves bullying and homosexuality. Well, I experienced neither, though I dare say both went on in Millfield's darker corners. Occasionally, some bright spark would let the tyres down on your bike, which was a bit irritating, but it was hardly 'Tom Brown's Schooldays'. Of course, fagging was rife, though my memory of it is tempered by the fact that the word has different connotations today.

Funnily enough, I was taking my daughter to Lapland just before Christmas when another father came running up to me and said, "You fagged for my dad at Millfield!" I thought, "Steady on – and keep your voice down a bit!"

"MY BUTTOCKS WERE RED RAW FOR DAYS AFTERWARDS."

Back then, fagging meant nothing more than polishing the boots of a senior boy and generally being a bit of a go-fer. Prefects had plenty of power at public school, so I was pleased when I was made second in charge of the Junior School within months of entering Millfield. I would supervise homework and make sure that my charges kept quiet while I did my own. It was all so awfully boring, so to liven things up a bit, I would tell a few jokes. This backfired spectacularly one day when the headmaster, RJO Meyer, who we all referred to as "Boss", walked past the room and heard the sound of uncontrollable laughter. Well, a bit of sniggering, at least. Rather shamefully, I didn't own up to the fact that one of my jokes had been the cause of such gaiety, and he caned the lot of them. Awful, isn't it!

A little later, I had my come-uppance. Lock-up time at the school was 6.30pm, so when I strolled back one evening at seven, I was duly reported and severely caned. It really hurt, and the raw swish-marks stayed imprinted on my buttocks for days afterwards. My clock-watching skills sharpened up immediately. I certainly didn't want to feel the rough edge of that cane again.

Millfield did little to awaken my interest in academic study, though I did take advantage of the school's reputation as a centre of excellence for sports. I captained the cricket team (again), joined the football team, continued to box (though I did my best to get out of it), and I was in the rugby Junior Colts. Fly half suited me well – I'd sling the ball deep into the scrum then get the hell right out of it! Self-preservation has always been important to me.

I was less happy about joining the Combined Cadet Force (CCF), which was depressingly compulsory. It meant that once a week we had to go through the rigmarole of polishing our shoes and the buckles on our belts until we could see our faces reflected in them. I thought it was a complete waste of time. We were given the choice of army, navy air force, so I chose the army because I thought that would be the soft option.

I would never join the Forces. I'm too much of a coward for that. I've never understood why anyone would want to put him or herself in the firing line. Or, for that matter, play around with guns and march around in a uniform. If all uniforms were made illegal, I'm sure the world would be a far more peaceful place.

My mistrust of religion didn't stop me from joining the local church choir in Street, the nearest town to school and one that had an amusing message for motorists: "Life is sweet, drive carefully in Street". There were two ulterior and decidedly God-less motives.

Firstly, the service lasted for half-an-hour, as opposed to the full 60 minutes we'd have to suffer at the school chapel. And then there was Mary Marsh. What a lovely name, and she wasn't a bad looking girl either. She lived nearby, but at that time there was little chance of getting to know each other properly because both her family home and the dorm at Millfield were strictly out of bounds. During our courtship we would walk for miles so it was just as well that the surrounding area – and Glastonbury was close by – was delightfully picturesque.

Surprising for the times, there were a few girls at Millfield, but most of them were 17 or 18 years old and had no interest in boys three or four years their junior. So with few opportunities to consort with the opposite sex, I would instead disappear, acoustic guitar under my arm, to a spare room in the dorm where I would write songs of love and loss based on absolutely no experience whatsoever. It didn't matter that the songs were second-rate. The important thing was that, at last, I'd begun to express myself.

While I'd shone at sports, and was more than happy to pick up the plaudits and a handful of cups, that was nowhere near enough for me. Since the age of four, I'd always wanted to be on the stage, to do – and be – something different. I didn't want to do the everyday things that everyone else did. Pillow fights in the dorm or going out with a gang of mates just didn't interest me. I wanted to do something for myself, like learning the guitar, writing songs, perfecting things.

I'd owned a guitar since my teens, together with a copy of Bert Weedon's legendary Play In A Day guide, which showed how to strum a few basic chords. I still bump into Bert at charity events and I always think that if his book didn't make him a millionaire then there's no justice in this world. Every star-struck teenager, from Marc Bolan in Hackney and future Led Zeppelin guitar hero Jimmy Page in Epsom to Antony Kenneth Blackburn from Lilliput in Poole, owned a well-thumbed copy.

I managed to find three other like-minded pop-mad pupils, one of whom played bass on a long broom attached to a tea-chest, and with them I made my performing debut at a school concert at Glastonbury Town Hall. It was a revelation, for while I'd virtually crumble at the thought of taking a solo in the school choir, I found myself entirely at ease when I stepped up to the microphone with a guitar hanging from my shoulders. That aside, my memories of that first appearance are dim now, though I'm guessing that we played skiffle-style versions of popular hits of the day with one or two of my own songs thrown in.

In truth, I cared little more for the Lonnie Donegan skiffle sound than I did being a full-time boarder at Millfield. And one happy day, some time during 1959, I left them both behind forever.

Twice a term, pupils were granted permission to be whisked off by their parents for the day. It was something I'd always look forward to, and we'd usually visit West Country beauty spots such as Cheddar Gorge or the caves at Wookey Hole, have a cream tea and then they'd drop me back. On this particular occasion, having cleared my 'family day out' with the headmaster, I simply hopped on a train and disappeared home.

"Millfield is an absolute a waste of time," I told my father, who couldn't hide his disappointment. However, I quickly won him round. "They just shove me out on a field to graze all day," I continued. "I don't think they take me seriously at all." It wouldn't be the last time I uttered those words.

But it was true. I had failed an IQ test miserably and was told that I'd never pass an exam in my life. That's why I'd been streamed into all these sporting activities, which was all very well except that I wasn't learning anything. I knew that I wasn't stupid, and my father agreed with me. So that was it. No more Millfield. We picked up my things, and I settled back at home. After a year's worth of private tuition, paid for by my father, I notched up 10 O-Levels.

It was such a relief to get my schooling behind me. It wasn't so much that I didn't enjoy it. It just bored me. I wanted to get out and pursue my dream of breaking into showbusiness. To please my encouraging parents I went along with the idea of enrolling on a business course at Bournemouth Technical College in autumn 1959. But I already knew that my real business would be making a name for myself around town.

* * *

TIME FOR (ANOTHER) BLACKBURN:
THE SISTER: JACKIE

I've always got on terribly well with my brother, but when people start describing him as a national treasure, I think, "What's all that about?" Of course he's done brilliantly, and the whole family has been behind him, but none of us have ever had much time for the celebrity world. I mean, someone like George Clooney . . . he's just an ordinary bloke, really. One of the nice things about Tony is that he's always been very grounded.

When we were young, we had our scraps like all children do, but we got on brilliantly. There was never any sense that he resented the fact that I needed a lot of special treatment until I was about five. In fact I know he didn't. Not that long ago, he told me that he wished he'd been born with my disability so that I could have led an easier life. I thought that was a lovely thing to say.

I don't ever recall Tony being cut out for an ordinary way of life even though he was hardly very 'showbiz' when he was young. In fact, he was fairly reserved and quite happy in his own world. Sometimes, if his friends turned up at the door, he'd get mum to tell them that he wasn't there. He seemed to prefer playing with me and my friends, possibly because we were all girls! There was a wood at the end of the garden, so when Tony had finished messing around with my wheelchair, he'd go and climb the trees there. In many ways, it was an idyllic childhood.

For as long as I remember, he's always been music mad. He loved the radio, and as a boy, he learned to play the piano by ear.

TONY: *That's right. Somebody taught me a few chords, then I went off and figured out how to pick out a tune myself. I did have a few lessons, but as piano teaching was always based around classical music, I soon lost interest. If I can find a short cut to anything, I'll take it! That's why I took up the guitar, because Bert Weedon's book promised that you could master it in a matter of days.*

He never did have any patience, and I think that's very much a family thing. I know I'm like that, and mum and dad were, too. We all have this sense that life's too short to dither about.

TONY: *I can't stand dithering. My wife Debbie's learnt to be very careful before suggesting anything to me. She knows that if she happens to mention, say, a holiday destination, I'll go and book it up without a moment's hesitation. In my world, if you're given an opportunity, you've got to grab it otherwise somebody else will. Imagine if I'd um'd and ah'd about doing* I'm A Celebrity. *Someone else would have been* King Of The Jungle *and I probably wouldn't be writing this book!*

Tony is much more like our father, while I take after our mum. My dad was more complicated, more into himself and generally a bit off the wall. He loved anything to do with cars, and was a stickler for making sure they ran smoothly. He also loved going to this local electrical shop called Bourne Radio where he'd try out all the latest radios and televisions. But we don't have to look far to see the best example of his desire for getting things absolutely right: it's this family home. I was only two or three when it was finished, but you can tell that a whole lot of love, sweat and tears went into the specially designed project.

Mum was easier to understand. She was very much a home-maker whose main concern was that everyone else was happy. Once she'd satisfied herself that they were, that's when she allowed herself to let her hair down and enjoy herself. She was such a lovely person, and contributed so much in making it a very warm and close family with a lot of love in the home. Our maternal grandparents lived next door to us for about 20 years, too. It was like one big happy family.

I know Tony's famous for his jokes, but I have no idea where that sprang from at all, because beneath all the hilarity and fun lies a very sensitive man. He thinks an awful lot, always has done, and if he's not careful he can let things get to him. I don't think he takes life lightly at all. Sometimes I think he feels a little bit too deeply for his own good. That side of him goes right back to when he was a young boy and saw that chicken being killed. He can't take cruelty of any kind, especially when it's directed at children and animals.

I'd be surprised if he hasn't been hurt when people have called him naff, especially in the past. It's not nice, is it! He seems to revel in the idea of it these days, but you do wonder if there's an element of self-protection going on there. I wouldn't say that I fully understand him. He's quite a complicated character.

TONY: *Am I? It surprises me to hear you say that. My mother said the same thing on that television documentary,* The Real Tony Blackburn, *and I never quite understood why.*

Just a little bit complex.

TONY: *In what way? I wasn't aware that I was complicated but you might well be right. Is it because my world is very different to yours?*

Yes, that's probably it. Plus the fact that I can never be entirely sure what's going on in your head.

TONY: *I can tell you there's nothing going on!*

That's just it. Of course there is. You're a complete contradiction.

46

Though Tony had this intensely private side, there was always this sense that he was a go-getter, too. So when he decided to pursue a career in the music industry, our parents were full of encouragement. Dad fixed up a huge aerial across the garden so that we could hear him. The reception was so poor in this part of the world. Mum followed every step of his career. Right to the very end, she never missed a show. The occasion that we can all remember was the day he opened up Radio One. All the family gathered round this big old radiogram in the living-room. It goes without saying that we all felt extremely proud of him that day – and most days since!

Even though he soon became a household name, Tony would come down and visit most weekends. We were by no means a showbiz family, and aside from the little bits of gossip we picked up, we had little real understanding of the kind of life he was living. But we trusted him to look after himself.

We all drove up to Southampton once, for the filming of one of his television shows, *Time For Blackburn*. Anita Harris, also from this area, was appearing in it. But the only time we really got involved in showbiz was when Tony was featured on *This Is Your Life*. The main change Tony's success had on us as a family was that we'd get a constant stream of girls ringing the doorbell and asking, "Is Tony in?"

Of course we worried about him, especially when he went through the sad times. We all knew that breaking up with Tessa would hit him hard. I thought she was lovely, and she still is, but the world knows how difficult it is to make a showbiz marriage last.

Dad, and particularly mum, were concerned because Tony began to spend so much time on his own. We knew he'd be sitting alone at *Hollycroft* going over and over what went wrong and what he could have done to save the marriage. In the end, though, you've got to give up and just get on with life. Eventually, the penny dropped – but it did take several years.

Part of the problem, I think, is that Tony likes things to be right. That's why he can't stand people being late. It's as if he's ruled by his own time-checks! As a professional, of course, he can't afford to be late – though I do think turning up two or three hours before the appointed time is overdoing it a bit. I mean, I was five minutes late today, and he was already on the mobile wondering where I was.

Mum and I were so pleased when he met Debbie. From that day, I think, Tony's life changed. I'd hardly call him relaxed, but he's a lot more settled now. That was just as well, because I knew that mum's death would hit him hard. Not that he'd always demonstrate it when I was around. In fact, he's very protective. I think he tried to put on a brave face so as not to upset me. But the whole awful experience certainly brought us closer together. We learned to express ourselves in front of each other, and share deep emotions that don't necessarily rise to the surface until something like a bereavement hits a family.

While mum was ill, I remember Tony telling her that he was going to write his autobiography. Her immediate response was, "Oh, God!" But she had a young attitude to life, which is why it's been such a shock dealing with the fact that she's no longer with us. Even on that last day, and after all the chemotherapy she'd been through, she told us: "I don't want to go".

Tony shares that same thirst for life. If I'm being really honest, I am dreading the day when the work dries up and he has to contemplate retirement. I know he adores his home life, but he's been cheering strangers up for all these years that I think he's hopelessly addicted to it. I know that he would never admit it, but a lot of people will be genuinely sad not to hear his voice any more in the mornings. And no one will be sadder than me. It's almost 45 years since he left the family home for his strangely public life on air, but I still listen to him every day, and there's a wonderful intimacy in that.

Even when he calls and says, "If you watch *Supermarket Sweep* tomorrow morning . . .", I'll be there tuning in. We're a terrifically loyal family, you know.

3
THE ENTERTAINER

Packing my bags and walking away from Millfield was probably the most rebellious act I committed during my teenage years. Although I was headstrong and determined to do things my own way, I was hardly a natural rebel in the classic James Dean mould. Whenever we played cowboys and Indians as children, I was always a cowboy. Cowboys were the forces of decency and order, not insurrection – or, at least, that's the way they seemed in those old John Wayne films. There was very little to rebel against. I liked my parents. My parents understood me, and on the rare occasion that they didn't, they certainly did their best to accommodate me. It's only when I come up against cold, monolithic establishments – schools, radio stations and suchlike – that my disobedient streak emerges.

I'm not one for conflict. I prefer films with happy endings. Melodies that bring pleasure. People that smile. I've always enjoyed making people laugh and having a pop at those who take themselves too seriously. The goodness in the world is continually being eroded by war and violence so I think it's important to create your own alternative universe otherwise life'll just get you down. I saw my father's mood deteriorate in his later years because he spent so much of his leisure time with his head buried in a newspaper. It didn't help him at all. There was absolutely nothing he could do about any of it, but I could see its paralysing effect on him.

I know I can't stop people killing one another in Iraq, but I wonder what would happen if I went over there wearing one of my ridiculous stage costumes. It wouldn't do any harm and might just do some good. Ask yourself: just where has armed action got us? If the American GIs put down their weapons for a day and walk the streets dressed up in silly costumes it would certainly confuse the enemy. Alas, the day when someone declares war and nobody bothers to turn up is a long way off. Not in my lifetime, that's for sure.

While my family was based in Poole, I spent much of my late teenage years hanging out in neighbouring Bournemouth, a thriving and – at least before the developers moved in – attractive tourist town that always promised fun. It's nothing like the stereotypical British seaside resort, with its pebbled beaches, tatty seaside hotels, miles of arcades and total shutdown during the winter. Bournemouth has golden sands, beautiful pleasure gardens, invigorating, pine-scented air and an all-year-round feelgood factor. Although famed for its ageing population, the place is actually remarkably cosmopolitan, attracting thousands of language students every year. And, according to various clubbing magazines, it has more nightspots than anywhere else in Britain outside London.

"BILLY FURY WOULD MAKE LOVE TO HIS MICROPHONE AND GRUNT AND GROAN AS HE PROWLED THE STAGE."

The town didn't buzz quite so loudly back in the late 1950s, though it always managed to attract a wide range of top-class performers to supplement a thriving local entertainment scene. I'd cherry-pick the best shows – which could be anything from comedian Tommy Cooper to one of those legendary Larry Parnes package tours. Just imagine: Cliff Richard, Marty Wilde, Billy Fury, Dickie Pride, Shane Fenton (later glam rocker Alvin Stardust) and The Vernons Girls all in one starry, starry night! The Parnes experience was worth every penny. All his protégés were iconic and fabulously lit, the audience couldn't stop screaming, and I left the Odeon along Westover Road knowing that I'd just witnessed something truly special. Cliff was like the British Elvis. Dickie Pride came on and vibrated a lot. Best of all, though, was Billy Fury. That man was way over the top for his time. He'd make love to his microphone, and grunt and groan while he prowled menacingly around the stage. I thought he was terrific, a huge, can't-take-your-eyes-off-him entertainer. Marvellous records too. So why doesn't *Halfway To Paradise* ever get played on radio anymore? (Actually, I'll explain why later on in the book.)

In the summer of 1961, Marty Wilde was back in town for a short season at the Bournemouth Pavilion. As many of the big stars often did, he rented a place in Lilliput, a house along Brownsea View Avenue. One afternoon, my sister Jackie spotted him driving in the area . . .

JACKIE: *He was driving this huge red-and-white American convertible, probably a Cadillac. I was with some friends on a street corner, spotted him passing, and called out for him to stop. He did. I was probably about 13 or 14, so Tony would have been 16 or 17. I wasn't shy. I told him, "I've got a brother, his name's Tony Blackburn, and all he wants is a chance. "Send him up to me," Marty replied, giving me the address where he was staying. So I did.*

* * *

I couldn't believe my luck: a big star on my doorstep requesting an audience with me! I wheeled my guitar and amplifier – which I'd bought with money I'd earned selling ice-creams on the beach – round the few streets to where Marty was staying, and sang him one of my songs. He sat on the sofa and listened. He seemed to like what he heard because he promised that he'd do what he could to help me. Unfortunately, that's the last I ever heard from him! His hits were just starting to dry up, so I presume that he was more interested in rescuing his own career than in launching mine. He also had a second child on the way, which by another coincidence, I found that out because my father was looking after his wife, ex-Vernon Girl Joyce Barker, while she was pregnant in Poole. That was Ricky Wilde, who enjoyed a brief stint as a teen heart-throb in the '70s before going on to produce several of big sister Kim's hits a decade later.

Once Elvis Presley had softened his act after going into the US Army, a new era of the teenage heart-throb had virtually wiped out the sound of tearaway rock'n'roll. I fancied a bit of that too, but once the initial excitement of seeing the Parnes show had died down, I felt mildly dispirited by the fact that nobody might ever discover me. I didn't dwell on it for too long. I had an inkling that I could present myself on stage just as well as some of the acts I'd seen. I knew that because I'd been watching myself in the mirror in the family lounge.

Frankie Laine's *Cool Water* was one of those songs I'd act out in front of my invisible audience. I'd throw out my arms and make all the right hand gestures to emphasise the drama in the song, carefully studying my reflection as I did so. It wasn't mere conceit. It was more akin to the way a ballet dancer continually monitors herself until she's satisfied that every movement and gesture is exactly as it should be. I see my 10-year-old daughter Victoria doing exactly the same thing now. Nobody has told her to do that. It's an instinctive thing that some people have and others don't. I knew right from the word go what I wanted to do, because I got such a kick out of rehearsing in front of the mirror.

I'd also begun to work a little harder on my image. With my thick dark hair and full complement of sparkling, Ultra-Brite teeth, I didn't look unlike Cliff Richard. And like Cliff, I was never a real Teddy Boy, nor would I become a Mod or a Rocker. If anything, I thought of myself as more like one of those clean-cut Bobbysoxer singers, more smart and casual than defiantly different. In a bid to jog a few memories, I dug out a box of old photographs the other day and was surprised to see myself all decked out in tight, dark trousers, offset by gaily patterned socks, white winklepicker shoes and a rather extravagant mohair jumper. The crowning glory was a quiff, stiffly Brylcreamed into shape. In my life, I only ever had one disagreement with my mother, and it was over those viciously pointed shoes. Oddly, she didn't object to the effeminate-looking mohair at all.

"SOME CLOT STARTED DEFACING OUR BAND'S POSTERS."

For anyone wishing to get work as a performer in those days, it was essential that you worked up versions of contemporary chart material. As Cliff was all the rage, I included a few of his earliest hits, though I can't say I was particularly fond of his music. I preferred the standard, Sinatra-style ballads, though I rarely got the opportunity to have a crack at them. Funnily enough, I wasn't big on Elvis. It's no doubt heresy in the street credibility stakes but I preferred Perry Como, a great singer whose *Magic Moments* and *Catch A Falling Star* were two of my favourite records from that era. Mind you, I've never given two hoots about street cred.

In 1960, while I was still studying for my Business Studies HND, I put my first proper group together. I called them Tony Blackburn And The Rovers, the name a nod to the Lancashire football team and the repertoire unashamedly populist. We'd originally gone out as Tony Blackburn And His Swinging Bells, but felt obliged to change it after some clot started defacing our posters (to 'Swinging Balls'!). At some point, I briefly restyled myself as Vernon Lawrence, in an attempt to sound more showbiz, but I soon saw the error of my ways and quickly reverted back to my own name. I was Tony Blackburn and I was determined to stay that way throughout my career.

I swear there was one genuine musical talent within the group. His name was Al Stewart, the lead guitarist, who always played rather too loudly in my opinion. Al later became a successful singer-songwriter, and enjoyed a huge worldwide hit in 1976 with *Year Of The Cat*. Back in the early '60s, though, I was the front man and my voice, pitched in a light ballad style, wasn't bad at all. We worked on our rudimentary skills in my parents' dining-room, four amplified young men in a confined domestic space, blasting the place out with enthusiastic versions of Buddy Holly hits. Incredibly, I don't remember the Sinclairs next door ever complaining once.

Another future world famous star who played the same circuit as us – from hotel ballrooms in Bournemouth to village halls in the Dorset countryside – was a young guitarist named Andy Summers. He later found fame and fortune with The Police.

I enjoyed fronting the group, but it was hard work, because we'd be required to play several sets that often totalled three or four hours per night. So I was pleased when a popular local danceband leader named Jan Ralfini asked me to join his 15-piece orchestra as the group's concession to the emerging new pop style. He had the house band at the Bournemouth Pavilion and was notorious for his unbending repertoire. In fact, you could tell the time by what particular tune was being played. If it was *Wheels Cha Cha*, then you knew it was 8.45pm, for example. One night, Jan dared to alter the running-order, prompting several disgruntled customers to come up afterwards and complain that they'd missed their bus.

While set-lists were firmly fixed in stone, the occasions would vary considerably. One night we'd be supporting a visiting beat group such as B. Bumble And The Stingers (one hit wonders from 1962 with that joyously daft instrumental *Nut Rocker*); the next we'd be entertaining the old dears at an afternoon tea dance. It never mattered to me what age the audience was. I was just happy to be up there entertaining them, especially when the orchestra took a break and I'd lead a smaller, beat-type combo through a few contemporary hits. One of my favourite parts of the act was getting the crowd to form a line and do the *Hully Gully*, which basically meant raising your arms and swaying them from side to side. Nothing much changes. I still do something remarkably similar in my act today.

I spent three years with the Jan Ralfini Orchestra. We interspersed our Pavilion residency with plenty of hotel dates, and I made pretty good money. More important still, being part of this semi-professional set-up encouraged me to improve my craft, both as a singer and as a guitarist. I took guitar lessons with a local jazz guitarist called Tony Alton. I later discovered that he also taught future King Crimson guitarist Robert Fripp, so he must have been pretty good.

But it was my singing that I really wanted to polish up. As an indication of just how serious I was about my voice, I took a train up to London every Saturday morning for several weeks to attend classes at the Maurice Berman School Of Singing, close to Oxford Circus. I'd seen an advertisement in *New Musical Express* and the venture seemed to promise imminent stardom. But we only ever seemed to practice one song, Bobby Vee's latest hit, *The Night Has A Thousand Eyes*. And that wasn't part of the Ralfini Orchestra repertoire anyway. I did have a rare brush with celebrity during one of my 200-mile round-trip journeys, when I spotted George Cansdale, host of a regular children's television programme called *All About Animals*. He was sitting in a first class carriage all alone with a squirrel on his lap. It was one of those moments you don't easily forget . . .

Being noticed is everything if you're in showbusiness. That's why, on one of my trips to London, I stopped off at Cecil Gee's in Shaftesbury Avenue and splashed out on a sparkling gold lamé jacket. Though the standard Pavilion show uniform was red jacket with black trousers, white shirt with black bow-tie, I thought it was important to stand out when I led the rock'n'roll interval band. I told Jan Ralfini that I didn't want to be an ordinary band member and he gave me permission to glisten. No one else seemed particularly impressed, though. I once spent an entire day wandering around Bournemouth in that jacket to see if anybody recognised me. No bugger did!

"COUPLES PRANCING AROUND IN THE NUDE PLAYING TENNIS? I COULDN'T THINK OF ANYTHING LESS AROUSING."

On one of these Saturday London sojourns, I sneaked off to the Windmill Theatre in Soho to see a naughty show. After plucking up the courage to buy a ticket and step into the darkness, I was sorely disappointed. Yes, there were naked women on display, just as advertised, but the laws of the day required that they stand completely still. It was about as erotic as leafing through an illustrated book on ancient statues.

I also pursued my awakening teenage interest in naked female flesh a little closer to home, too, thanks to the flea-pit known as the Continental Cinema in Winton, a fairly nondescript part of Bournemouth. Once again, I was sorely disappointed by what was on offer – just a handful of dreary Health & Efficiency films that showed couples prancing around in the nude playing tennis. I couldn't think of anything less arousing.

Sex and pornography is virtually mainstream in today's society. But back in those pre-Beatles, pre-contraceptive pill days, it was all kept remarkably well hidden. So were the girls, virtually invisible beneath all those calf-length skirts and layers of crinolene.

My interest in women was first aroused by going to the cinema with my father and watching Doris Day films. He was a big fan, but I took it much, much further. I simply adored her and still do. If there's one person in entertainment I regard as a genuine icon and one I'd have loved to have met, it's her. Doris Day is my archetypal woman – fresh, feminine, fabulous. And she's devoted her later life to looking after animals. Just perfect. At the time, Marilyn Monroe was the big female star, but she just didn't do it for me. Had she lived, I'm sure she would have gone to pieces. But good old Calamity Jane – still going strong!

I adore the elegance of the late '50s/early '60s woman. I'm probably sounding dreadfully old-fashioned but I find it far more appealing than Jade Goody's effing and blinding. Sally McKenzie, my first real love, was very much cast in the classic mould. She was my girlfriend for six years, from 1958 until shortly after I'd started work on the pirate ships in 1964. And I was the classic teenager in love – doe-eyed but dreadfully insecure. In fact, it's only in later life that I've finally managed to let go of my insecurities, but not before several relationships, including my first marriage, had been ruined.

Before Sally there was Annabelle McCrostie, my partner in a memorably cinematic romantic clinch one night on top of Evening Hill, overlooking Poole Harbour. I don't think it was my first kiss, but it was the first one that meant something to me. We each put one end of a blade of grass in our mouths – like that scene from *Lady And The Tramp* – and gazed into each other's eyes, drawing ever closer until out lips met. It was lovely. There wasn't too much fumbling around under each other's clothes in those days, at least not in my world, though I certainly made up for it later on.

I was 18 when I lost my virginity, in a wood close to the college during a lunch break. The "lucky lady" wasn't Sally but a friend from the college. I'd secretly hoped that it might have cured me of my jealousy towards Sally but it didn't. I now had an added burden of guilt to carry round with me. On top of that, I knew just how powerful male sexual desire was, which only added to my suspicion that every man who even dared look at Sally was a potential suitor.

Most of the time, Sally and I did the usual teenage things – skating at the ice-rink in Westover Road, followed by a trawl of the nearby coffee bars, a walk along the piers. I don't recall anyone hitting passers by for kicks which seems to have become a national pastime in recent years. The early '60s were good times. As I said goodbye to my teens, in January 1963, I got rid of the Lambretta scooter I'd had since I was 16 and upgraded to four wheels. The MG Midget Sprite, a gift from my father, soon became my pride and joy. He bought it secondhand, but it was a first-class car, cool, sporty and something of an emblem for the new decade.

The '60s weren't yet in full swing, but something undeniably new and powerful was starting to happen on the streets: The Young Generation. No one epitomised the new mood more than The Beatles. I can still recall walking around the streets that autumn and hearing their hysteria-inducing chorus, "She loves you, yeah, yeah, YEAH!", sung and whistled by everyone – young and old. I think it's wonderful when a whole nation latches on to one particular song, though with the sorry state of the singles market, it tends to happen less frequently now.

On November 16, 1963, The Beatles rolled back into town headlining another one of those package tours, together with The

Vernons Girls (again), The Brook Brothers and Peter Jay And The Jaywalkers. The Beatles had played three shows at the Gaumont in Westover Road during the summer, and that's when Jackie caught a glimpse of them on the balcony of the Palace Court Hotel where they were staying. The story didn't end there. The band sent one of their roadies down to take her and her friend upstairs for tea with John and Ringo. My sister was a Beatles groupie! Recounting the tale again for me recently, she insists that the pair were actually very well behaved young gentlemen.

By now, Beatlemania had moved into full swing, and a film crew darted about as the Fab Four played to a packed, ecstatic Winter Gardens crowd. I can't comment on the music; it was impossible to hear for all the screaming. I couldn't even tell what songs they played. For all we knew, they might not have even been plugged in! The kids just went wild. I've never experienced anything like it again.

It was impossible not to like The Beatles, but if I'm perfectly honest, I'd say that I seeing Bobby Vee at the Winter Gardens was far more enjoyable. He had great songs – *Rubber Ball*, *The Night Has A Thousand Eyes* and *Devil Or Angel* – and an impressive stage manner, too. I was far more interested in being Bobby Vee than a Beatle.

Many years later, I went to see Bobby in cabaret in London and he was tremendous, even better than I remember him being first time round. He came out bouncing a rubber ball, and after the show, I was surprised to discover that he was actually two years younger than I was. You often expect performers to disappoint when they're on the comeback trail, but Bobby, who had his two sons with him in the group, did nothing to tarnish his reputation.

* * *

"THERE WAS SOMETHING SECRETIVE AND VAGUELY ILLICIT ABOUT LISTENING TO THESE UNFAMILIAR SOUNDS FROM ACROSS THE ATLANTIC."

Away from The Beatles, away from my growing anxieties about Sally's fidelity, away from those nights when I sparkled on the stage alongside Jan Ralfini at the Pavilion, I would retreat into my own private world. With the radio by my side, pumping out Radio Luxembourg, I was never alone. Radio was far more important, especially to me, than television in those days, which is why the late '50s and early '60s are so often described as the Golden Age Of Radio. I'd tune into the Light Programme for *The Goons* or *Round The Horne*, both of which were hilarious, then I'd defect to Luxembourg where Pete Murray and Alan Freeman were playing the best assortment of contemporary sounds.

That's really where my early interest in American black vocal music, nurtured by my Jackie Wilson-loving father, was massaged into a raging passion. Don't get me wrong. It wasn't wall-to-wall doo-wop and R&B – black music was still very much a minority interest back then. But every once in a while, you'd hear the wonderful harmonies of a vocal group such as The Crests or The Cascades, whose *Rhythm Of The Rain* was a particular favourite of my father's. The orchestration on The Drifters' *There Goes My Baby*, for example, was daringly unusual for its time; the strings on *This Magic Moment* simply majestic. There was something secretive and vaguely illicit about listening to these unfamiliar sounds from across the Atlantic. When I heard The Shells' *Baby Oh Baby*, for example, I felt absolutely sure that I was the only person in this country that fell in love with it. But I could never really understand why that was. So much of this music was so beautifully melodic – it was pure pop music, really, though it's taken all this time for urban black music to truly emerge as something other than a minority taste genre.

In time, of course, I realised that other forces were at work. When I arrived at the BBC, a bastion of the white middle classes, the cultural chasm between the sound of black America and the stiff suits at Broadcasting House was painfully obvious. That's why I'll always be extremely proud that I helped popularise black music in this country.

I created the first ever soul music radio show while at Radio London, and have been pushing black music ever since. I can't say that I'm the world's biggest rap and hip hop fanatic, but even some of that, such as the more melodic songs of LL Cool J, has found its way onto my shows. To me, it shouldn't be categorised as black music. It's popular music, plain and simple.

The Beatles were all right but I'd already heard a lot of the songs they were singing because they'd been hits in the States for black American groups. I don't think I was alone in thinking that The Beatles had been cheating just a little bit. But John, Paul, George and Ringo's runaway success seemed to herald the arrival of a golden era, when everyone began to feel good about themselves and the world in which they lived. Yes, it might well have all been a mass delusion but it was tremendous fun while it lasted. And all I really wanted was to be a part of that.

I'd been scouring the pages of the music press for several years, not just for news of the latest discs and concert tours, but for hints on how I might better fulfil my ambition. I'd always found the classified pages at least as interesting as the articles, and one early summer's day in 1964, one advert in particular in the pages of *New Musical Express* caught my eye. It was a request for aspiring disc jockeys to send in their demo tapes. I promptly recorded a four-song mini-show, featuring four Beatles songs linked together with some snappy banter, and shoved it in the post. The address was Caroline House, Chesterfield Gardens, London, the on-shore home of the newly launched pirate station Radio Caroline South.

As I placed the reel-to-reel tape in the envelope, and posted it off, I knew that the job was mine. Strange isn't it? There was absolutely no doubt in my mind that I'd just done something that was about to change my life for good.

My mother was especially encouraging. She knew that, for all my aspirations as a singer, I'd always had a natural inclination to be a DJ. She'd spotted that very early on, when I used to ask for "moo-moos" as a two-year-old, which was my infant way of demanding that she put some music on. By the time I was 13, I'd taken it much further, inspired, no doubt, by my father's fondness for gadgets. During one of my holidays from Millfield, I set up my own primitive DJ sound system to entertain my mother while she did the housework. I played records on the family radiogram, introduced them on my new microphone, and relayed the sounds into the hallway via a giant speaker. A few years later, while earning some Christmas cash at the sorting office in Parkstone, I went public with a few jokes over the post office internal communications system.

Talking into a microphone came more naturally to me than singing into it – and I already had the rejection slips to prove it. Always thinking big, I'd managed to get myself an audition for Decca Records during my days with the Jan Ralfini Orchestra. Unfortunately, they said I looked too much like Cliff Richard and sang too well. They'd just signed The Rolling Stones, so they were looking for something a little less tuneful. I think the man who denied me stardom was Dick Rowe – who'd previously turned down The Beatles. Two gross errors of judgment in as many years – he must have been kicking himself for the rest of his days.

Bournemouth wasn't exactly the epicentre of the emerging British beat scene in 1964, and I had a feeling as I boarded the train bound for Waterloo one midsummer's Monday morning that I would soon be leaving it. I knew all about Radio Caroline, which had started broadcasting on Good Friday, March 21, 1964. There had been several stories about the newly emerging pirates in the press, though when I tried to tune into the station, all I heard was buzz and crackle because the reception in Poole was notoriously poor. Caroline had also featured in a 'World In Action' documentary which had made the idea of playing pop records from a ship three miles off the coast of Britain seem like the most exciting thing in the world. I wanted that job, and by mid-afternoon on July 23, 1964, I'd got it!

4

THE PIRATE

Caroline House was a seven-storey building based in the heart of London's Mayfair, which I thought was an oddly inappropriate location for the head office of the country's leading pirate radio station. As soon as I arrived, one June mid-morning, a receptionist ushered me up the grand, winding staircase and into the office of Radio Caroline's Programme Director, Chris Moore. As she held the door open, I caught first sight of the man on whom my future rested. He was standing on his head throwing darts at a dartboard. I knew I'd come to the right place.

After a brief introduction, he whisked me down to a small basement studio, left me with an engineer, a small pile of records and instructions to record a 30-minute dummy broadcast. I did the best I could, but when he came back and played it through, he wasn't particularly impressed. "Your voice is too flat," he said. "This is radio. It's got to sound more exciting than that. Put some energy and laughter in it." I was relieved when he gave me a second shot, and as I went through the playlist again, I could feel myself relaxing into the part of an affable, easy-listening DJ. It was wonderful advice and I've not looked back since.

Visibly happier with my second attempt, Chris then sent me away for a long lunch, while my audition was discussed with the other Caroline executives. It was a beautifully sunny day, so I sat in nearby Hyde Park and agonised as my fate was so delicately poised in the balance. When I returned, Chris simply said, "Can you start tomorrow?" I had the small matter of giving some notice to Jan Ralfini, but we agreed that I'd have a day to sort that out, and that my career as a disc jockey would start on Wednesday July 25, 1964. For that, I would be paid the grand sum of £15 per week.

My parents were delighted for me, even though they'd assumed that my passion for pop was a phase I'd eventually grow out of. Four decades on, everyone's still waiting... My girlfriend Sally McKenzie was less impressed by the news. Within a few months of my leaving for the cool waters of the North Sea, I'd met with a similarly icy reception from her during one of my weeks of shore leave, and it was obvious that our seven-year relationship had finally gone aground. I was hurt. First love is especially painful. But in some ways it came as a relief. I'd been driving myself fairly mad with jealousy whenever we were apart, and though we'd been very close, I was always convinced that she was being terribly unfaithful. It wasn't just my insecurity. I'd caught her out on a couple of occasions and I think that her infidelities may have continued once I was away at sea for two weeks in every three.

"THE PIRATE SHIPS HAD EVERYTHING: YOUTH, MUSIC AND REBELLION."

Having started out from Poole at something like five in the morning, I'd met Chris Moore at Liverpool Street Station at 8.30am, as arranged. I had with me my suitcase, my guitar, a hooped nautical-style shirt that my mother had bought as soon as she heard the news, and, most important of all, my passport. From there we took the train to Harwich on the Essex coast where Colin Nichol, one of the first batch of Caroline DJs, was waiting for me. After the bizarre formality of going through customs (ostensibly our destination was Holland), we were on a tender ship sailing into internationally protected waters some three and a half miles off the coast of Frinton. The vessel from which Radio Caroline broadcast was anchored in territorial waters under the protection of the Panamanian flag, and at the end of our two-hour journey, I was politely informed that I was no longer under British jurisdiction. I could almost feel the freedom.

My first thought when I saw the *Mi Amigo*, a beat-up 160-ton ex-passenger ship dominated by a huge 130-foot radio mast, was one of great excitement and more than a little surprise. Could this little ship really be the cause of so many headaches for the British government? How wonderful to be part of all this! It was a relatively calm day so I hopped off the tender with little difficulty – in high seas that could be a pretty scary experience – and onto the ship that would become the focus of my life for the next two years.

Radio Caroline has always been regarded as one of the foundation stones of the Swinging '60s and rightly so. It pioneered independent, commercial radio and changed the face of British broadcasting in the process. It shoved two fingers up to authority. Above all, it had everything central to the dynamics of the era in abundance: youth, music and rebellion.

I thought it was wonderful and enjoyed my time on Caroline immensely. But there are a few truths that have got lost amid all the myth-making. For a start, like Radio One in its early days, Caroline was by no means a 24-hour continuous pop station. In fact, during its earliest months, it mixed fashionable Merseybeat sounds with programmes almost entirely devoted to easy listening and light music from film soundtracks. As for its politics, Caroline was actually more pro-Conservative than Labour, because it was felt that the Tories were more receptive to the arguments in favour of commercial broadcasting. None of that mattered much to me. I was simply grateful for being given the opportunity to talk nonsense for a couple of hours every day and get paid for it. That's what I've been doing for the past 43 years, and I'm even more grateful to be able to do it now than I was then!

It was a precarious existence aboard the *Mi Amigo*, though, and I'm not just talking about the rough seas and terrible gales we so often endured. As I've discovered over the course of my career, you're always at the mercy of those who control the purse-strings, whether they understand radio or not. Apparently, an Australian named Allan Crawford had the original idea to broadcast offshore, and to that purpose, he began fitting out the *Mi Amigo*, which lay forlorn and decrepit in an Irish shipyard. Ronan O'Rahilly, an Irishman who ran with the fashionable Chelsea Set centred on the Kings Road, got wind of this and quickly started refurbishing his own converted ferry, *The Frederica*. It was O'Rahilly who dropped anchor first, launching Radio Caroline several weeks before Crawford followed suit with his own Radio Atlanta.

The pair quickly reached an agreement whereby Crawford's *Mi Amigo* would stay anchored on the East Coast and become Radio Caroline South. Meanwhile *The Frederica* was packed off to the Irish Sea, just off the coast of the Isle Of Man, where it was renamed Radio Caroline North. Crawford, the man who had the final say in giving me my job, supervised Caroline South, O'Rahilly the ship in the north. Obviously, money was the basis of the alliance – O'Rahilly had convinced Crawford that by covering both regions, a combined Caroline North and South could bring in a much bigger advertising yield. I'm sure he was right. The bad news for the DJs was that the pair never really hit it off, and the constant factionalism caused much insecurity on board. When one business partner had the upper hand, he would sack staff hired by the other, and vice versa. While Caroline usually worked with a core of around half a dozen, I think the station got through over 60 DJs in just over four years, all of whose names were added to a roll of honour on the wall in the mess room.

When I joined Radio Caroline, O'Rahilly and Crawford had only just joined forces. I kept out of the politics as much as I could and spent most of my first few weeks on the *Mi Amigo* familiarising myself with the bare bones of broadcasting. Not that time was particularly on my side. Within 24 hours of being on ship, I was on air, hosting an afternoon show called *The Big Line-Up*. I found it a totally relaxing experience. I've never suffered from nerves on the radio, and I can only assume that's because I was born to the job.

The first record I played that day was The Four Seasons' *Rag Doll*, one of hundreds of songs that became hits thanks to the pirates. I know that because it was well over a month later before that particular song even entered the pop charts. Listing all those pirate-sponsored successes would fill the rest of this chapter, but two songs from Caroline's early days merit special mention: The Honeycombs' *Have I The Right*, and *It's Not Unusual*, the infectious, fresh-sounding hit that set Tom Jones off on his underwear-strewn path towards Vegas and international superstardom. One song that Caroline couldn't work its magic on was Booker T & The MG's *Green Onions*. It was apparently a big favourite of Ronan O'Rahilly's, and while we were all encouraged to play this instrumental as often as possible, it never became anything more than a club hit. But we got it right: *Green Onions* is still filling dancefloors well into the 21st century.

Unfortunately, neither Tom Jones or Booker T made the short hop into Panamanian waters to show their appreciation. However, we did receive a visit from Twinkle, a young, blonde singer from Surrey who was plugging her controversial death-disc, *Terry*. In fact, she enjoyed her time on the *Mi Amigo* so much that she stayed the night. This was a wonderful publicity stunt, and the record – dreadful though it was – went on to become a surprise hit.

Station Controller Ken Evans usually selected the Caroline playlist, though we were usually permitted to slip in a small handful of our own favourites on each show. As my days on the *Mi Amigo* coincided with the rise of the fabulous Tamla Motown from Detroit, I eagerly awaited the daily arrival of the midday tender boat in the hope that it might bring the latest Supremes, Temptations or Four Tops 45. During my early pirate days, I also developed a huge passion for Dionne Warwick, who sang some of the first Bacharach and David hits such as *Anyone Who Had A Heart* (which knocks spots off Cilla's version!) and *Don't Make Me Over*. I thought her voice was absolutely gorgeous – and I still do all these years later.

"SO WHAT IF ONE OF MY JOKES INDUCED A COLLECTIVE GROAN AMONG MY LISTENERS?"

At first, the Caroline studio was always manned by two DJs, one to provide the links and sometimes read out the commercials, the other to put the discs on the turntable. Initially, I was paired with the breakfast show host Doug Carr. Doug was already losing his hair, and he spent much of his spare time gobbling molasses and pills in a bid to reverse the situation. My thick, Beatles-style barnet was obviously a source of great envy to him, and one day he blurted out that it looked like a tea-cosy. From that moment on, he always referred to my programme as the Tony Tea-Cosy Blackburn Show, and I'd often keep the joke running on air.

Playing the fool has always been an integral part of my radio style. That was what had impressed me about Pete Murray's broadcasting manner, and now I had the chance I was determined to carve out my own comic niche. For many years, decades even, my style has been a fairly constant string of corny one-liners. I'm not sure that many people have cottoned on yet, but I don't do them any more, and haven't done for years. Their sell-by date has long past, though I should admit that it probably took the arrival of Harry Enfield and Paul Whitehouse's Smashie and Nicey characters to ram the point home to me. In the mid-'60s, when the Carry On series of films represented the mainstream of British popular culture, corn was cool – well, almost. And so what if one of my jokes induced a collective groan among my listeners? I've always believed that it's better to be loved or loathed rather than have an audience that was indifferent to you. At least it meant that people were talking about you.

To begin with, I made up jokes on the spot. These usually involved things such as masts and portholes, anything with a nautical theme. Very soon, though, I realised that even corn needed to be executed with a bit of finesse. I very quickly filled a pile of exercise books with jokes and carried them everywhere. Later on, when I was presenting three-hour shows on Radio London, then Radio One, I used the Robert Orbin joke books, which I had to order in from America. I also subscribed to his bi-weekly updates. This resource also proved invaluable to quite a few of my contemporaries, too. I know Bob Monkhouse was a keen Orbin admirer. The only problem was that his jokes were geared towards the American way of life, which meant that you often had to given them a British twist.

Within months, my name started to pop up in those "Top DJ" polls in the press, despite the fact that Radio Caroline South could only be heard in the southern and eastern parts of the country. I'm sure my humorous approach helped get me noticed ahead of some of my colleagues, and I don't think my middle class accent – a much rarer commodity on the pirate ships than at Broadcasting House – did me any harm either. I suspect that when I was interviewed for the Caroline job, they were actually looking for someone who sounded just a little bit BBCish, which was probably why they snapped me up. I don't think many ex-public schoolboys had walked through their doors.

At least as important in the DJs armoury, though, was the catchphrase. All the big names had one. Jimmy Savile, who had just started making a name for himself presenting *Top Of The Pops*, BBC TV's new pop show, uttered "Now then, now then, now then", followed by a daft braying donkey noise at every opportunity. In the more refined corner of broadcasting, Jimmy Young would always sign off with the words, "Ta-ta for now". My signature in those early days was to start a programme with a hearty "Let's away – with the first record of the day!", and end it with the words, "Have lots of fun, be good and 'bye for now . . . Goodbye everyone!". I had also chosen a theme tune for the show, a cool, jazzy instrumental called *Beefeater* by Johnny Dankworth, that I spiced up with two barks from my imaginary dog Arnold, from a tape in the sound effects library. Gimmicks like that are crucial in giving a show its own particular identity.

The Caroline studio was well equipped considering its location. We had a turntable console, fitted with a microphone and volume controls to fade the music and voices in and out; a bell we'd ring to remind the audience they were tuned in to "Radio Caroline on 199 meters"; a bulky reel-to-reel tape machine from which we used to blast out the pre-recorded commercials and a cartridge machine for playing jingles. On the face of it, jingles were just another form of station identification, but to me they were a crucial element in creating a cohesive, smooth-running radio show. I quickly learnt my way around the studio in an effort to make my programme as energetic and entertaining as possible though, with the grumbling generator outside the studio door, that wasn't always easy on the *Mi Amigo*. To make matters worse, the studio was housed above the waterline which meant that as soon as the sea got rough, so did the shows. We'd often place a heavy coin on the stylus arm to stop it slipping across the discs. When conditions got rough, we'd often play it up a bit, throwing ashtrays and things around to make it sound as if we were really braving it against all the odds.

Though we'd often make light of the situation, conditions could be genuinely dangerous. In a really bad gale, the boat swung like a pendulum (the huge radio mast didn't help) and on many occasions I'd peer through the porthole while on air and watch giant waves crashing over the side of the ship.

On one occasion, in January 1966, the engines faltered and the *Mi Amigo* ran aground on the beach at Frinton. It was a serious situation that, without the speedy actions of local lifeboatmen, could have ended in death and disaster. I kept my wits about me. Knowing that the press would be there waiting for us as we scrambled to safety, I made sure I was first off the boat, and the next day it was my face that was splashed all over the papers. The *Mi Amigo* was hauled off to Holland for repairs, and we were rehoused on a replacement ship, *Cheetah II*. But things were never the same, not least because we were often off air due to various technical difficulties.

One reason we lost our signal was because some rope became snagged at the top of the mast. I was so fed up with the forced intermissions that when Ronan offered £50 to the person whc'd climb up and disentangle it I immediately volunteered. Halfway up the mast, I looked down and cursed myself: "You stupid idiot! What the hell are you doing this for?" One slip and I was a goner. I did get us back on air but, of course, I never received my £50.

* * *

"THE CREW CONSIDERED ALL OF US HOMOSEXUALS AND WEIRDOS SIMPLY BECAUSE WE WERE IN SHOWBUSINESS."

Shimmying up that mast was really a job for the mainly Dutch crew who manned the ship, but they valued their lives enough not to be tempted by Ronan's offer. There was always a bit of friction between them and us, especially during the early days of Caroline. They used to find us rather amusing, I think, as we walked around in our pink shirts and Beatle haircuts, and were forever sending us up. This one particular Dutchman considered all of us homosexuals and weirdos because we were in showbusiness – not at all the thing for a hardy seaman. We took it in good part, but whenever we hit back and gave them a dose of their own medicine, they couldn't take it at all. Who knows? Perhaps we touched a raw nerve.

The crew might have imagined that we were effeminate fools, but to the nation's teenagers, we were heroes. "Nobody Loves The Pop Pirates – except the listeners," ran one newspaper headline. And there were a lot of them, usually young, working class and in possession of one of those new fangled portable transistor radios. Culture was moving fast, and unlike the BBC, pirate radio was keeping up with it. We were the "Radio Caroline Good Guys", a guise we adopted when making personal appearances at hip hangouts like the 100 Club in London's Oxford Street. On our arrival, we'd be mobbed like pop stars. The sacks of mail that arrived via the tender ship further confirmed our immense popularity.

The first superstar DJ of the pirate ships was Simon Dee. With his pop star looks and relaxed style, he was the first face of Radio Caroline and the man who opened up the station. Simon was a nice guy who was very helpful to me during my early days on air and I had a lot of respect for him. I didn't get to know him too well, because by spring 1965, he'd quit and joined forces with the enemy over at Broadcasting House. It was only the next stage in his meteoric rise to fame. By 1967, he was hosting his own twice-a-week television chat show, with a revolving door of world famous guests. In fact, I was one of them – and the experience taught me an even more valuable lesson about showbusiness than anything Simon had showed me in the radio studio. But more about that later...

The great thing about the pirates was that, with such a small staff, they provided a great training ground for all of us eager young hopefuls. I remember once when the transmitter suddenly came on again after a long lay-off, I was the only one around to man the studio. I seized the microphone and broadcast continuously for eight hours. Wonderful!

That wouldn't have been possible a few months earlier, when radio broadcasting was invariably a two-man job. Even in the early days of Caroline, one DJ was at the microphone, while the other span the records. It was a large and rather loud DJ named Dave Lee Travis who changed all that. I shared a cabin with DLT (as he was better known) for a while and it wasn't always easy. But DJs in this country owe him a lot because he was the first to master the art of doing it all himself. The technique became known as self-op and within a couple of years everyone at Radio One was doing it.

Space on board the *Mi Amigo* was too limited to let anyone's bad habits get on top of you. There was a kind of siege mentality about the place that kept everyone relaxed and dedicated to the job. Off-air, we'd congregate in the mess room and play cards, watch television and barter with our weekly rations of beer, cigarettes and soft drinks. We'd also have a bit of fun teaching Rosko's pet mynah bird some choice phrases. Emperor Rosko – the son of Hollywood film producer Joe Pasternak – was one of Caroline's key personalities. He came across as this mad, fast-talking American with plenty of 'D' factor. Rosko was definitely different, though he was oddly peaceful off air. His pet mynah bird was the exact opposite. It wouldn't shut up at all, but shove a microphone under its nose and it dried up completely. Nevertheless, Rosko – *"The host with the most from the California coast!"* – persevered with his feathery sidekick, at least until the thing began to blurt out "Rosko is a wanker!" on air. He wasn't, of course, but it was great fun teaching his bird to say that.

Twinkle aside, women were remarkable rare on the *Mi Amigo*. That, in addition to the very real threat of cabin fever, was one of the main reasons we looked forward to shore leave – which was one week in every three. There were just two female colleagues, Marion and Maureen, who worked in the record library. I once had a brief clinch with Maureen, but that aside, there was very little of what Mick Jagger once called "girl reaction".

It was difficult to enjoy anything like a meaningful relationship when two thirds of your life was spent at sea. No sooner had you met someone, you'd be back, bleary-eyed, at Harwich flashing your passport at a customs man again. By the time you came back ashore, the new love interest was nowhere to be seen. It was like being in the Royal Navy, only without the brawls and the brothels.

The only woman that kept me awake at nights was the Italian landlady of my £4 per week bedsit in Earls Court Square. She was considerably older than I was, and though I found her incredibly attractive, that particular liaison started and finished in my over-active mind.

I had more luck with a woman who worked at Caroline House. As a matter of fact, I think she was Ronan O'Rahilly's personal assistant. She had one of those high-rise Dusty Springfield beehive hair-do's and for some inexplicable reason always wore clogs. She wasn't even Dutch. We had one terrific night back at her place, but though she was lovely, we never got round to repeating the experience.

I also enjoyed a six-month fling with the wife of one of Caroline's other DJs. It all started off so innocently, with a coffee after a chance encounter at Caroline House. Pretty soon, though, it had developed into regular sex sessions back at my cramped Earls Court pad. I didn't feel too guilty about it because I knew the couple weren't getting on at all. But eventually, as with most affairs based on sex, it fizzled out.

The bitter truth was that London can be a lonely place when you're single. Of course, I had a few offshore affairs in my three years on the pirate ships. But mostly, when I wasn't broadcasting, I'd be alone. One day, while killing time idling around Piccadilly Circus, a policeman approached me. He glanced at me suspiciously and asked for my name. "Tony Blackburn," I replied, a little nervously. "Oh, Tony Blackburn from Radio Caroline?" he said. His manner changed instantly. I told him about life aboard the pirate ship, and explained that while I enjoyed the job immensely, it played havoc with my private life. That's why, I said, I'd find myself wandering aimlessly round the streets of Central London. When I returned to my bedsit, the first thing I'd do was to tune in to Radio Caroline, just so I could hear my friends.

"I KEPT HEARING THIS ONE PARTICULAR JINGLE, *WONDERFUL RADIO LONDON*, AND THAT PRETTY MUCH SAID IT ALL."

One morning, while I was hosting Caroline's Breakfast Show, news came through that another pirate ship was on the way. There were other pirates in the area, such as Radio Sutch and Radio City, which both operated out of the old sea forts in the Thames Estuary. But those were generally shoestring operations and often a magnet for genuine rogues and ruffians. In fact, it was the subsequent death of Radio City boss Reg Calvert, fatally wounded in June 1966 during a scuffle at the home of a sea fort owner, which marked the beginning of the end for the pirates. Days later, the Government set in motion the legislation that would, a year later, bring us all back to dry land. Back in November 1964, though, news of the imminent arrival of Radio London panicked everyone on Caroline for all the right reasons.

I still remember the moment the London ship first came into view, this massive American minesweeper with a huge radio aerial mast, slowly forming into a recognisable shape as the early morning sea mist lifted. Now, size isn't everything (my partner of choice back then was invariably blonde and petite), but I was hugely impressed by what I saw. Compared to the ship that hosted *The Big L*, Caroline's *Mi Amigo* seemed so small and insignificant.

As soon as Radio London began broadcasting test transmissions, I knew the game was up. I kept hearing this one particular jingle, *"Wonderful Radio London"*, and that pretty much said it all. This was slick, American style commercial radio at its best – coherent programming, interspersed with regular, professional advertising and the best jingles I'd ever heard.

By the end of 1965, Radio London was up and running and poaching listeners and advertisers off Caroline in huge numbers. I wasn't at all surprised by this. While Caroline would start the day with hip and contemporary pop on my breakfast show, the schedules later went all over the place, from show music, back to pop, then to big bands and jazz. By the end of the day, we'd lost virtually all our listeners. Radio London was the real deal. The station played non-stop pop, interspersed by these wonderfully distinctive jingles bought in from the States, and knew instinctively how to win an audience and keep it. Everyone on Caroline felt intimidated by *Big L*'s slick professionalism. And anyone with any sense of ambition would have fantasised about defecting to the other side. I know I did.

It wasn't too long before Radio London came knocking. Tony Windsor, who'd briefly worked for Radio Atlanta in its pre-Caroline days but was now London's senior DJ, signalled me over one afternoon when I was on the tender going back to Harwich. Leaning over the side of the 750-ton *MV Galaxy*, he quietly suggested that I pay a visit to London's onshore HQ at Curzon Street in Mayfair, round the corner from Caroline's head office. It was, at last, the opportunity I'd been waiting for. Unfortunately, as it turned out, I had to wait a little longer before I could – literally – jump ship.

As Tony Windsor had suggested, I made an appointment to see the Programme Controller, who offered me a job there and then. There was just one snag. He told me I would be known as Mark Roman – Radio London's latest addition to its own fast-growing empire. I didn't like that at all. I was Tony Blackburn, and wasn't going to throw away all the goodwill I'd earned on Caroline broadcasting under my own name. But it was in-house policy, and common practice in the States, that when a DJ switched stations he was also obliged to change his name. It was several months before the powers that be had a rethink and finally relented.

"MIMING TO A VIRTUALLY EMPTY ROOM SAVE FOR A BARMAID AND HALF A DOZEN CLEARLY DISINTERESTED CUSTOMERS..."

For the time being, though, turning down Radio London was the right decision. Besides, Tony Blackburn, a name I was already starting to perceive as a marketable product, still had a second career in the balance. Some months after I joined the station, Caroline's co-owner Allan Crawford had signed me to his music publishing company, and he put me in touch with Fontana Records' Artist & Repertoire man Jack Baverstock. Very soon I found myself working alongside Les Reed, a hugely successful songwriter who did much to get Tom Jones' early career off the ground.

It was a pity that Les's magic didn't work quite so effectively on the song we worked on together, called *Don't Get Off That Train*. Don't get off that ship, more like! I remember the thrill of hearing Sam Costa play it on the Light Programme, and I plugged it as much as I could on my breakfast show, but still the beat-fixated public managed to ignore my first single. After a second flop 45 for Fontana, *Is There Another Way To Love You*, I decided to put the singing career on hold for a while.

I didn't particularly like what I'd seen during my brief encounter with the recording side of the music industry. For a start, it seemed rather ungentlemanly. When I thought I'd found the hit song I'd been searching for, a mid tempo ballad called *Come On Home*, my enthusiasm got the better of me and I mentioned it to one of the Fontana A&R men. A few weeks later, one of his artists, Wayne Fontana, was on his way up the charts with a new hit single titled . . . *Come On Home*.

Far more soul-destroying, though, was the week I spent traipsing round the country's beer-stained club and cabaret circuit promoting my first record. Miming your song to a virtually empty room save for a barmaid and half a dozen clearly disinterested customers was an experience I'd never want to go through again. Although I was well-known in London and the south-east, Caroline's signal didn't travel beyond the home counties so perhaps it was hardly surprising that no one showed up north of Watford.

Hosting *Discs A Go Go*, one of many short-lived pop television shows that sprung up in the mid-'60s, helped to raise my profile in the UK, but I think the single had been and gone by then.

For some obscure reason, my records always sold better on the continent in Holland and Belgium, where I occasionally did a bit of club DJ-ing, than they did here at home. A little later, Belgium's *Humo* magazine presented me with an award in recognition of my work on Radio London.

London came knocking again in June 1966. This time, they were ready to take my name as well as my DJing skills. But Tony Windsor, who I liked and respected, dropped a bombshell as we sat in a pub close by Radio London's Soho HQ. He said that my voice was too high-pitched and my jokes were rubbish so I should drop them. With two years' experience as a broadcaster under my belt, I was angry, but Tony was spot-on about the voice. By the time I'd settled into the Radio London studio, I'd lowered it to something akin to the relaxed, warm tones that everyone now knows and loves. Or loathes!

" 'HERMIONE' HAWKINS WAS A BIG, BRAWNY AUSTRALIAN WHO WALTZED AROUND WEARING THE SKIMPIEST SHORTS YOU COULD POSSIBLY IMAGINE."

Tony Windsor was one of the great unsung heroes of British broadcasting. He was a big, butch Aussie and as camp as a row of tents. I'd heard that he ended up broadcasting over here because he'd told his listeners in Australia that he had cancer or something, then used the money he'd raised to pay his passage to England. Nevertheless, he was a wonderful broadcaster with a distinctive voice, one of those rich, deep, relaxing radio voices. I've never heard anyone make the word 'Hello' sound as engaging as Tony did. He really split those syllables down the middle each time he delivered his winning catchphrase: "Huh-low, it's the TW show." I could sit and listen to him say that all day long.

Unlike us younger pirates, Tony's style wasn't particularly slick, but that was part of his charm. He'd cough and splutter and there'd be these enormous gaps on his programme. "Ladies and gentlemen, boys and girls, right now we have Number 17 on the Fabulous 40!" But, no, there would just silence, because Tony had forgotten to cue the record up! He'd seek to remedy the situation with a hastily added, "Er, in a moment . . ." while he desperately scrambled to find the disc. Despite absolutely no organisation whatsoever, *The Tony Windsor Show* nevertheless worked beautifully.

I learned a great deal about broadcasting from him. He had this thing about being in "the smile business". It was the same every morning. "Ladies and gentlemen, boys and girls. Join me, Tony Windsor, in the smile business! It worked for me and it'll work for you . . ." He was an old bullshitter really, and all over the place, but I thought he was absolutely brilliant. Best of all, the tea break on his morning show was sponsored by a company called Camp Coffee.

It was Tony's idea that everyone on *Big L* was given a girl's name. It was all very silly, but it was one of those things that helped keep us sane, and probably kept one or two egos in check too. As the station's head DJ, Tony was known as the Queen Mother. Or Mother Superior. Or just plain Mum. The sign on his cabin door read, somewhat inevitably, "Windsor's Castle". To me, though, Tony was always Wendy.

For no reason other than the joys of alliteration, I was dubbed Bessie Blackburn and my quarters duly christened "Bessie's Bunk". Other Radio London 'lasses' included Chris "Christine" Denning, Keith "Samantha" Skues and Richard "Sally" Swainson. I don't think Ed Stewart, who later took over from Tony as the station's chief DJ, had a feminine alter-ego.

This girlish tendency wasn't restricted to DJs. One engineer with a peculiar fondness for flamboyant dressing gowns was Mike "Mother" Howell. Another was "Hermione" Hawkins, a big, brawny Australian who waltzed around wearing the skimpiest shorts you could possibly imagine. In the mess room where we ate, a red light would flash whenever there was a problem with the transmitter, and this was the cue for "Hermione" to dash past in his short-shorts to a chorus of wolf whistles. "Pack it in, sports," he'd complain, but there was no let-up. The butch buccaneers rarely had the upper hand on Radio London.

"KENNY WAS CERTAINLY THE MOST INVENTIVE DJ I'VE EVER HEARD ON RADIO."

The most complicated colleague on board was "Edith". You'll know him better as Kenny Everett. In 1966/67, most of us earned a standard fee of £50 per week on Radio London, and no one deserved it more than Kenny. He was something else: super quick, crankily creative and one great big jumble of confusion. Leading a double life as the most exciting DJ in the country was probably more than enough for such a slight, incredibly shy man. But that wasn't all he had to deal with.

Most of Kenny's younger days were spent covering up the fact that he was gay. I'm afraid that, for all their permissiveness, the '60s weren't ready to embrace homosexuality. Kenny himself fought it, too, for a while. He even married Lee Middleton, the long-time ex-partner of Billy Fury, although many of his friends advised him against it. I suspect that he hoped it might actually swing his sexuality but of course it didn't. He was in denial, I suppose. But his public life complicated matters further. Had the press got hold of the story, his career might well have ended right there.

As it turned out, Kenny made a pretty good job of doing that himself. The man was quite brilliant, but he just couldn't stop himself from wisecracking his way into trouble. I can't think of a DJ in this country who has been sacked more often than dear old Kenny Everett.

One of his earliest brushes with the authorities was when he sent up one of his Radio London programme sponsors. That was The Radio Church Of God, whose representative on air was an evangelist who went by the rather splendid name of Garner Ted Armstrong. Kenny had trained as a Catholic priest at college, but gave it up when he remembered that he didn't actually believe in God. "A bit of a drawback, Bessie!" I remember him telling me.

When his sponsors complained about his customary irreverence, the management at Radio London had to let him go, albeit with great reluctance, because as a commercial station, it was the sponsors and advertisers' money that kept everything going. Kenny moved over to Radio Luxembourg, but by the middle of 1966, he was back on *Big L*, and that's the period when I got to know him best.

After all that, he still couldn't keep him mouth shut. "Every time he hears Diana Ross on air, Ed Stewpot has an orgasm!" he announced to his surprised listeners one day. That indiscretion resulted in a severe reprimand rather than a sacking but that's the way Kenny conducted his career, from London to Radio One, Capital and beyond.

For all his headline-creating outbursts, Kenny was remarkably different away from the microphone. In fact, he's the perfect example to back my theory that those who are strangely shy in private often make the best radio DJs. It's as if they've stored up all that energy for the moment they're sat in that broadcast studio hot-seat. That's certainly how I remember him at *Big L* on The Kenny And Cash Show, the programme he co-hosted with Dave Cash. It drew an incredibly large and loyal audience, eager to hear Kenny's repertoire of crazy characters, including the infamous Captain Kremen who stayed with him for much of his career.

Kenny would spend hours putting his shows together in his makeshift studio at home. In that sense, he was like an experimental musician, so no one was particularly surprised when The Beatles later asked him to put together their fan club Christmas records – which got increasingly more bizarre towards the decade's end. He was forever fiddling with long strips of recording tape, cutting it up then splicing bits back together again. Whereas most of us had our own favourite themes and jingles, which we would use every day, Kenny would practically rebuild everything he used in his show on a daily basis. He was certainly the most inventive DJ I've ever heard on radio, that's for sure. The only person who came anywhere near him was Jack Johnson, a largely forgotten Light Programme broadcaster from the post-war era. His special trick was to edit bits of songs together, then add random sounds such as a cat meowing, and talk over the lot of it. I'm sure Kenny must have heard him as a schoolboy.

I ran into Kenny not too long before he died in 1995 and out of the blue he said, "You've never liked me have you, Bess." I made a joke of it at the time, saying something along the lines of, "Come on, Edith, you know that's not true!" But I was hurt by that, not least because I had absolutely no idea what I'd ever said or done to make him say it.

With major talents such as Kenny to contend with, there was a keen competitive spirit at London, though this rarely developed into the outright rivalry that would occasionally erupt at Radio One. I put that down to our alter egos. After all, it's not that easy having a showdown with someone when they're calling you "Bessie".

Perhaps that's why "Mother Superior" eventually backed down when I pleaded to keep my jokes. It was the right decision. Within weeks of me taking over the *Big L* breakfast show, Tony Windsor said, "Fair enough, sport. Your jokes are crap but you're doing well!"

It almost backfired, though, the day I read out a joke that had been sent in by a listener. "Why don't fairies have children?" I said, without giving the joke a second thought. "Because they're always going to goblin parties." Others quickly spotted the sexual connotations, and after the show, I was torn off a strip or two.

That aside, the transition to Radio London went remarkably smoothly. I was even given an occasional second show where I could play the soul records that were starting to make inroads into British pop consciousness. I was aware of discrimination and the race riots that were raging across America, but there wasn't a lot I could do about it. My mission was simply to give more people the opportunity to hear the music of urban black America and the show was the first of its kind over here.

The professionalism that ran right through the *Big L* set-up inspired me. I soon learned how to sell ads on air, casually throwing in the brand name after the pre-recorded commercial had played out. I also applied the same philosophy to the fast-growing Blackburn brand by doing something that not even Kenny Everett had thought of. One afternoon, I hired a small studio in Denmark Street, London's Tin Pan Alley, and with a group of session musicians I recorded a handful of my own jingles. Though I have absolutely no idea who played on the session that day, it could of course have been anyone from Jimmy Page to Elton John, both of whom were session men before hitting the big time. A future Led Zeppelin legend strumming away behind a troupe of sirens extolling the virtues of *"The Tony Blackburn Show"*? What a deliciously perverse thought! Whoever it was, I certainly got my money's worth out of them, because I took the jingles with me when I moved on to Radio One.

Something else I'd honed to perfection during my wonderful 12 months at Radio London was livening up those inevitable timechecks. "It's 20 *Big L* minutes past . . ." later became "20 fundable minutes past . . ." by the time I'd arrived at Radio One. I continued with this right the way through to the '90s when I was at Capital Gold, though I've given it a rest in recent years. Richard Park, television's latest Mr Nasty thanks to his hilariously churlish performances as The Headmaster on 'Fame Academy', once admitted to me that when he was a young DJ in Scotland in the late '60s he adapted the idea. In his thick Scottish brogue, he'd say, "It's now 20 Richard Park minutes past . . .". Even I didn't go that far!

Much of the criticism directed at the pirates, and at Radio One in the early days, was that we were part of an insidious Americanisation of British culture. I saw little wrong in that. In fact, I was so impressed by what I'd heard of American commercial radio that in 1965, I went over to WBAC in New York to see it first-hand. I was disappointed. Dan Ingram, a big name at the time, just seemed bored by the whole thing and sat there with his head buried in a newspaper. If you're a DJ, then surely the first rule is to listen to the music you're playing.

Radio London was doing it all so much better. That wasn't surprising. After all, it was an American owned company steeped in hard-nosed business practices that had been honed to perfection over the years. I see nothing wrong in earning a lot of money, while at the same time having plenty of fun, though in Britain we still tend to be a bit sniffy about that. I suppose it proves that the class system is still very much alive and with us. Radio London was a model business venture that enabled me to have the time of my life. Set up to usher in a new era of commercial radio, the station made a fortune, though the dream of commercial radio went unrealised – at least, until a watered-down version was rolled out during the '70s.

Big L was a cash cow, and as the presenter of its flagship breakfast show – *The Tony Blackburn Show,* no less – I was one of its prize assets. I genuinely believed in the station, so much so that on my days off, I'd help distribute T-shirts at promotional events, which took place anywhere between the Marquee in the heart of Soho to the Brand's Hatch motor-racing circuit. Rummaging through my old boxes of photographs, I even found myself posing with a chicken wrapped in cling-film in the Radio London studio. I'd stop at nothing to help raise the station's profile – save for eating that poor chicken, of course.

Two things marked out Radio London from its competitors and helped define the golden age of pop radio. What was known as the station's '*Fab 40*' format provided the blueprint for pop music broadcasting as we still know it. As I'll explain later, it's actually had a negative effect over the past decade or two, but in the mid-'60s, it was a revelation.

Essentially, the American-style formula went like this. Seven records would be played every half an hour – two from an A-list

89

selected from the Top 10, two from a B-list consisting of records from Number 11-40, plus a climber, an American hit and an oldie, what we called a 'revive 45'. Each disc would be plucked from a box, spun, then placed at the back of the box so it didn't come round again for another three hours. Rotating that simple formula throughout the day lent a remarkable consistency to the station. My only reservation was that the *Big L* sales team was so successful in pulling in advertising that sometimes we only had time to play three records in one half-hour slot.

> "I WAS MILES AWAY, LOST IN THE MUSIC OF THESE
> BITE-SIZED MASTERPIECES, MOST LASTING
> NO LONGER THAN 10 OR 15 SECONDS."

But for me, what really clinched it were those jingles. Just days ago, I decided to celebrate the arrival of the spring sun by digging out a CD that includes more than 100 of those era-defining jingles. It was the second occasion during the writing of this book that I found myself wiping tears from my eyes. I turned to my 'ghost', the writer who's been helping me on the book, and said, "This is what I joined Radio London to play". And that was absolutely true. Most people now know me as *King Of The Jungle*, and that's something I'm extremely proud of. But when it's said I'm a *King Of The Jingle* too, that truly makes me feel like radio royalty. I'm not sure if anyone's really worthy of that but those jingles are pretty hard to beat!

As one nostalgia-packed jingle followed another, many of them featuring that distinctive, electronically enhanced Sonovox voice that sounded like Sparky's *Magic Piano*, the lump in my throat kept growing. I turned to my wife, who'd just walked in the room wondering what all the noise was about. "You can never stop playing these," I said. She could see I was in no mood for talk. I was miles away, lost in the music of these bite-sized masterpieces, most lasting no longer than 10 or 15 seconds. Beautifully crafted, they are in their own way, works of art. I know I'd much rather sit and listen to these than the many thousands of records I've played over the past 40-plus years. Even Marvin Gaye's *What's Going On*, my favourite record of all time, doesn't make me feel like this.

These blink-and-you-miss-'em treasures of radio station branding came out of PAMS, the legendary jingle factory based in Dallas. PAMS had jingle writers who'd come up with a concept and tailor it to fit the station's brief. There were composers who'd dream up the incredible hooks and the studios where a team of musicians and arrangers would record the jingles. It was actually Radio England, a third pirate ship based off Frinton, which introduced the PAMS jingles to this country. Though intended for the exclusive use of a particular station, these wonderfully fresh and exciting between-song sounds were immediately pirated by Radios Caroline and London.

Jingles had been a distinctive feature of American radio since the '50s, and the essential idea was that they utilised a musical style entirely different to the music played on the station so they'd stand out. The PAMS jingles had their own particular style; essentially brassy and jazz-tinged, overlaid with fast, Easy Listening vocal harmonies. The company was very secretive about its methods, though I always thought one of their key weapons was this one particular woman who sang with an amazingly strong falsetto voice. Another, of course, was that extraordinary electronic voice effect. Many years later, I bought a machine and tried to replicate the watery vocal effect at home. It came out sounding like an amateur cluelessly fiddling about with some half-baked musical ideas in his garage – which is exactly what it was.

Knowing how to work with the jingles on air was something of an art in itself. As a vital slice of broadcasting history continued to pour out from my living-room speakers, I was all at sea, and back in that radio London studio once more. When one of the old 'doughnuts' started up – a doughnut was a jingle designed specifically for a DJ to talk over – I found myself back on air. "Hi, it's Tony Blackburn here and welcome to the wonderful sound of *Big L*. That's right, Radio London, on 266 meters medium wave . . ." Just as the doughnut ended, my finger instinctively jabbed at the imaginary turntable. I got the timing exactly right. All that was missing was the evocative hit record to follow, something like Nancy Sinatra's *These Boots Are Made For Walkin'*, a pirate station favourite back in 1966. Just as one of those jingles so tunefully claimed, *Big L* really was, *"The station with the happy difference"*.

Working with jingles is very much like piecing together a jigsaw puzzle. All the pieces are there. All that's missing is the technical know-how to create the bigger picture. And if you really knew what you were doing, like Kenny Everett, you'd bring a bit of creative flair to the table, too.

The arrival of each season's jingles was always an event on the pirate ships. The basic package would consist of between 20 and 30 jingles. But with some clever editing, you could create up to 60 or more customised jingles tailored to your own taste. Kenny was brilliant at that. He'd take one basic phrase, *"Swinging Big L"*, for example, splice it with another, say, *"It's a positive charge"*, then run the two together. It was like an early form of hip hop!

Life on the *Big L* ship was a lot of fun. Unlike at Caroline, we each had our own cabin. The vessel was big and sturdy so there were relatively few cases of sea-sickness. And the wonderful sense of unity about the place was helped by the fact that the shows were piped throughout the ship. One rumour went round suggesting that we'd all become sterile due to the massive amounts of radiation emanating from the huge aerial. Happily, I can confirm that it proved to be false.

* * *

" 'HAVE A LISTEN TO THIS,' PEEL SAID IN HIS CUSTOMARY DRAWL. 'WHAT A LOT OF CRAP!'"

One DJ who didn't quite fit into all this was John Peel. A public school-educated Liverpudlian, he'd been to the States and had done fairly well there, not least because his accent gave Anglophiles the impression that he was the fifth Beatle. And if you knew The Beatles, you were in! When he joined Radio London, around spring 1967, he no longer stood out because, apart from Dave Cash and Pete Brady, who both had connections with Canada, most of us were English.

He quickly found a new niche. Popping down to the studio one day, I came across Peel sitting alone surrounded by all these records. "Have a listen to this," he said in his customary drawl. "What a lot of crap!" But he seemed simultaneously to undergo some kind of instant revelation, because he added, "Hey, I think can make a programme out of this lot." That's how he came to create a show that was different from everything else. Days later, he was hosting a new, late night show called *The Perfumed Garden*, where he spoke in a soft, monotone voice, and read out the blurbs from the back of record sleeves.

While John Peel went underground, Kenny's sidekick Dave Cash was always desperately trying to go in the opposite direction. He was a Walter Mitty-like character, full of big ideas that never seemed to come to fruition. I think I'm right in saying that he went to Canada for a two-week holiday and came back with this big-time accent which he never quite lost! Years later, when Dave and I were at Capital Gold and he was doing the night shift, he'd still be talking about the multi-million dollar deal with The Fox Network that was just round the corner. One day, I couldn't resist saying, "Well, you're obviously gonna to chuck in the night-time DJ-ing with all that money about to come in."

"Oh no," said Dave. "Better keep my hand in . . ."

One time, though, he surprised us all. For years, he'd been telling everybody about this great novel he'd been working on. When he turned up with a dust-jacket for it, we all assumed he'd had it specially printed up for himself. We were wrong. Dave had not only finished writing it, he'd found a publisher and the book went on to become a best-seller. That was his cue for packing in the radio job, but when the follow-up didn't sell half as well, he was soon back behind the microphone again.

When The Marine Offences Bill was going through its final stages, and the writing was on the wall for the pirates, I felt particularly sad, both for Radio London and for Tony Windsor, who had taught me so much while I was there. It was always a great disappointment to me that London wasn't granted a licence to broadcast. The management even offered to bring the ship into port while they built a new studio on land, but the authorities were committed to granting the BBC a total monopoly.

Personally, after three years on the high seas, I was ready to accept the Beeb's offer and come aboard what was in many ways a dry pirate. I also wanted to bring Tony Windsor with me. It was clear to most of us at *Big L* that Tony had a drink problem and when he left to become a wine taster, that seemed to be really asking for trouble. "I don't spit it out," he told me proudly, "I drink every single bit of it!" After I'd settled in at Radio One, I wangled him an audition, hoping that the responsibility might give him a lift. But he turned up drunk and blew it. I don't think Tony really recovered after that, working mostly for hospital radio. He died in 1985.

Not all the pirates met such a sad, unnecessary end. But after the initial euphoria of those first few days at Radio One had passed, there were certainly more than a few storms for many of us in the years ahead, myself included.

* * *

TIME FOR ... BLACKMORE
THE PRODUCER: TIM BLACKMORE

The '60s witnessed an incredible music revolution supported by an equally amazing radio revolution. And, ludicrous though it may seem, Tony and I were two young men in our early 20s thrown right into the heart of it. I was producing the biggest radio programme in Britain, The Tony Blackburn Breakfast Show. He, of course, was presenting it. That was an incredibly powerful position. We regularly had audiences of 12 to 14 million, up to 20 million if you read the figures over a monthly period.

Tony was Radio One's golden boy, no doubt about it. Getting him in and out of places in the late '60s required considerable subterfuge. I remember a particular Wednesday lunchtime when he was booked to host Radio One Club or something similar at the BBC's Paris Theatre. I went down with him because it was dangerous for Tony to go places on his own back then. And the crowds outside the stage door were seriously deranged. Eventually, we managed to bundle him through the door, but I recall his light blue jacket being, if not ruined then at least seriously damaged by all those pens being waved in his direction. The Beatles were obviously top of the league in terms of national hysteria, but in the early days of Radio One, Tony was certainly hovering around the Number Five or Six mark.

I didn't produce the breakfast show from the word go. Johnny Beerling was Tony's producer for the first few weeks while I was a Production Assistant. Then, after Johnny was shunted upstairs to become an Executive Producer on December 3, 1967, I was installed as Tony's right-hand man. That meant organising his playlists, suffering his interminable jokes, trying my best to keep him off the subject of politics and – when he got his way – making the teas.

Tony and several of the other leading ex-pirate DJs, brought so much that was exciting and innovative to BBC Radio. By dispensing with the idea of a scripted show, they had more freedom to express their personalities spontaneously. The jingles added more fun. And the introduction of the rotational system, where we created our own weekly Top 40 format, gave freshness and consistency to the shows. It was our way of staying ahead of the game because, while a record might take three or four weeks to drop out of the sales chart, the moment it lost impact, we'd drop it from our own chart and replace it with something new. It meant that the DJ was always leading from the front, giving the listeners something new to talk about.

The first potential conflict I recall was over a 1968 single called *Eloise*, sung by Barry Ryan and co-written with his brother Paul, who just happened to be the stepsons of Tony's manager Harold Davison. Tony, who heard it first, said, "We really ought to make it our record of the week." I said, "Are you kidding? If the press get wind of you heavily promoting your agent's stepson's record, you're gonna get shit left, right and centre."

I knew that Tony believed it was simply a great song, though Barry and Paul's mother Marion Ryan would no doubt have been expecting some support. Tony probably thought I was being a bastard by putting my foot down, but I was only protecting him. Luckily, it was a brilliant record and went all the way to Number One, so every DJ – Tony included – was able to play it without fear of being accused of unfair patronage.

I know we all think of Tony as an 'entertainment first' kind of DJ, and for good reason, but he has left his mark on popular music. The work he did on behalf of Motown was phenomenal, championing that kind of music when many of the other DJs were seeking out more esoteric sounds from the domestic market. But what he doesn't really receive any credit for is digging out the Phil Spector *Christmas Album* every year. We always hear its wonderful songs played now each Christmas, but there was a time after its release in '63 until Tony picked up on it when it was virtually ignored.

My parents, Pauline and Ken, on their wedding day, in 1942.

The earliest surviving photo of me, at around 18 months, doing my bit for the war effort.

I won a sports scholarship to Millfield, where I soon captained the cricket team.

"Here's lookin' at you, kid!" With my dorm mates at Millfield, circa 1957.

Aged 16 in 1959. An aspiring Teddy Boy strips down to his trunks.

Move over Alvin Stardust and Shakin' Stevens! Mean and moody with my first love Sally McKenzie.

Spiv-like and accompanying my girlfriend Sally McKenzie, the first lucky lady in my life!

This is how the *Mi Amigo*, home of pirate radio station Radio Caroline, looked from the tender ship as we were about to board for another two-week stint on ship.

On board the *Mi Amigo* with, to my left, the engineer known only as 'The Child Scientist' and two members of the Dutch crew.

Spinning the sounds of the Swinging '60s aboard the *Mi Amigo*. It was 1964, and it was my first job in broadcasting.

Cruising along the Bournemouth seafront in my new MGB sports car. I was 21, and had just joined Radio Caroline.

On the good ship *Mi Amigo* with the Radio Caroline Good Guys. That's me with Keith Skues on the far left. Singer Twinkle provides a rare touch of glamour on board.

The MV *Galaxy*, the converted US minesweeper, that for a wonderful year during the mid '60s became my home as a DJ for Radio London.

Move over David Bailey!
A publicity shot for a camera
by the looks of things.

My *Big L* colleague, the quite
brilliant Kenny Everett, in
characteristically "zany" pose.

Inside the *Big L*'s studio.
The set up was far more
professional than I'd been
used to on Caroline.

Robin Scott (centre back) with his Rogues' Gallery of new Radio One DJs, on the steps of All Souls Church, September 1967. Front row from left: Pete Murray, Ed Stewart, Pete Drummond, Mike Raven, Mike Ahern, John Peel.

Middle row: Bob Holness, Terry Wogan, Barry Alldis, Mike Lennox, Keith Skues, Chris Denning, Johnny Moran, Pete Myers. Back row: Me, Jimmy Young, Kenny Everett, Duncan Johnson, Robin Scott, David Ryder, Dave Cash, Pete Brady, David Symonds.

Lapsed would-be priest Kenny Everett gets down on his knees and prays that the new station will be a success. It was!

In 'Continuity A', my studio at Broadcasting House, preparing for the first day of Radio One – just another fun day at the office.

A staged publicity shot for the opening up of Radio One. I'd have to be up at 5am for my breakfast show – but with up to 20 million eager listeners, it was worth it!

Preparing to open up Radio One with my producer Johnny Beerling. He later became the station's Controller – despite being associated with me!

A publicity shot taken in Hyde Park during the early days of Radio One. Quite painful by the look of things!

Taking my job judging a mini-skirt contest extremely seriously.

Someone said, "Leg it!", so I did. Definitely a perk of the job.

On the London to Brighton vintage car race, with four-wheel enthusiast Lord Montagu (left).

With my Playboy Bunny Girl girlfriend Lynn Partington, on holiday in Spain in the late '60s.

At a book-signing session for *The Tony Blackburn Annual.*

Another superstore opens! Cutting ribbons provided a useful second income for me during my radio heyday.

Tony's in town. There's nothing like a good mobbing!

At the faders in the old Radio One studio. It's a late '60s shot, as the shirt, a Carnaby Street special, loudly confirms.

It was typical of Tony to make a big thing of Christmastime. Fun was integral to his style, although I can't say I laughed at every joke he made on air. Or any joke he made on air! You'd think; 'For Christ's sake, that was appalling'. But the point is it worked because he knew they were appalling. And, of course, everyone would arrive at school, or the office or the factory floor saying, "Did you hear what Tony Blackburn said this morning?"

That self-deprecating approach has been a very clever move. In a way, it's a form of protection. If you make yourself appear vulnerable by putting yourself down all the time, you can hardly be accused of being arrogant or pompous.

The reality is that, in his heart of hearts, Tony knows that he's actually a bloody good broadcaster. The testimony to that is the fact that he's in his 60s and he's still working in frontline radio. Many of his colleagues from the '60s and '70s have disappeared without trace. The fact that Tony's still there says that he knows what he's doing and that he's getting it right.

There are times when he doesn't get it right; usually those aberrations when he decides that he wants to become a political commentator. It's always a mistake. He's crap at it! He's an entertainer who, fundamentally, works in the area of candyfloss. And he does that magnificently. In British broadcasting, balance must be achieved, and you knew that Tony, given his personal political views, was never going to offer a balanced view on anything. Just don't do it! He's Mr *Daily Mail*.

TONY: *I've never said what political party I'm with.*

You don't need to! I'm not accusing you of being a fascist . . .

TONY: *It's middle England.*

It's an attitude, a belief that most things can be summed up in simple black and white. I believe that most truths can be found in an infinite range of shades of grey.

> TONY: *Whereas I'd say, for example, if someone takes somebody else's life, hang 'em . . .*

. . . And I'd want to debate the circumstances.

> TONY: *You don't need that. You only need a rope!*

Don't you think we should talk about our Records Of The Week? We'd always choose the Record Of The Week together, and the statistics show that we had something like a 50% success rate. That was pretty damn good, bearing in mind that out of all the records released in any given week, only 3-4% would make it into the Top 40. It's fun leafing through some of our comments on the old paperwork. Here's a sheaf of notes from 1970. Tony on Canned Heat's *Future Blues* – "Drag". That doesn't surprise me. They were hairy white bluesmen. Bread's *Make It With You* is rated "Beautiful", Elton John's *Rock'n'Roll Madonna*, "Terrible", Melanie's *Lay Down*, "Terrible", Joni Mitchell's *Big Yellow Taxi*, "Terrible", Lulu's *Got To Believe In Love*, "Very irritating" and Jethro Tull's *Inside*, "Very ordinary". Want more? Hotlegs' *Neanderthal Man* is declared "a hit but hate it", though my favourite is the comment beside Sly & The Family Stone's *I Want To Take You Higher* – "Rubbish!" You seemed more interested in Pickettywitch's *That Same Old Feeling. . .*

> TONY: *A Top Five hit, that one! I must add that I thought the little blonde singer was quite beautiful. It was terrific fun trying to spot the hit records. And I'm still playing some of them 40 years later . . .*

On my station! Until very recently, when we were bought out, I was the chairman of the company that owned Classic Gold, where Tony's been hosting the breakfast show for several years. We hadn't worked together since the summer of '71 when I got moved on to work with Noel Edmonds, Jimmy Savile and Stuart Henry. I also worked on my own radio documentary series, *The Story Of Pop.*

In many ways, it's clear that Tony and I are chalk and cheese. There's much we don't agree on. But I am an enormous admirer of what he's achieved over the past 40 or so years. Take it from me: he's nowhere near as daft as he looks!

5

THE BIGGEST BREAKFAST

From the late '60s to the mid-'70s, Radio One was the nation's jukebox. It notched up incredible audiences, with up to 20 million listeners for the breakfast show, a figure that would slowly, inevitably tail off as the day progressed. As a consequence, a Radio One disc jockey became at least as famous as many of the pop stars he – or in the case of Anne Nightingale, she – played on air.

The opportunities to let this power go to you head were manifold. There was an endless stream of record pluggers eager to wine and dine you in the hope that you'd play one or two of the records from the box they'd generously brought along with them. Wherever you went, and invitations galore would always be rolling in, there'd be a generous supply of women ready to throw themselves at you. You'd be fussed over by administrators at BBC Radio, flattered by the press, and treated like a hero whenever you rolled into a provincial town to open up a club or a supermarket. I'd always found it the most natural thing in the world to keep my feet on the ground, and – jokes about being "a living legend" aside – was unusually self-deprecating for a young man in my position. But it was observing at close quarters the incredible rise and calamitous fall of the era's most talked about DJ that taught me the perils of stardom. He was the shining star who one minute had it all before him, and the next was a yesterday man queuing up to sign on at Fulham Labour Exchange.

When I first met Simon Dee, he was the rising star at Radio Caroline and an utterly charming man. I liked and respected him, and wasn't at all surprised when his defection to the BBC soon resulted in him being given his own television chat show, complete with his own personal hair stylist. The programme was called *Dee Time*, and it was televised twice a week, prime time, throughout 1967 and '68. In a matter of months, Simon Dee had become a household name.

Just weeks into my new career at Radio One, one of the many offers that came flooding in was the opportunity to resume my recording career. And that's how, one evening at BBC's Television Centre in White City, I found myself in close proximity to Britain's most talked about personality. I say 'in close proximity' because by this time, the television host did not encourage face time.

The recording of the show started off well, with the warm-up guy building it all up in the traditional manner: "Ladies and gentlemen, welcome to Television Centre. And now, your host for the evening, Mr Simon Dee!" And on he strolled, looking every inch the perfect, self-made '60s man – tall, handsome, cool and attractively blond. If he'd had stopped there, he would have won a standing ovation. But he didn't. "Right, tickets are difficult to get for this show," he said, deadpan. "So if I say something funny, laugh." No one was quite sure if he was actually trying to be funny. He wasn't. With a look of bored disinterest in his face, Dee turned away from the audience, said, "Gimme a camera", and that was it. Everybody in the room took an instant dislike to him, and I can't say I blamed them.

It wasn't long afterwards when, on route to see my agent in Regent Street, I spotted Simon sitting in a café. I couldn't resist getting to the bottom of his extraordinary personality change. "Why is it that you're terribly rude to people?" I asked once we'd exchanged a few pleasantries. He didn't quite get my meaning at first. Then I reminded him of his offhand studio manner, how he'd showed absolutely no warmth to the audience, and then treated the cameraman like dirt. He said, straight-faced, "But I'm Simon Dee". "Yes, but Simon, these are work colleagues doing their job. The audience is there because they like you. Don't you see that they'll talk behind your back and say how awful you are?" I might as well have been talking to a deaf man. "But I'm Simon Dee," he repeated.

He was still Simon Dee as the '70s got underway, but by then, everyone was past caring. His monstrous ego had done for him, and Simon simply slipped out of the public eye and into anonymity. A little later, Radio Two stepped in to help rescue his career, but his old ways were still intact and before long he was gone again. Then a local station, decided to give him a go. On the first day, he was supposed to interview Gary Glitter, but he flatly refused. "I don't like Gary Glitter," he said, and stormed off. (Perhaps he knew something we didn't. This was years before Glitter's career was ruined by his convictions for underage sex.)

Simon Dee's meteoric rise and fall was a masterclass in how not to play the celebrity game and I memorised it. When I ran into him again, long after he'd faded from public memory, I asked him why he thought it had all gone wrong. "I just couldn't take the publicity," he said. That mystified me. "What was there not to take?" I asked. "Well, pretty much everything," he said, his voice trailing off.

Although Simon chose to believe the hype, I also blame the people around him for letting it get out of hand. Both his agent, Bunny Lewis, and Billy Cotton Jr, Head of Light Entertainment at BBC-TV, were all, "Yes, Simon, no, Simon, three bags full, Simon." That's no way to treat a normal human being, let alone a highly paid celebrity, who if anything ought to be more grateful than most for their elevated standing in life. My agent Harold Davison would never have allowed me to lose sight of who I was – even if I'd wanted to.

"TAKE EVERY OPPORTUNITY THAT COMES, BECAUSE IT MIGHT NOT COME AGAIN TOMORROW".

That didn't mean I was without ambition, or that Harold wasn't doing his best to build me up as one of the country's most recognised personalities. Far from it. Obviously, there had been an element of luck – right place, right time – along the route to Radio One, but you have to possess talent to pull it off. The listening figures seemed to indicate that I had had some of that too. But I was acutely aware that I'd been handed a golden opportunity, and I had no intention of passing up anything that came my way so long as it wouldn't harm my career. In that respect, Harold Davison was right behind me. His attitude was always, "Take every opportunity that comes, because it might not come again tomorrow". And for the next ten years, until Harold left London to work on the American West Coast, that's exactly what I did.

Harold Davison was one of the most important men in British entertainment, an agent, manager and promoter who handled everyone from Frank Sinatra and Liza Minnelli to The Dave Clark Five and Engelbert Humperdinck. He promoted tours featuring Jimi Hendrix and Pink Floyd, and as the agent for Kenny Everett, Ed Stewart and myself, he'd gained a firm foothold in the DJ business. But I was the only one of the three he chose to manage. Even though singing brothers Paul and Barry Ryan were his stepsons, via his marriage to '50s vocalist Marion Ryan, he treated me like a favourite son. And I regarded him very much as my second father.

Whenever we went to dinner or a function, such as a major boxing match, he would always have me sit beside him. To those who were paid to take note of entertainment industry etiquette, which usually meant the heads of TV and radio channels, that counted for a lot. His patronage certainly helped smooth things along when Harold decided it was time I was seen on television a bit more often. He'd say, "Get Tony on *The Eamonn Andrews Show* and I'll see what I can do about that *Sinatra Christmas Special.*" He had tremendous bargaining power, and together with Lew (later Lord) Grade, it often seemed as if the pair of them had the British entertainment industry sewn up.

They even looked alike. Both were Jewish and had that classic showbiz agent look – well built, a little tubby even, with this massive great cigar stuffed in their mouth. Harold smoked cigars that were so long that, on my way out of his office one day, he shut the door on it. I had to knock on the door and hand him back the lit half!

During autumn 1967, and with my Radio One career settling down, offers started coming in from all angles. It wasn't all night club appearances and supermarket openings either. I judged beauty contests, wrote columns for a national newspaper, signed off a Tony Blackburn Annual and handled endless requests from my fan club secretary, Mel. There was major league stuff to deal with too. I became a regular presenter on BBC-TV's flagship pop programme, *Top Of The Pops*, which I continued to appear on for the next two decades. Most exciting of all were two quite unbelievable offers. One was a lucrative recording contract with MGM Records. The other was to present my own television show.

* * *

"AS THE OLD JOKE GOES, I ALWAYS FELT AS IF I HAD THE PERFECT FACE FOR RADIO."

Sitting down in front of the television is my favourite past-time. I love it; I could watch it for hours. Remember that character Peter Sellers played in *Being There*, the one who sat in front of the box all the time? Well, that's me! When I lived alone in Kensington during the 1980s, I'd sometimes watch it for 17 or 18 hours on the trot. In that respect, I'm a natural couch potato. And I don't go along with those self-styled experts who reckon that television is the root of all evil, either. I've learnt a hell of a lot – about nature, politics, the world, people – from it. It's enormous fun, too, especially *Coronation Street*. I've hardly missed an episode since the series began, in 1960. It's brilliantly written, often hilariously so, and it's given us so many wonderful small screen characters over the decades. The only one I didn't take to was the blonde bombshell barmaid Bet Lynch. In interviews, the actress who played her, Julie Goodyear, obviously thought of herself as Queen Of The Street. As all Corrie addicts know, no one character is bigger than the Street itself – and of course the show has continued to flourish in her absence.

One of the great things about the soaps is that everyone watches them. They give people something to talk about the next morning, and I rather like that, the feeling that you have at least something in common with your workmates. I love the fact that Sky has revolutionised our way of watching television in recent years, especially with SkyPlus, which just has to be my favourite televisual invention ever. But it is sad that with so much choice, we're all doing different things in our spare time now. I suppose it's inevitable that this has contributed to the breakdown of our sense of community.

Back in 1967, everyone young and old knew exactly who Michael Miles and Hughie Green were. That's because everyone watched their massively successful light entertainment quiz shows, *Take Your Pick* and *Opportunity Knocks*. Me, too. These relatively unexceptional middle-aged men were huge stars but they weren't necessarily naturals. I mean, Michael Miles looked extremely awkward as he supervised the 'Yes/No' game ("And the next one please!"). Eamonn Andrews, too, was far from relaxed. He hosted one of the top talk shows of the day, and was a terribly nice man, but you couldn't have a proper conversation with him on camera because he stuck so rigidly to his questions. I remember him perspiring a lot, too, hardly a hallmark of a TV natural. But as I was soon to discover, television was not nearly as easy as it looks.

When Harold Davison told me he'd lined up pilots for me to present two different television pop programmes, I was ecstatic. The ink was barely dry on my initial, one-year contract with Radio One (almost everyone else worked on the basis of eight-week trial contracts at the start) before I found myself talking into a camera. If I'm being ruthlessly honest, I wasn't totally comfortable being chased around by a cameraman on wheels or memorising my lines, but Southern Television seemed to like what I did and commissioned me to present my own series.

Pilots and working titles such as *New Release* and *As You Like It* were soon discarded. Instead, I was to host a new 13-week television series titled, quite simply, *Time For Blackburn*. Screened at 9.30pm every week through spring and summer 1968, the advance publicity claimed it to be "a new style pop show". In truth, it was little different to most other television pop programmes. I'd host a discussion of the merits of the latest pop 45s, and stars such as Sandie Shaw and The Amen Corner would come in and plug their latest releases. The most memorable guest was a singer called Arthur Brown, something of a cult hero on the hippie underground circuit, who chose my show to debut his dramatic new act for the wider masses. Backed by his sinister looking group The Crazy World, Brown was part way through his new song, *Fire*, when we suddenly realised that the blazing helmet of fire he wore on his head had got out of control. The singer literally had caught fire, and if it wasn't for the quick thinking of one of the security guards who quickly located a fire extinguisher, that could have been it for crazy Arthur. But we managed to save him, which was just as well because *Fire* went on to become a massive hit that summer.

In fact, the song fared rather better than my television career. The show ran for the best part of two years, but it was really hard work. And, unlike radio, I never felt completely at ease with the medium. That was primarily because I was under a lot of pressure during the late '60s. I'd be up at 5am to prepare for the breakfast show, I was also hosting a programme for Radio Luxembourg, putting in plenty of personal appearances during the daytimes and evenings. Finding time to prepare for a weekly television show, which was difficult because it would involve a full team of people, was not easy.

I was doing so much during this period that, in one exhausting week, I was getting just two hours sleep a night. It was getting like a treadmill, and though I tried my best to get on with it, my body eventually gave up and I collapsed with exhaustion. It was obvious to the TV show's producer Mike Mansfield (another Harold Davison protégé) and his team that I was starting to crack up, because I couldn't remember any of my lines. I wasn't particularly happy with their solution, which was that we drop the section of the show where I'd sing one of my songs, but I understood that something had to give.

The other problem was that, despite all those "Most Eligible Bachelor In Britain" headlines, I was never really confident with myself in the looks department. I always felt as if I had the perfect face for radio, as the old joke goes. I get an odd feeling flicking through those old scrapbooks now and coming across some of the generous comments about me by some of the era's leading entertainment writers. Here's Lionel Crane in the *Sunday Mirror*, October 8, 1967: "[Blackburn] is good looking, very good looking, with wide spaced blue eyes that thousands of girls are already longing to look into." A wonderful writer, obviously! And good old Lionel wasn't the only one. I have absolutely no recollection of reading any such thing at the time, but I suppose I must have done.

What I do clearly remember is experiencing the most terrifying self doubt whenever someone wheeled a television camera in my direction. When I catch a rare sighting of some old black-and-white footage from the show, I notice that I tended to hop about from one leg to the other and nod my head a little too eagerly, both obvious signs of nerves. I was extremely self-conscious, always had been, and continued to suffer from the awful delusion that I wasn't God's gift to women after all for many years afterwards! It doesn't bother me in the slightest now, of course. Stick me in front of a television camera and I'll not even know it's there. It does makes me laugh when I'm visibly collapsing in front of the nation on Supermarket Sweep or something equally daft and fun, and some young production assistant will come up and say, "It's remarkable! You haven't aged at all." All very nice, of course, but I always want to say, "Put your glasses on and you'll see that the picture's not quite as good as you think!"

"NOT EVEN I HAVE BEEN GRIPPED BY AN UNQUENCHABLE DESIRE TO HEAR MYSELF SING THE WHITE CLIFFS OF DOVER."

Despite the private pitfalls, television was wonderful exposure for me, and I hoped it would be the key that would at last unlock this ex-pirate's best-concealed treasure – the Tony Blackburn singing career. On October 24, 1967 I signed a three-year recording deal with MGM that, it was reported, would earn me £50,000 a year. I think that last statistic was a bit of myth-making on Harold's part, but everything else was deadly serious. Even the record label had high hopes that I'd become a top-selling balladeer. If that sounds unlikely in an era when Jimi Hendrix was burning his guitar and The Rolling Stones were regularly in court answering drug charges, think again. The three best-selling singles that year were all by Engelbert Humperdinck. Anita Harris, Frankie Vaughan and Tom Jones each had entries in the year's Top Ten best sellers. The phrase on everyone's lips might have been 'All You Need Is Love'. But all they needed on the radiogram at home seemed to be good old-fashioned ballads and melodies.

There seemed to be room for everyone in the charts that winter -- except for me. It was all rather unfortunate because the record company had predicted that my first single, a romantic ballad titled *So Much Love*, was a contender for the Number One spot. I'd appeared on several prime-time television shows, including *Juke Box Jury* and *The Val Doonican Show*, to promote the song. Early demand for the record was terrific, and in its first week, it zoomed straight in at Number 31. It was just my luck that staff at the pressing plant chose that moment to call a strike and bring production to a standstill. All that exposure, and yet no records in the shops. By the time the machines started turning again, my moment of one-hit-wonder pop glory had passed.

Instead of being a fondly remembered golden oldie like Engelbert's *The Last Waltz*, *So Much Love* provides a mere footnote in *The Guinness Book Of Hit Singles*. But at least it's there, alongside *It's Only Love*, which made it to Number 42 in spring 1969. Elvis Presley covered the song too, though he had a little more success with it than I did.

I'm not suggesting I would have given Elvis or Cliff Richard, two singers whose styles I told interviewers I was hoping to emulate -- anything to worry about. Actually, I can't believe I ever mentioned their names alongside mine in the same breath. That's got to rate as one of the most conceited things I've ever said! In truth, I have a very average singing voice, I can hold a tune, and that's about it. When the subsequent album, *Tony Blackburn Sings*, failed to induce mass hysteria among the record-buying public, I knew that singing would be little more than an entertaining sideline to my career. Well, entertaining for me, anyway . . .

I dug a copy out the other day. It didn't look as if it had seen much turntable action in years. Not even I have been gripped by an unquenchable desire to hear myself sing *The White Cliffs Of Dover*. But I did enjoy the liner notes, which I'd completely forgotten about, written by my good friend Richard "Sally" Swainson. After a preamble that refers to my habit of inventing songs on the spot in my cabin on the pirate ships, Richard soon got to the real point of the piece:

> *"I think Tony's main appeal has always been due to the sincere attitude he's put into everything he does. He really enjoys his work as a disc jockey and enjoys singing, as you will hear when you listen to his first album. Many of the numbers found on this album I think will surprise a lot of people but this is another young personality who I think could develop into one of the year's best sellers on record."*

Nice one, Richard! But I don't think even that I fell for that one.

"COMPARED TO THE ROLLING STONES, I WAS A NO DRUGS, NO CIGGIES, LIGHT DRINKING GOODIE-GOODIE."

I knew what I did best, and that was presenting the Radio One breakfast show. It was the most popular weekday programme in the country, and as the listening figures continued to rise, so too did my popularity. Robin Scott, Controller of Radio One and Two, famously kept a league table of fan mail that would arrive by the sackload at Broadcasting House. Within a month of the station's launch, I topped the table comfortably with 2,500 letters. My nearest competitor was Jimmy Young with 2,000. Next up was David Symonds with 1,000, closely followed by Pete Brady. When the *News Of The World* ran its own poll in October 1967, the paper reported that I'd picked up two-thirds of the total votes cast, and that I'd trounced second-placed Simon Dee by a ratio of six to one. I rather enjoyed researching this part of the book! Just as I was about to close the file, another poll revealed itself, this time for *The Daily Mail*. Once again, I was firmly in first place, this time followed by my old Radio London colleague Kenny Everett.

Much of my publicity concentrated on apparent wholesomeness, and I went along with it, describing myself as "so clean I almost squeaked", and as "a kind of Cliff without the religion". None of it was entirely true, of course, but I was in the hands of the best public relations man in the business, a real gentleman named Les Perrin. I was in no position to argue with his cleanliness first strategy. Les was a short, round jolly man, who moved slowly but was as sharp as a pin when it came to looking after the public lives of his clients. He also handled The Rolling Stones, then the most troublesome group on the pop scene, so I suppose he must have enjoyed the contrast when he sat down with me – a no drugs, no ciggies, light drinking goodie-goodie in comparison – to discuss new publicity angles. They were the bad boys of British pop. I was the golden boy from Radio One.

Les, who introduced me to all the national journalists at his favourite watering hole, *The Wig & Pen* in Fleet Street, built me up like a pop star. I was on the cover of glossy magazines such as *Fab 208*, admiring the scenery at glamorous events such as the *Gorgeous Girls Gala*, and putting the pop world to rights in my regular column for *The Daily Sketch*. Actually, Les wrote that himself, though he'd always run the topics past me each week. Revisiting these in the scrapbooks lovingly kept by my mother, I was particularly surprised at how outspoken I was, thanks to Les. I advised Elvis to pack up and quit, described Sinatra as "a bit dated", and dismissed jazz music completely! I came out as "an unashamed pop man", and named The Temptations, Four Tops, The Miracles, The Supremes, The Hollies, The Beatles, The Small Faces, Cliff Richard and The Bee Gees as the cream of the Class of '67. Forty years later, I'm still happy to stand by those names.

DO YOU KNOW, I THINK IT'S TIME FOR A TOP TEN...

If I was choosing a list of favourites today, I'd no doubt include names such as Luther Vandross, Spandau Ballet and Beyonce. Fear not. I will be inflicting my contemporary tastes on you later on in the book. But because we're at the point that coincides with what many people regard as a golden era of pop, I've dug out a dog-eared list of my ten favourite records as selected by me late in 1967 for a music paper. And so, in no particular order . . .

MY SHIP IS COMING IN
The Walker Brothers

This was the last record I played on Radio London before I left to join Radio One. It was a great one to finish on, wasn't it? This was one of the group's last hits before their lead vocalist, Scott Walker, began a solo career. He was a complicated fellow, didn't like the limelight at all. But he had the most magnificent singing voice. Still has, probably.

YOU'RE THE ONE I LOVE
The Miracles

I have no idea why I chose this. There are plenty of other Smokey Robinson songs I'd go for above this one. In the original article, I described it as a minor hit, but also the best record on the Tamla label. Perhaps I was trying to show off a bit.

REACH OUT, I'LL BE THERE
The Four Tops

Now this truly is one of the best Tamla records ever. It's got so much energy, both in the stop-start beat and the vocals, and it's one of those records that just never sounds dated. I still use it in the act today – I put it on and encourage the crowd to raise their hands in the air and reach out. Never fails!

YOU'LL NEVER GET TO HEAVEN
Dionne Warwick

This is a beautiful song, especially written for Dionne by my favourite songwriter, Burt Bacharach. Her voice is magnificent, the music quirkily catchy, and the lyrics, as so often with Bacharach & David songs, are memorable and beautifully romantic. That's pretty much everything you want from a pop ballad. I once went to see Burt Bacharach in concert. He comes out and plays the piano, but he's got an awful singing voice, so often out of tune. It was like watching an episode of Fame Academy! But his songs are so good it doesn't matter. He's got real presence on stage, too. Oddly, that's just what Dionne lacked when I saw her in concert. She sang beautifully, but I don't think she managed to touch her audience emotionally. It was all a bit cold. Her version of Burt's *Walk On By* was tremendous too, but it's one of those songs that gets rotated endlessly on the Gold radio stations, and that's killed it a bit for me. I'd much rather listen to the album Burt recorded with Elvis Costello, proof that he's still got that special touch. Perhaps he should be writing for Joss Stone. She's got an incredibly soulful voice, but I don't think she's picked the right songs yet.

YOU'VE LOST THAT LOVIN' FEELIN'
Righteous Brothers

When I hear a song as good as this, I always wonder whether everyone in the studio realises that they've just recorded a masterpiece. I suppose a lot of the power of this pirate ship favourite comes from the unique sound created by producer Phil Spector. He's turned out to be yet another pop eccentric, but he really knew how to make unique sounding records, as his hits with The Ronettes and the Crystals prove. The Spector Wall Of Sound is as distinctive as the Motown Sound or, in the early '70s, the Philadelphia Sound. It's never the same when someone else re-records one of his hits.

DON'T WORRY BABY
Beach Boys

The fascinating thing about The Beach Boys is that while the sound they make is full of fun, their private lives seem to have been a total mess. God only knows how they managed to notch up so many hits! I've been going to see them live since the '60s, and their concerts became more enjoyable as they got older. When I last saw them a few years back, everyone turned up dressed in shorts, Hawaiian shirts, throwing beach balls around the venue, the whole bit. It was an absolute party. The group send themselves up, even Brian Wilson. I love it when an audience turns up determined to have fun, rather than sit back with that "Entertain me" attitude. I don't think the group quite hit those high notes like they used to, but you're having so much fun you'd forgive them anything. And besides, they're The Beach Boys, the group that more than anyone else sum up the happy-go-lucky vibe of the '60s era. I'd take The Beach Boys over The Beatles any day.

FLOWERS IN THE RAIN
The Move

Back in 1967, I described this in my usual manner – "Terrific!" I suppose I had to. It was the song I'd chosen to open Radio One and one with which I'll forever be associated. It's not something I'd necessarily sit down and listen to for pleasure, but it's a bright, cheery record that certainly fitted the bill that first Saturday morning. I particularly liked the fact that it began with that crashing rainstorm effect, and its opening phrase, "Woke up one morning half-asleep", was just the job for a 7am start! It was important, too, that we launched Radio One with a British record. Yes, for the first time in my career, I think I actually put a bit of thought into something. Never happened since, of course!

WHISPERS
Jackie Wilson

I played this on air only last weekend. Jackie Wilson is the man who turned me on to soul music, and for me it's always a close call between this and Lonely Teardrops, which has that incredible note at the end.

It's the orchestration that gets me on these records, and some of The Drifters' early songs too, quite advanced for the era. In the original 1967 interview, I described Jackie Wilson as "the best artist in the world". I have to say that I've changed my mind since. Marvin Gaye's the one for me. He's the undisputed king of soul music.

STRAWBERRY FIELDS FOREVER
The Beatles

While their early Beatlemania hits were obviously very effective pop songs, I thought The Beatles became a lot more interesting after they started taking drugs. Strawberry Fields Forever was a truly beautiful single, though I could've done without that long, drawn-out ending. A Day In The Life was another good example where the drugs worked. I couldn't tell you anything about the LSD experience, though. No one offered me any drugs until I was in my 40s!

WHAT THE WORLD NEEDS NOW
Jackie DeShannon

I chose this back in '67 because it chimed perfectly with The Summer Of Love, but it's a lovely song with a message that's probably even more relevant today. It encourages me to fantasise about my dream world, free from cruelty and violence. I think instead about an English country garden, a clear blue sky, and the sun beaming down brightly on Doris Day in her prime serenading me with *Secret Love*. Now that would be wonderful. But as 1967 turned into 1968, it was obvious that the world needed a lot more of Jackie DeShannon's "love, sweet love" and rather less of the anger and violence that seemed to erase all the peace vibes preached by the hippies.

"KENNEDY WAS YOUNG, DYNAMIC AND DETERMINED TO MAKE POSITIVE CHANGES. AND THEN SOME IDIOT SHOT HIM."

Now, this might surprise some of you, but I was at the mass demonstration outside the American Embassy in Grosvenor Square that spring – not to vent my anger, but to see what was going on. I didn't like too much of what I witnessed. I detest war, and it annoys me that politicians often act before they think, with the result that thousands of innocent civilians get caught up in their dirty work. But what I didn't like about this famous anti-Vietnam War demo was the depth of anti-American feeling. As a nation, they are generally a get up and go people who think positively and are not held back by class snobbery as we still are.

John F. Kennedy epitomised many of the good things about America. He was young, dynamic and determined to make positive changes. And then some idiot shot him. I mean, what a stupid thing to do! His peace-chasing brother Robert suffered the same fate five years later, in spring 1968. But you only have to see how Tony Blair has changed over the past decade to understand that however good the original intention, power eventually corrupts everyone. I'm sure the same would have happened to Kennedy.

I'm afraid that I'm rather fatalistic when it comes to politics. The world seems far too complicated a place for any one person to come in and do something about it. One minute, America is selling arms to a country that it regards as a friend. The next, the same country has been demonised as an enemy. Where's the sense in that? It might sound simplistic, but I can't help thinking that they all talk a load of old rubbish – probably a lot more even than I do!

There was one brief moment, fairly early on in my Radio One career, when I feared that I was caught up in a something beyond my control. It was a little after five in the morning, and I'd just shut the door of my flat in Knightsbridge, and was about to get in my car and drive to work. I suddenly found myself surrounded by a group of youths, who bundled me into the back of a car. They roughed me up a bit, actually, and I had no idea what was going on. It turned out that they were students who decided to kidnap me in the hope of getting a message read out on air. It misfired because after driving me out to Heathrow, they rang up the BBC and insisted that they'd hang on to me until their message was broadcast. The Beeb flatly refused, and I thought, "Thanks a lot. So that's how much my employers value me!" I'm not a big fan of practical jokes, especially those that interfere with my work, so I wasn't particularly pleased by the episode.

"I NEVER UNDERSTOOD IT WHEN CRITICS COMPLAINED THAT I TALKED TOO MUCH."

For all the publicity about my corn-loving, on-air persona, I took my job very seriously indeed. Fun and laughter was integral to my show, but I kept a tight reign on the humour, never letting it stray into smut or cheap jibes at other people's expense. Some might say that didn't leave room for much else, and they may well be right. But with children getting ready for school, one liners such as "I saw a dog the other day that was so lazy its fleas had to scratch themselves" were, I thought, exactly what was required. Oh, it was a terrible business, but someone had to do it!

From start to finish, *The Tony Blackburn Show*, as it was soon known – the Beeb had quickly woken up to the fact that their new roster of DJs were stars in their own right – was intended as fun, energetic and informative. And between the jokes, the jingles and the most ludicrous contests we could think of (we once held a Miss Knobbly Knees competition – on air!), I'd squeeze in one or two records as well. The show's original title, *Daily Disc Delivery*, was as uninspiring as its concept. What's the point of a DJ if he's just going to spin one record after another and say little more than the bare minimum in between?

I never understood it when critics – and it was usually only critics – complained that the Radio One DJs, me especially, talked too much. In particular, they seemed to hate it when we spoke over the first few bars of a song. But they didn't have a clue what they were talking about. There was a very good reason for that, which was that the show would sound very sluggish if you didn't. The art is to finish speaking just as the singer's voice comes in.

"IS IT RIGHT THAT THIS MAN IS BEING PAID MORE THAN THE PRIME MINISTER?"

I was not in a position to be able to answer that question, posed in one of the broadsheets shortly after the launch of Radio One. But I do know that the late '60s and early '70s was the heyday of the big image broadcaster. On my Radio One breakfast debut, I'd joked, "You know that expression 'the worst is yet to come'? It's not true. I'm here." Once I'd settled in, though, I began to playfully wrestle with the idea that I was God's gift to broadcasting. It was the biggest joke of all, of course, because though we all were potential Simon Dee's in the making, I don't think I've intentionally refused to sign an autograph in my life.

Being surrounded by a heaving crowd with a police escort struggling to hold them back? There's no point in being blasé about it – I loved every minute of it! There's nothing like a good mobbing. That's what I can't understand when I meet someone in the business who says, "Oh, it does annoy me when somebody comes up and asks for an autograph". Or these people who complain when they're being photographed as they're leaving a club. If you don't want any of that, there's always someone else who does, and who'll appreciate it too. It's when the paparazzi don't want to take your photograph that you've got to start worrying. It's the audience that keeps you where you are. Without it, you're nothing.

I wasn't stupid. I was well aware that my Mr Nice image wouldn't go down well with everyone. I'm not mad about that miserable ex-Smiths singer Morrissey, but I think he touched a nerve with one of his song titles: *We Hate It When Our Friends Become Successful.* Envy is a very British thing, and for every few thousand happy listeners of my show, there was always one person in the Radio One Roadshow audience who took it upon himself to boo me.

Part of my act was to walk on and say, "I'll stand here for a moment and let you admire me". It was so obviously tongue in cheek, but there were always a few blockheads who didn't get it and had to respond. Their girlfriends always seemed to, which I suppose only made matters worse.

Ah, girlfriends! Well, there was the bubbly blonde household name, the Dairy Queen, the high-flying PA, the Paper Doll (easy, Tiger!), and plenty more besides. But there was only one that mattered: Brandy. My bachelor status was continually advertised all over the papers, but the truth, at least during those first months at Radio One, was that I'd fallen happily in love.

I met Brandy, whose real name was Barbara, while she was working for a fashion company housed within Harrod's. She was a well-educated white girl from Rhodesia (now Zimbabwe) who was pretty and kind. We had a wonderful courtship for several months. Marriage was clearly on the cards but when I mentioned this to Harold Davison, the colour drained from his face. "It'll ruin your career," he said bluntly. He knew what he was talking about. Very few pop stars were brave enough to admit to marriage in those days because so much of the fanbase was female. It was the same principle as far as DJs were concerned, so with a heavy heart, I put my career first and ended the relationship.

Years later, after I'd divorced my first wife in the late '70s, Brandy contacted me again and we met up but it didn't amount to anything. Had we married when we were both very much in love, I'm sure we could have had a happy relationship, but one of the major downsides of being a public figure is that it's not always conducive to maintaining stable relationships. You tend to mix with other showbusiness people who, like you, are more interested in their careers than truly caring about someone else. And, as anyone who reads the celebrity magazines knows, that's a recipe for disaster.

"MARY MADE HER EXCUSES, LEAVING HER FRIEND TO MAKE A SPEEDY ADVANCE. 'I 'EAR YOU WANNA FUCK ME!' SHE SAID IN HER FAMOUS MARKET-STALL VOICE."

Although I was alone again against my will, I soon got into the swing of being single once more and made the most of my 'Eligible Bachelor' status. I have absolutely no regrets. As a recognised face wherever I went, there was no shortage of opportunities to meet and mingle with desirable representatives of the opposite sex. I thought it quite natural at the end of an evening for two consenting adults to go home together and make love. I was never brazen about it, though. The era of prying paparazzi and cheque-book journalism might only have been in its infancy, but I still had a public image to protect. The usual routine so as not to set tongues wagging was to leave a function separately from my companion for the evening.

We'd reconvene back at my bachelor pad in Kensington, with its furniture arranged to face the turntable in the middle of the lounge, and wardrobe crammed with clobber from Carnaby Street.

If they weren't otherwise distracted, they might also have noticed the pad and pencil on the bedside cabinet, for when I woke up in the night with a joke just itching to get out of my head.

Occasionally, I'd play away, most often at girlie flats where the floors would be strewn with Biba dresses and half-thumbed copies of *Nova* magazine. One night, though, I found myself playing strangers in the night with an older woman in Frank Sinatra's exclusive London lair in Grosvenor Square. That was Mary Titmus (she suffered a regular chorus of "Merry Titmus to you!" every December!) Harold's personal assistant, who had a habit of making a beeline for anyone in trousers. She was not exactly my type, but I often found myself escorting her at celebrity functions.

Because Harold represented Sinatra, Mary had the keys to his flat, which is how we ended up there together one night after watching The Supremes play The Talk Of The Town. She asked if I'd stay with her in the flat overnight because she was afraid of being alone. The next thing I knew, she was standing before me stark naked and demanding manly caresses. Afterwards, I felt as if I'd been on some kind of casting couch, and a pile of photographs under the bed of other likely conquests did nothing to ease that suspicion. I think she'd been through the entire agency – with the notable exception of Kenny, of course!

One of Mary's best friends was a bubbly blonde actress and a household name with two distinctly famous assets. I'd joked that I rather fancied her pal, not realising for one minute that the pair of them would materialise on my doorstep later that evening. Mary quickly made her excuses, leaving her friend to make a speedy advance. "I 'ear you wanna fuck me!" she said in her famously shrill market-stall voice. "Well, the idea had crossed my mind," I replied, a little embarrassed by the bluntness of the approach.

Little Miss Muffet found the bedroom, took off all her clothes and said, "Well, come on then!" Actually, I couldn't. In the flesh, her figure seemed a little more boyish than buxom, and besides, I just couldn't perform to order.

Every time we've met since, the pair of us always have a good laugh about the incident. In fact, she always greets me with a "Hi, Tony!" wave, then slowly lets her middle finger drop in memory of that floppy late '60s evening.

Most of my late night personal performances came to a more satisfactory conclusion than that particular encounter did. But one night in 1969, while filming one of the last episodes of *Time For Blackburn*, the revolving door of London lovelies was about to come to an abrupt halt. On the set was a beautiful, leggy blonde who had been filming a small part for another show. I was taken aback by her magnificence and invited her for a lift back to London later that night in my new E-Type Jaguar. Her name was Lynn Partington, and for the next two years, she was the love of my life.

"I SPENT MUCH OF THE RELATIONSHIP OBSESSED WITH THE IDEA OF WHETHER SHE WAS BEING FAITHFUL OR NOT."

Lynn and I made a great couple. I was at the height of my career and she was a glamorous Bunny Girl who worked at the prestigious Playboy Club in Park Lane. Years later, when Lynn was interviewed for a television documentary, *The Real Tony Blackburn*, she said something along the lines of, "I don't think he realised how much I loved him". But because of her obvious desirability, and the fact that her work brought her close to some of the wealthiest and most important men in London, regretfully, I spent much of the relationship obsessed with the idea of whether she was being faithful or not.

On the face of it, Lynn and I had a wonderful two years together. We sealed our relationship with a two-week holiday in Torremolinos and, unusually for someone so beautiful, she had a generous personality and was a lot of fun. We made each other very happy. Lynn smartened me up fashion-wise, and when I bought my own two-bedroom flat in Albany Street near Regent's Park later that year, she offered plenty of advice on the internal design and furnishings. I never took to the black leather sofa, which squeaked incessantly, though. She, in turn, could never quite understand my ever growing collection of television sets. I couldn't get enough of them – and I was one of the first people in the country to have a video recorder, too.

Funnily enough, it was when Lynn finally moved in with me, around late 1970, that our relationship began to crumble. It wasn't, like many relationships, because we spent more time together and realised we couldn't stand each other. It was because she rolled back at four or five in the morning, just long enough to catch me getting ready for work. I began to start my day feeling dreadfully insecure, and even before Lynn left me unexpectedly, I think I knew it wasn't going to work.

The manner of her departure was shocking for me at the time, but in retrospect, now seems rather sweet. I'd driven down to the West Country for the day, putting in one of those lucrative but exhausting personal appearances. When I got back home, Lynn was gone, but she had left a little memento. Neatly laid out on the bed were her bunny girl ears and tail.

And that was it. No note, no phone call, nothing. The next I knew, I opened up a newspaper and there she was on the arm of singer Jack Jones, a man with considerably more money and celebrity clout than I had. Secretly, I'd always thought she'd end up with someone like that, and she did. Lynn's now married to the head of the Fabergé Corporation and lives the good life somewhere in America.

* * *

"AFTER OUR FIRST SUCCESS, THE NEXT THREE BREAKFAST SHOW RECORDS OF THE WEEK ALL FAILED MISERABLY."

Ironically, at the moment I felt most powerless in my private life, I was probably at the peak of my influence professionally. On December 1, 1969, my producer Tim Blackmore and I launched *The Tony Blackburn Show Record Of The Week*. People always speak in hushed tones about the influence of John Peel's late night programmes, and it's true: Marc Bolan and David Bowie did eventually break through after John had spent years plugging their records. But the breakfast show's *Record Of The Week* spot was in a different league entirely. One week, we could be playing, say, Diana Ross And The Supremes' *Someday We'll Be Together*, and the next it would be well on its way towards the Top 20 or higher.

In truth, by choosing The Supremes' latest as our first Record Of The Week was hardly sticking our reputations on the line. When Tim recently showed me the paperwork for the following three weeks, I was shocked to see that our subsequent hat-trick of predictions all failed miserably.

Mama Cass's *Make Your Own Kind Of Music* hardly lived up to the promise of her previous hit, *It's Getting Better*. The US duo of Nino Tempo and April Stevens were way out of date by the time they released their *Sea Of Love/Dock Of The Bay* medley. And we were a bit too quick off the mark with Bread's *London Bridge*, which wasn't a patch on their gorgeous breakthrough record, *Make It With You*, released in summer 1970.

With the *Record Of The Week* slot up and running, Tim and I became even more of a magnet for the pluggers. They inundated us with discs delivered by the box-load, though we were always our own men. On the rare occasion that we completely disagreed, we would nominate two Records Of The Week. More often than not, we hit the jackpot, and our selections had a clear impact on the early '70s pop chart. During 1970 and '71, we had numerous Top Ten hits, including Bob And Marcia's *Young, Gifted And Black*, Brotherhood Of Man's *United We Stand, Divided We Fall*, and two apiece for Ray Stevens (*Everything Is Beautiful* and *Bridget The Midget*) and the wonderful Andy Williams (*Can't Help Falling In Love* and *Home Lovin' Man*). Among those we sent spinning all the way up to the Number One spot were two personal favourites, The Carpenters' (*They Long To Be) Close To You* and Freda Payne's *Band Of Gold*, as well as Matthews Southern Comfort's *Woodstock*, Dave Edmunds' *I Hear You Knockin'* and Middle Of The Road's irresistible bubblegum classic, *Chirpy Chirpy Cheep Cheep*. What a wonderful playlist that lot would make for one of today's Gold stations!

But before we all get too carried away on a nostalgia trip, I'd like to remind readers that for every hundred or more records that came through our tiny office in Egton House each week, we'd be lucky if we found more than two or three that were worth hearing a second time. The '60s and '70s certainly witnessed so many unforgettable hits, two and a half minute gems that stand as a testament to the fine art of pop songwriting. But it's important not to look back and imagine that every song was great, because it just wasn't like that.

One song from this era that remains a pop classic and deservedly so is Diana Ross's *I'm Still Waiting*. Now, on the breakfast show, I could make or break a record, simple as that. On this occasion, though, I went way further in my enthusiasm. I first heard the song on an LP, its beautifully sad sentiment striking a cord with my own miserable mood. I just couldn't get it out of my head. I called up the guy who was running Motown's British office, and told him, "There's a surefire hit record on this new Diana Ross album". He listened to it and said, "I think you're right". Motown rang her up, she granted permission for the song to appear on 45, and *I'm Still Waiting* gave Diana her first Number One in this country in seven years.

It was an honour for me to give something back to one of the great Tamla artists, and become a small part of that label's illustrious history. It wasn't too long afterwards that I was able to see a bit more of Diana Ross in person, when I was asked to compere her first British solo tour. After introducing her to wild, yet respectful applause, I'd stand at the side of the stage completely mesmerised. It wouldn't be too long before another public performer had a similar effect on me. So much so that I married her.

6

MARRIAGE, MARVIN AND ME

Within ten minutes of my first date with Tessa Wyatt, I'd asked her to marry me. She turned me down. Twelve months later, she'd changed her mind. The year after that, we had our son, Simon. Three more years and it was all over.

My first, failed attempt at creating a family topped and tailed the '70s for me. The heady rush of courtship was played out to the fabulous sounds of superfly soul and the frivolous sensationalism of glam rock. The fall-out, though, was like a scene from one of those miserable modernist plays that were fashionable at the time. Alone and in the grip of morbid despair, I saw out the decade with the sound of punk rock resounding round the country. I hated the music, and everything about punk culture, but there's no denying that it provided a fittingly angry and desperate soundtrack to the mess I'd found myself in.

I'd first set eyes on Tessa while I was having dinner with a friend in a restaurant along Brompton Road in Kensington. A male friend, luckily enough. I was utterly captivated, so much so that I instructed the waiter to pass on a message to her. The words she heard were that she was "the most beautiful woman" I'd ever set eyes on. I'd had the good fortune to have rubbed shoulders, and much else besides, with some of the most gorgeous women in the country since I'd become a DJ. But her almond-shaped eyes and blonde hair, delicate face and petite figure, fun-loving smile and intelligence suggested some kind of perfection for me. I had marriage in my sights, and I'd not even uttered a word to the woman yet!

When the waiter returned, he had in his hand a piece of paper. I knew exactly what was on it – her telephone number. That was always a good sign, and while I couldn't wait to give her a call and find out more about the mystery blonde, it took me two weeks to pluck up the courage. Initially, the news wasn't good. "I'm just watching myself on the telly," she said. Hmmm, so was I. I've a feeling she was appearing in an episode of *Doctor At Large*. It must have been a Thursday because I was watching myself presenting *Top Of The Pops*. My heart sunk a little. A partner in showbusiness and a successful marriage were mutually exclusive in my book. But I bit the bullet anyway and invited her out for an Italian meal at a nice little place near the Embankment. She'd barely had a chance to look at the menu before I proposed to her. She must have thought I was a complete idiot, but I meant it. I noted that she smoked, which didn't impress me much, and that she drank in moderation. But nothing I heard or saw distracted me from my pursuit, not even the blazing rows we sometimes had during our first few months together in 1971. Most of the time, though, we had great fun. I even broke one of my cardinal rules and threw in an occasional mention of "the mystery woman Tessa" during my breakfast shows.

Though she'd land the occasional role in a television drama or sitcom, Tessa had her sights set on a film career. She'd got off to a flying start with parts in a couple of Irish productions, *I Can't . . . I Can't* (1969) and *Wedding Night* (1970) when she 21. Alexandra

Bastedo, from the hit TV series *The Champions*, and a young Dennis Waterman also featured. She also had a small part in a crime thriller, *The Beast In The Cellar* (1970), alongside two grand old dames, Beryl Reid and Flora Robson.

A few months into our relationship, Tessa was offered a more substantial role in a big screen version of a Graham Greene novel, *England Made Me*. Peter Finch and Michael York were set to star. Shooting was to take place over several weeks in Yugoslavia. My initial trepidation at losing her for such a long period eased when I began to sense that her loneliness made her increasingly receptive to my daily phone calls. It was during one of these long distance conversations that once again I asked her to marry me. This time, she said yes, though I did it all over again in person when she returned home, after I'd compered The Supremes in concert. Six weeks and one £300 triple diamond engagement ring later, we were married.

I was more than happy to have a Registry Office wedding, which took place at Caxton Hall in Westminster, where hundreds of confetti-throwing fans turned out to wish us well. The bride wore a cream dress suit, with thigh-length black boots and a single orchid, the groom a fashionably slim-line maroon suit with a rounded collar Brutus shirt. It was Thursday March 2, 1973 and as I placed the ring on her finger, I knew that this was the happiest moment of my life. I was full of hope that it would be like my parents' marriage, and that we'd be happy and together forever. I hadn't reckoned on my old enemies, self-doubt and insecurity.

Looking back, I can see that something was already amiss that evening, when I found myself a stranger at my own wedding reception. Held in a function room at the Hyde Park Hotel, it was a costly affair, so to keep Tessa's parents' expenses down I'd decided not to invite any of my DJ friends. Derek Chinnery, Controller of Radio 1, was the only representative from my professional world. I regretted it later, not least because halfway through the evening, I'd spotted that one of Tessa's ex's had been invited, which choked me a bit.

I'd also gone along with a church blessing earlier in the day, at the Holy Trinity Church in Knightsbridge, because her parents were adamant that the marriage required God's blessing. However, just as I expected, when the day of judgement approached, even He could do little to save our marriage.

Although I was by no means from a deprived background, there was a significant cultural gulf between my family and Tessa's. When I was first introduced to her parents, at the family home in the village of Mayfield, Sussex, I walked into an antique table and accidentally broke off one of its legs. The Wyatts were very much the Barbour-wearing hunting, shooting and fishing brigade, their fortune made in the City, their lifestyle that of affluent country people. I remember getting into an argument with one of her in-laws after he'd come back to the house bragging about all the game birds he'd just shot. I thought he was a heathen, and I suspect the feeling was mutual. Tessa's golf-playing mother, in particular, didn't seem to regard DJ-ing as a profession befitting a future son-in-law. I suppose she was right!

Our honeymoon began with a night at London's exclusive Savoy Hotel. On our arrival, the manager recognised us – or should I say, saw us coming. "Ah, Mr and Mrs Blackburn! I have a much, much better room for you," he said. He certainly did. It overlooked the River Thames. "That's very kind of you," I said, before closing the door. As we gazed out of the window, drinking in the starry moonlit scene, we were both naively grateful for his generous gesture. But when morning came, and with it the bill, I noticed that we'd been charged a fat sum for the Savoy's hospitality.

C'est la vie. We were very much in love and about to take off on a three-city continental break for ten days. Given the choice, I would have much preferred a honeymoon on a gold, sandy beach in the

Caribbean, sharing fresh pineapples and drinking coconut milk from its shell, but it was Tessa's wish that we lap up a bit of old fashioned continental city life and culture. We fell asleep at the Opera House in Venice, and got huffy in rude Rome, where every moment seemed like rush-hour. Happily, things picked up in Paris, the perfect city for springtime lovers, with its beautifully lit riverside vistas and wide, romantic thoroughfares. Nevertheless, by the end of the honeymoon, I was exhausted and grateful to be back in my BBC Radio studio chair.

"IT WAS IMPOSSIBLE TO TELL WHETHER SAVILE FELT THREATENED BY THE NEW GENERATION OF YOUNGER UPSTARTS."

While filming *Time For Blackburn* had been a strain, I was devastated when the series came to an end in 1969. But there was some compensation. By that time, I'd established myself as a regular host on *Top Of The Pops*, the most popular music programme on television. The show's original presenter was Jimmy Savile, who was probably around 40 back then. By the early '70s, he'd hardly changed at all, his long blond hair and wide-eyed, slightly manic delivery ("Now then, now then, now then!"), still oddly in tune with the times.

In 1966, before the days of Radio One, the Big Four of the DJ world had been Pete Murray, king of the old guard, Simon Dee, fast snapping at his heels, Alan Freeman, who presented the Light Programme's chart rundown show *Pick Of The Pops*, and Jimmy Savile. Alan, who died in 2006, was one of the most professional and universally liked characters in the industry. He had his own favourites, too, and apparently I was one of them. At one of Diana Dors's legendary showbiz parties – where, I'm afraid to say, I saw no evidence of her infamous two-way mirrors – she'd apparently asked Alan who he had his eye on that particular evening. "Tony," he said. Some time later, we were hosting an episode of *Top Of The Pops* together, I was suffering from a bad bout of flu. Just as the cameras were about to roll, I fainted, and Alan managed to catch me before I hit the ground. "I am sorry about that, Alan," I said, as I collected my senses. "Oh, not at all," he smiled. "That was the most wonderful moment of my life!"

While Alan Freeman was certainly shy, I don't think any of us knew what went on behind Savile's impermeable front. In autumn 1967, when *Top Of The Pops* producer Johnnie Stewart began to bring in new faces, such as myself and Stuart Henry, it was impossible to tell whether Savile felt threatened by the new generation of upstarts. There can't be a person over 30 that isn't familiar with his repertoire of catchphrases but that's about all Jimmy would ever give of himself, even off-air. It was a mask that few have penetrated, not even the bemused TV reporter Louis Theroux who made a documentary about Savile in 2000. Even when he's constantly surrounded by people, Savile is strangely wrapped up in his own universe.

It was a real pleasure to interrupt those blissful early months of marriage by hosting *Top Of The Pops*. Although I'd been co-presenting the show on and off since '67, it seemed to come into its own during the early '70s thanks to the arrival of a new kind of pop star – the glam rock idol. Marc Bolan, David Bowie, Gary Glitter and Slade's 'Super Yob' guitarist Dave Hill – each desperately trying to look more daft than the other. It was pure theatre and just the tonic pop needed after it had gone a bit stodgy at the end of the '60s. The programme even had a new producer, Robin Nash, who seemed perfectly in tune with the era, forever camping it up with his booming, over-the-top voice, garish shirts that invariably left his nipples exposed, and his trademark 'tache.

There are a lot of myths about behind the scene shenanigans on set at *Top Of The Pops*, and almost all of them are false. The atmosphere was always professional, performers and audience had little opportunity to mingle and the presenters were little more than glorified bingo callers: "And now, this week's highest climber, it's Chicory Tip with *Son Of My Father*!"

There's a story from that time, apparently stemming from The Who, which maintains that drummer Keith Moon once threw a cymbal at me in revenge for my claim that their record *Pinball Wizard* was "sick". I still don't particularly rate the song, about a "deaf, dumb and blind kid" who can operate a slot machine. But I'm sure I would have remembered if a heavy cymbal had come crashing in my direction.

The most unpleasant act I encountered on the show were Mott The Hoople. It was spring 1972, and the band were climbing up the charts with *All The Young Dudes*, a song David Bowie had written. It had this middle section where it all went a bit quiet, which was the cue for us DJs to talk over it, just to liven things up a bit. In a break between recording the show, the ringlet-headed singer Ian Hunter came up to me and said, "I wish you'd stop talking over our bloody record". "Fine," I said. "I simply won't bother playing it anymore." He wasn't expecting that. "You can't do that," he snapped, "you don't even select the songs." One of the other band members came over and tried to patch things up, but I told the Mott man that I'd withdraw the record from the playlist for two weeks, and I did.

It takes quite a bit to make me angry, and incidents like that thankfully have been few and far between. But I do remember saying, "Look, I'm gonna be here in a year or so, and where are you gonna be?" And I was right. A few years later, while making a personal appearance in some provincial nightclub, I saw a poster and there was the name, Mott, in small letters. These one-time big shots were now the support act.

Sticking to the subject of unfriendliness, *TOTP*'s resident dance troupe Pan's People were on the show even more often than I was. I always found them a bit full of themselves, but for no good reason, really. I mean, I still occasionally bump into Babs Lord, the blonde one, who's married to Robert Powell these days, and she's fine now. But they were little more than a dodgy dance act choreographed by a real cold fish, Flick Colby.

They did help boost ratings, though. In those glam rock days, you're talking about 18 or 19 million viewers. That's almost half the country bang up to date with this week's highest climber, the exact number of new entries and, of course, the excitement of a new Number One. Today, there's absolutely no sense of occasion to the chart rundown and that's a real pity. I enjoyed it immensely and I didn't even like half the records!

One of the joys of presenting *TOTP* was that I'd often get a chance to say hello to one of the visiting Tamla stars. I'd always get an invitation to join Diana Ross And The Supremes, The Four Tops and that little genius of a man Stevie Wonder in their dressing rooms. It couldn't get much better than that for me, although for entirely different reasons, I have particularly fond memories of meeting Petula Clark on set too. To me, she's second only to Doris Day in terms of womanly perfection. I first lost my heart to Petula when I was a teenager and she was in *Goodbye Mr Chips* with Peter O'Toole.

Olivia Newton-John was just as lovely as she looked, too, though I didn't get on with the barefoot girl from Dagenham Sandie Shaw at all. On one television show, the subject of *Puppet On A String*, her 1967 Eurovision Song Contest hit, came up and she said, "Oh, that's not me anymore" and got an immediate smell under her nose. I thought, "Actually, that song is you, and it's the only thing we'll remember you for."

The one Brit girl with the truly amazing voice was Dusty Springfield, the white soul queen from West London. I met her several times over the years, and she was another of the shy ones, not really sure of herself at all. So often those turn out to be the interesting ones, and of course, Dusty ended up having this rather complicated love life. Her live-in girlfriend for some time was the incredible Madeleine Bell – amazing voice, amazingly big smile! In fact, she sang backing vocals on one of my records, though I much prefer to hear her on Blue Mink's terrific 1970 Top 3 single, *Melting Pot*. That song's message is no less relevant today, with its joyous prediction of a future world free from racial tensions because we'll all be "coffee-coloured people" one day.

WHY I HATE THE UNDERGROUND

In October 1970, Melody Maker sent a reporter to quiz me on my attitudes towards the emerging alternative culture centred on hippies and loud rock music. Here, in essence, is what I told them . . .

"I went to the Isle Of Wight [festival] and I saw two guys there play and afterwards tell the audience to fuck off. The whole act of groups like these is based around being vulgar and rude to their audiences, and I feel this is unprofessional.

They are dirty as well. Some of them look as if they have not had a bath for six months, and people don't want to see this. They want a certain amount of glamour, and those who are trying to give them it will be dragged down with them if it goes on."

"When I was young I enjoyed seeing The Beatles and reading about their glamorous lives and that sort of illusion is now being killed off by this sort of behaviour. If people want to take drugs, for instance, it's not for me to prevent them, but

these underground groups have influence among the young. Drugs do harm and kill, therefore I don't think it's good to take them."

"It's not good to get away from showbiz. It's a glamorous business, and it does you good to take you out of ordinary day life."

"There's enough of this sort of thing as it is, without underground groups making it worse. You can go down any side alley and see dustbins. Take television, for instance. What people want to see is something glamorous, like The Golden Shot *– something that's professionally run, is smart, and has respect for the audience which has come to see it."*

"If I'm going into a ballroom, or opening a shop, then it gives me a kick that people have come to see me, and I take the trouble to show up moderately smart to see them. Put on a certain false front, if you like, because that's what all professional business do. You don't go to Carnaby Street to see behind the scenes, you go to see its front."

"I'm not generalising, but I've come up against the underground, and although I've tried to appreciate them, they're just not interested in what I'm saying, so why should I bother?

It's the 'in' thing to like that kind of music, but it's not what the majority want."

"Does the public want to be taken down to earth with a bump like this? I'm certain the kids in the provinces, in Manchester and Birmingham, don't want to be. It's good to see

fellas coming over with smart suits and a clean appearance. I just don't like dirt; it's a lack of professionalism. Let's give the public a nice show."

"The ratings show that when underground shows are on Radio One there's a slump, so I think this type of music should be on Radio Three, and the underground DJs agree with me. Most people would rather hear this type of music on VHF* anyway, and in some areas they even have stereophonic sound, so that's my answer. Great Britain isn't renowned for giving the people what they want, but it'd be easy to get a few more VHF receivers.

We haven't seen the possibilities yet of VHF. Put something on VHF that they want to hear and can't already get on the usual station, and people will go out and buy them."

"But if I'm to get the maximum audience, I have to cater for the mums and dads and they don't want heavy music. There's no time to listen to heavy music in the morning. There's lots of underground programmes on Radio One at present, you know, but they have never made it commercially. It's got minority appeal."

"[These groups] don't come on Top Of The Pops *because we're not on their wavelength. Dammit, these people asked us if they could be on it! And then [Humble Pie's] Steve Marriott says after the programme, 'It was just a joke, nothing personal'.*

I told him, 'You try to make me look like an idiot and then want us to play the record'. Anyway, it's a bad record [the

*VHF (Very High Frequency) was the term used before FM entered the popular vernacular. With kind thanks to Michael Watts, who dutifully filed this story first time round.

band's 1970 flop 45, Big Black Dog], I think, and a lot of other people think the same. It's not got anywhere."

"I don't like the way they go on talking to someone else while you're shaking hands. They have done it to [Jimmy] Savile a couple of times as well. They put up the barriers on us. They get on a pop programme and make themselves look idiots."

"I've nothing personal against underground music, or most of the musicians. It's just that I'm interested in commercial music, like Tamla Motown. But you'll never put that in your paper, will you, because it's not progressive."

"I DON'T THINK WE'LL EVER BE SEEING GARY GLITTER ON A STAGE AGAIN, LET ALONE AT ANOTHER 'CHILDREN IN NEED' CONCERT."

In general, though, I wasn't a big fan of "message" songs. The people who wrote or sang them tended to take themselves far too seriously. Though he's been accused (and convicted) of far more odious things since, you could never have said that about glam ham Gary Glitter. I know it's unacceptable to play his music now, and I understand why, but I do think it's a shame. Perhaps someone should go in and re-record his old songs again so we can hear them without having to hear him. Over the top hits such as *Leader Of The Gang* were simply brilliant, the best possible party music you could possibly ask for.

Only Slade could compete with Glitter when it came to generating a real sense of excitement in the *TOTP* studios. Glitter's act was true pantomime, as he tottered awkwardly on his ludicrously high platform boots without giving two hoots about how daft he looked. Some years later, I had him on as a guest on my Radio One children's show, and he came in blind drunk wearing a sailor's cap. Later still, at a Children In Need event, he was doing the old act, yelling "Come on, come on!" at the top of his failing voice. By the end of the show, he was in a dreadful state, perspiring badly and needing to be helped into a chair.

Of course, that was nothing compared to the tattered state of his reputation now. None of us had any idea what he was up to. I met his son once and even he told me his dad was a bit weird. I don't think we'll ever be seeing Gary Glitter on a stage again, let alone at another Children In Need concert.

Oddly enough, I didn't think much of the two singers credited as key architects of the glam rock era, David Bowie and Marc Bolan. I'd first heard of Bowie several years earlier, when he was copying Anthony Newley on a gimmicky 45 called *The Laughing Gnome*. It was a complete flop and Bowie hates being reminded of it. Two years later, in 1969, things began to change for him. His record company had thrown a lunchtime reception in his honour, I think, at the Revolution Club in Mayfair. Everyone was sat around waiting to hear what position his latest record, *Space Oddity*, would enter the chart at.

He seemed like a nice guy, a little fazed by all the razzmatazz, and with a sense of style that was by his standards remarkably normal. Bowie's music was not my kind of thing, though, and neither was Marc Bolan's. The T Rex star was a huge sex symbol and sparkled brightly on stage, but . . . Well, sod Ziggy Stardust! I'll take Alvin Stardust over Bowie and Bolan every time. Much more fun.

While all eyes were on the men in the Bacofoil outfits, it was easy to forget that a slow change had been taking place that was splitting the pop world in two. Partly inspired by the hippie underground, and preached endlessly at the BBC by John Peel, the Rock Revolution had divided youth culture down the middle. That was a terrible shame, because the serious-minded rock music fans would simply dismiss the teenybopper groups, while the pop-minded among us simply felt patronised by those who wanted to elevate pop to the level of classical or art music.

In many ways, I was the whipping boy for the hairy progressive types, as Michael Watts, in his October 1970 profile of me for *Melody Maker*, carefully explained. "Basically, [Blackburn's] problem is that he has become the personification of Radio One and *Top Of The Pops*, and all the commerciality associated with it. He is the Tin Pan Alley target who has set himself up for the sharp barbs of the heavy music brigade, and they hate him because he epitomises – through his musical tastes and public image – all the attitudes and ideals that the underground thought it had got rid of."

It was all pop music to me, except the stuff that John Peel tended to play was almost without exception completely awful. I mean, ELP? Extremely Loud and Pretentious. Er, no thanks. Led Zeppelin? Lead balloon, more like. Here was I waking up the nation with the most uplifting sounds you could possibly hear, and there was John, bless him, at the end of the day sending them to sleep with a load of old codswallop dressed up as something clever and arty! We were the Yin and Yan of Radio One, and though we were pleasant enough to each other when we met at radio functions, I always felt an undercurrent of animosity from John. Once in a while, our differing ways would explode into a public spat.

While I headed up the initial intake of Radio One DJs, John was one of many names that the new station were testing out before dishing out longer contracts. As a kind of philosopher DJ, who played rare and esoteric records from the outer margins of the pop world, he found a niche and soon became a regular presenter on a weekly programme called *Top Gear*. Initially broadcast on Sundays, it soon switched to weekday late evenings, where its regular live sessions helped conserve the station's valuable needle time.

One of the strengths of the BBC was that it could justify a show that had so few listeners – no doubt part of its 'education' brief that goes back to the days of BBC pioneer and ideologue John Reith. In fact, the regular General Evaluation Figures (GEF) confirmed that Peel's audience was remarkably faithful to his show, unlike those for the daytime broadcasts. Even so, I always felt that his programme was out of place on Radio One and probably far more suited to Radio 3. That's because teenagers who came home from school wanted pop music and I didn't think that Peel's show really catered for them.

I casually mentioned this during an interview one day, not to be nasty, but simply because I believed Radio One should be a Top 40 station pulling in a mass audience 24 hours a day. And John never really forgave me for that. From that time on, he saw me as the devil incarnate, never missing any opportunity to snipe at me. True, I did once tell a local newspaper reporter that *Top Gear* should be taken off the air, that it spoilt my weekend listening and that it appealed only to undesirables. But to me it was a disagreement about aesthetics, whereas John continually personalised it. I sincerely believed in Radio One as the nation's jukebox and yet there was Peel every night playing the most ungodly racket imaginable by the oddest characters he could find. I accidentally tuned in once just in time to hear him say, "And now another one from Captain Beefheart". I thought, "B-fart" – that really says it all!

Our strained relationship was a perfect metaphor for what was happening in the pop world at that time. John was onside with the long haired, the drop outs, the students, all those who regarded the three-minute pop single as a blot on the face of culture. I was the happy-go-lucky dispenser of the kind of song that an audience only had to hear once before rushing out to buy it – which they did in their thousands. Records that people loved, in other words. I saw no crime in that at all.

The only time I made an attempt to go to a rock festival, I managed to get there late and missed the entire thing. I wasn't sorry at all. It was one of those sprawling three-day marathons held on the Isle Of Wight, and all that I missed were a load of interminably loud heavy rock groups such as Taste, The Who, Jethro Tull and Jimi Hendrix. All wonderful if you wanted to take all your clothes off and dance while out of your mind on LSD, I'm sure, but I couldn't see anything in it at all apart from people trying rather too hard to be different. Odd, then, that they all seemed to be dressed in the same uniform – blue jeans and tie-dye T-shirts!

"SOME INSIST THAT SOUL MUSIC IS SPIRITUAL. I CALL IT BEING DEEPLY IN TOUCH WITH ONE'S OWN FEELINGS."

Being different didn't appeal to me at all. For a start, it would cut me off from my audience, and besides my tastes have always been unashamedly mainstream. That's who I am and I like it that way. Yet, without even trying, in the early '70s I found myself as a crusader for a style of music that still fell somewhat short of mainstream acceptance. Today, Marvin Gaye's What's Going On LP regularly features highly in those 'Greatest Album Ever' polls. But in November 1971, when Motown first released it in Britain, both the LP and the single stiffed. That was quite extraordinary, really, because there was nothing particularly abrasive or difficult about the record.

What's Going On was a truly remarkable piece of work, and one of those rare instances when something of real quality is grossly overlooked by the public. Over 35 years later, it's still my favourite record. For me, it's got everything. It's a truly complete collection of songs that works as a continuous piece of music – and with absolutely no filler either. Above all, it's made from the heart, surely the definition of a genuine soul record.

Like many of the great American soul singers, Marvin learned to sing in church. I'm not at all religious, but I can certainly hear a depth of feeling in his voice that most other singers cannot hope to achieve. Some insist on calling soul music spiritual. I prefer to describe it as being deeply in touch with one's own feelings. If anyone in popular music has been able to connect with those most private sensations, then that person has to be Marvin Gaye.

By the early '70s, Marvin was dismantling the characteristic Tamla sound and giving it his own brilliant, personal twist. He wasn't alone. Stevie Wonder was doing it too, diving deep into a new funk sound with songs such as *Superstition* and *Higher Ground*. I wasn't surprised at all. Every time I'd meet Stevie, usually behind the scenes at a television show, he'd be tapping out a rhythm the whole time. Music was everything to Stevie, who had been blind since he was an infant.

"My life is all sound," he once told me. "I can see everything, I can imagine everything, it's all in the sound." That's what made him such a great musician. Put him in front of that keyboard and he's like a hyperactive Ray Charles, and as immaculately dressed, too.

The early '70s saw a shift in soul music, away from the more abrasive Stax/Atlantic stars such as Otis Redding and Sam & Dave, towards a softer, more sophisticated sound. I found myself giving it even more airtime, especially as a new wave of vocal groups such as The Chi-Lites and The Stylistics broke through. This wonderful music was impervious to the petty rock versus pop debates. And unlike so much progressive music and glam rock, the '70s soul sound has endured without really sounding dated. It's not hard to draw a line from Diana Ross and Marvin Gaye, through the Philly Sound era and George *Rock Your Baby* McRae, on to Luther Vandross and Alexander O'Neill and right up to, say, American Idol winner Jennifer Hudson. Her version of *And I am Telling You I'm Not Going* in *Dreamgirls* had me in tears. Timeless music, the lot of it.

I'm proud that I've played my part in bringing the smoother end of soul music into the mainstream where it belongs. What's more, I was told recently that in his later years, John Peel would occasionally let slip to journalists that he secretly admired my unswerving belief in black music. It was nice to hear that after all those years of unkindness.

I suppose I should also own up to my brush with fame as a soul star. I'd released a second solo album in 1972, this time for Polydor Records. Once again, it was largely a collection of light pop and ballad material, and it didn't really get anywhere. However, in my enthusiasm, I managed to smuggle a couple of soul songs on it. I do wish I hadn't. One of the songs I'd chosen was The Four Tops' *Baby, I Need Your Loving*. My version was awful. I'd desperately wanted to record a soul classic, but it just didn't work because unfortunately I just haven't got the soul!

Someone out there obviously did appreciate my blue-eyed soul stylings because, one day in 1973, I got a call at Radio One saying, "Did you know you're a hit at the Wigan Casino? It turned out that one of the DJs on the thriving Northern Soul scene, which prided itself on playing the most obscure dancefloor fillers, had enjoyed my version of *I'll Do Anything* by the great soul singer Doris Troy and had it pressed up on a white label 45. Because everything was so elitist and secretive on that tight-knit scene, the record was credited to 'Lenny Gamble', in a bid to throw other DJs off the scent. Very soon, copies began changing hands for £25 or more – crazy, really, because once again, I thought I'd totally ruined a perfectly good soul classic.

For the first time in my life, I had a genuine hit record. OK, so the only chart it figured in was the specialist Northern Soul Top Ten, but to know that crowds of cool young things were dancing wildly to it . . . I mean, how could I not put in a personal appearance at the Wigan Casino, the hub of the Northern scene? The only problem was, the crowds didn't want me, they wanted the legendary Lenny Gamble! When I started to sign a few autographs, the signature they wanted was 'Lenny Gamble'. I remember saying to one of them, "You do know I'm Tony Blackburn, don't you?" "Yeah, Lenny, yeah!" he replied. For one night only, I really was Northern Soul legend Lenny Gamble.

"MY FIRST THOUGHT WHEN I SAW MY SON WAS, 'MY GOD, HE LOOKS THE COMEDIAN CHARLIE DRAKE!'"

It was a particularly beautiful spring in 1973. Tessa and I were now living happily in The Marlowes, an impressive three-storey townhouse in St John's Wood. The O'Jays were riding high in the Top 10 with the fabulously slick *Love Train*. And on April 8, our son, Simon Anthony Blackburn was born. I don't know why we called him Simon. He certainly wasn't named after Simon Bates. I didn't even know him then.

Men weren't encouraged to be present at the birth of a child back in those days, so I'd been waiting patiently at home for news, with my father on hand to steady my nerves. As soon as the call came through, I was straight round to Queen Charlotte's Hospital, a large bouquet of flowers under my arm, to see the new product of my love for Tessa. Simon had next to no hair, and my first thought was, "My God, he looks like the comedian Charlie Drake!". Thankfully, he's changed a bit since then...

At last, I had everything I'd wished for. My own perfect little family, a gorgeous wife and son, and a beautiful home furnished in a classy, traditional style by the ever tasteful Tessa. There was one niggling blot on all this. I was about to lose my other pride and joy: the Radio One breakfast show.

7

ON THE ROCKS

One spring morning in 1973, a proud father-to-be signed off on air at 9am with his customary "Bye-bye everyone!". I was looking forward to rushing back to The Marlowes to be with my beloved Tessa, who was heavily pregnant at the time. But first I had an appointment with my agent, Harold Davison.

"Tony, Derek Chinnery has decided to freshen up the schedules a bit," he said." "Great," I thought. "I'm going to get an extra show. Perhaps a specialist soul programme at the weekend . . ." That wasn't quite what the Beeb had planned for me. "Derek has decided to move you to the mid-morning slot," he said. Harold was not a man to joke about serious matters, so I knew this was no wind-up. For a rare moment, I was completely lost for words. It was as if something had died in me. I'd been presenting breakfast shows for almost a decade. That was me, the wake-up-and-smell-the-coffee man. Ratings for my Radio One breakfast show were as high as they'd ever been. I was still the highest profile DJ in the country. The decision made no sense to me whatsoever.

Money was hardly an issue because the proposed switch to mid-morning didn't come with the added humiliation of a cut in my fee. Prestige certainly did play a huge part in my reaction to the news. The breakfast show was the ultimate prize for every broadcaster. Having worked so hard to make it my own, the thought of giving it up and playing second fiddle to someone else made me feel angry. I found it difficult to talk to anyone about it without losing my cool.

What no one seemed to appreciate was how it feels to lose your audience. For six years, millions of people had been waking up with me on Radio One, setting off to work with one of my daft one-liners ringing in their ears. It was like losing a bunch of friends – all 15 million of them. In the weeks after the announcement was made, my mailbox at Broadcasting House was swamped with letters of support. I was too heartbroken ever to read more than a handful of them.

Everyone did their best to soften the blow. Those closest to me, like Tessa and Harold, knew that behind my put-on-a-happy-face grin was a fragile ego that needed emotional support just like everyone else does. While I appreciated their concern, their words did little to console me.

I still had another decade left at Radio One, and had a lot of fun – as well as more heartbreak than I'd ever bargained for – during that time. But looking back, I can see that my time there was never the same after I was forced off the breakfast show. Once I accepted that the decision had been made, and that there was no going back, I did my best to make a success of my new show. But it left a deep scar, and the residual anger and resentment that remained ate away at me during my most vulnerable moments.

I've since learned that coping with the knocks is at least as important as accepting the accolades. For all its apparent glitz and glamour, showbusiness is a desperately tough world to be in. You have to be thick-skinned in order to survive, and if you're not when you start out, then you'd better develop that hard outer layer pretty damn quickly. It doesn't matter who you are. Take Bruce Forsyth. For decades, that brilliant man has been at the heart of the British light entertainment industry, presenting everything from *Sunday Night At The London Palladium* to *The Generation Game*. Then, during the '90s, he was suddenly deemed too old for television and couldn't get a look in anywhere. I don't care how strong anyone is – that must have hurt. (Happily, those who make the decisions eventually realised the error of their ways, because Brucie's been back where he belongs for some time now.) All failure hurts, especially for those who put themselves in the public eye, because ultimately that's all about craving affection, attention, call it what you like. I don't believe it when certain stars say, "Leave me alone!" They're usually the most vain, arrogant and emotionally demanding ones of all.

When I was called in to Derek Chinnery's Radio One office to discuss the nuts and bolts of my new role, I found it difficult to hide my hurt feelings. On the one hand I wanted to make it clear that I was shocked, mystified and disappointed at losing the programme I'd presented for the past six years. At the same time I knew I couldn't overplay the drama because I needed to assure him that I was more than happy to bring my characteristic enthusiasm to the mid-morning slot. It was a lie. To know that I was no longer the golden boy of Radio One hit me bad. Worse still, that accolade had now been passed on to someone else: Noel Edmonds.

" 'THERE'S ONLY ROOM FOR ONE PERSON TO TELL BAD JOKES ON AIR AND YOU'RE LOOKING AT HIM,' I TOLD NOEL EDMONDS."

Back in 1973, there were none of these 'hot seat changeovers' you get in the cash-strapped commercial radio today. While Noel Edmonds was wrapping up the breakfast show in one studio, I'd be in another readying myself for my new mid-morning slot, broadcast from nine to midday, five days a week. There was no glass through which we could even see each other. But during those first few weeks, I think everyone could feel the tension between the two of us as Noel handed over to me each morning. We kept the banter as friendly as possible, perhaps too much so, because it was only natural that there'd be an undercurrent of awkwardness and tension lurking behind all that "Hello, Tony!" and "Thanks, Noel!" repartee.

I'm not proud of the way I treated Noel in the early days. I took an instant dislike to him the moment I first heard him broadcasting on Radio Luxembourg some time during 1967. Tony Windsor, my good friend and mentor at Radio London, had switched to Luxembourg after the pirate ships closed down, and it was he that had discovered Noel and got him his first job there. I was doing a programme for the station, too, as a lucrative sideline to my Radio One show. One day, Noel and I happened to bump into each other at the Mayfair studio, where the shows would be recorded before being sent over to the Grand Duchy.

I didn't mince my words. "There's only room for one person to tell bad jokes on air and you're looking at him," I said. It wasn't the warmest welcome I'd ever given someone, but I'd heard him on air telling gags like mine, and I wasn't about to surrender my crown as the undisputed King Of Corn.

By 1969, Noel had started to make the occasional broadcast for Radio One, usually filling in on some minor show while one of the regular DJs was sick or on holiday. If I'm truthful, I think I was already keeping an eye on him, though at that stage only Stuart Henry seemed to provide any real competition. And Stuart, with his thick Scottish accent and general air of flamboyance, was always going to be an acquired taste rather than a family favourite. Besides, there were those within the corporation who took a dim view of his endless championing of environmental concerns on his weekend shows. Stuart was not only way out; he was way ahead of his time in that respect.

It was the sacking of another old Radio London colleague, Kenny Everett, that gave Noel Edmonds his big break at Radio One. Kenny had always been at the sharp end of the broadcasting spectrum, prodigiously talented but a law unto himself as soon as he opened his mouth. He was forever being hauled in to Derek Chinnery's office and asked to explain the reasons behind his latest tirade against "Auntie", the name he'd invented for his paymasters which has since passed into popular parlance.

Kenny knew he was playing with fire but he just couldn't help himself. In 1969, he was given a severe dressing-down for referring to a BBC executive as a "pin-striped prune" and mouthing off about the curse of Needle Time. Most of us pretty much agreed with him on both counts, but we valued our work and our livelihoods far too much to say anything publicly.

When it came, Kenny's final undoing was not, as everyone expected, for biting the hand that fed him. It was for a seemingly innocuous, off the cuff comment in response to a rather insignificant news story. The newsreader had just announced that the wife of the Transport Minister had passed her driving test. It was an odd story to share with the rest of us, I know, but it must have been a slow news day. Seeing the funny side of the tale, as he inevitably did, Kenny suggested that perhaps the Minister had offered a bribe to the examiner. It was so obviously a joke, but I don't think the timing was too good. A new Government led by Edward Heath had just been elected, and in its eagerness to placate its paymasters, the BBC management felt obliged to sack its improbably gifted DJ.

While the rest of us had seen it coming, Kenny Everett simply couldn't believe it. He went straight to Harold and said, "They've sacked me!" Harold told him straight: "You've already had two or three warnings. I'm not going back to them and ask for your job back because, frankly, you deserve to be sacked." Kenny sat there, like a badly behaved little boy forced to contemplate the consequences of his actions. "They don't mean it, Harold, do they?" he pleaded. But they did. And the lesson was a warning to the rest of us, too – a warning that I, in my increasingly agitated state, ignored at my peril.

Noel, who'd been given his own two-hour Saturday afternoon show in the spring, took over from Kenny's mid-morning Saturday show in July 1970. He made such a success of it that a year later, he was moved to the popular Sunday morning slot, from 10am to midday. He started to appear on *Top Of The Pops*, too. Though few realised it at the time, it seems obvious now that he was being groomed as the new face of Radio One.

Young, good-looking, and most important of all, single, Noel Edmonds first warmed the seat in the breakfast show studio in June 1973 and stayed there until April 1978. It was difficult to accept that someone else was now Number One at Radio One, but Noel did a fantastic job, no doubt about it. Management got it exactly right. Noel was a clean-cut guy, handsome and with a good head of blond, wavy hair, sharp-witted and an excellent broadcaster. And he turned out to be even better when he popped up on television. Oh, don't you just love to hate him!

Despite my suspicions, I like to remind myself that I actually helped Noel on the way up. During the late '60s, I had a business interest in a club in Corfu called, naturally, Beeb, and Noel was one of the first DJs who worked there. I don't think I sent him down to the sunny Med as a way of keeping him out of harm's way – at least, that's what I tell myself. In fact, Corfu was where Noel and I first perfected our classic perma-tan look, though his gold, flowing locks probably gave him a head start in convincing the local women that he was actually a modern-day Greek God.

Back in the bowels of Broadcasting House, I buried my true feelings and set about transforming the British mid morning. I did my best to hang on to my confidence. I had no doubt about my abilities – the regular ratings figures neatly confirmed that. Instead, the move prompted me to take a hard look at myself. It was, I realised, all about image. I'd just hit 30, and had a wife and a baby. Of course I was no longer the energetic, ever-popular young man about town. Chinnery and the others were right: I epitomised a cosier, more settled way of life – just right for those millions of housewives who'd tune in once they'd got their children off to school and husbands to work.

I made several changes, most notably introducing the *Golden Hour*, which I'd first developed for the breakfast show to help boost the Friday ratings, which for some reason were always the lowest of the week. Simon Bates inherited the *Golden Hour* when he took over mid-mornings in November 1977, and though some people now associate it with him, it was a Blackburn initiative.

"I SPENT MORE TIME OBSERVING THE DOGS' BEHAVIOUR THAN I DID ON THE DYNAMICS OF MY MARRIAGE TO TESSA."

It had been an emotional few months – a new baby and a new radio slot. Thankfully, life at home was blissfully good. Some days, when I'd sit beside Tessa on our sofa taking turns to bottle-feed Simon, I couldn't give a damn about anything else. But obviously I did, because I was soon spending rather more time water-skiing at a club out near Heathrow than I was performing dad duties. A neighbour had encouraged me to go, and I took to it like a DJ to water. That all came to an abrupt halt after someone pointed out to me that my voice was being adversely affected by all the water I'd been swallowing.

There were more changes afoot. Tessa and I had driven out to the Wogans for dinner one night, and on the way back, we realised just how blissful life in the stockbroker belt could be. They lived in a village outside Maidenhead, and almost immediately, we started hunting for a property in and around that area, way beyond the suburbs of north west London. For the price of our home in St John's Wood, we could virtually own a mansion house in the country, and that's exactly what we decided to do early in 1974. Besides, we both wanted Simon to be able to roam around safely in a decent-sized garden, and we adored the peace and simplicity that a country home could offer us.

As soon as we set eyes on *Hollycroft*, an ivy-clad, 100-year-old period house in Cookham Dean, Berkshire, we knew it was ours. Set in one and a half acres of magnificent, tree-lined grounds, with a gravel drive and gorgeous rosebushes, *Hollycroft* had four bedrooms, three bathrooms and plenty of period features such as old bay windows. Later on, we added a swimming pool. Thanks to the technical know-how of "Mother" Howell, my old friend from the Radio London days, I soon had a small studio built above the garage, too, where I would work on jingles for my show. A gardener and a cleaner looked after the basics, while Josie, our Maltese nanny, tended to Simon. With two adorable Dachshunds, Winifred and Clara, the picture of domestic bliss was complete. What could possibly go wrong?

Well, for a start, I probably spent more time observing the interaction between the dogs than I did on the dynamics of my marriage. Clara, who we'd usually called Cluck, was meant to be a wire-haired Dachshund but for some reason the wire hair never grew. Winnie was a long haired Dachshund, absolutely adorable, but completely indifferent to exercise. Whenever we'd call out "Walkies!", Barbara Wodehouse style, she'd always hide in the same place behind the chair. Clara, who we brought home a little later, announced that she was boss as soon as she came through the door, despite being the youngest of the two. Earlier than we would have liked, Winifred was put down after suffering a painful back problem.

Three years later, my marriage to Tessa also had to be put out of its misery, which is something I'll always regret because I hate failure of any sort. Of course, I'd never want to turn the clock back. When I think back to those times, I realise that neither of us were really prepared for marriage. Nor did we know enough about each other – or even life itself – to give the union much of a chance. If I look at it dispassionately, I think I fell in love with an image. It takes far more than that for a relationship to work. Still, I learned something from it, and later in life I've managed not to make the same mistakes. The way things were for me in the mid-'70s doesn't bear comparison with the life I have with my second wife Debbie and our daughter Victoria.

"PANTOMIME IS THE ARISTOCRACY OF LIGHT ENTERTAINMENT."

As early as November 1967, just weeks after made my Radio One debut, I'd made it clear where I wanted my new found fame to take me. "Actually, my big ambition is to do a pantomime," I told one reporter. The papers may have been full of tales about my lucrative record deal and imminent television series. Harold Davison was busy telling them, "The next natural progression for Tony will be into films". And all the while I was really just hoping for my first offer to appear in panto.

Forty years on, I can proudly say that I've been in around 20 pantomimes, and I've loved every one of them. It's a make-believe world filled with larger-than-life caricatures, kindly goodies and evil baddies, but that only makes it more watchable and entertaining. Unlike serious theatre, where everyone sits there bored out of their minds, thinking only of the cigar and glass of wine that awaits them in the intermission, panto is a rollercoaster ride of fun and high spirited emotion that involves everyone right from the start. To my mind, it's simply the aristocracy of light entertainment – wrestling is probably the nearest thing to it – and I always regard it as a privilege when I'm asked to do it.

It's certainly not an easy option. Unlike my wife, Debbie, who has no trouble at all memorising her lines, I struggle with that. But when I'm on the stage, more often than not in a ludicrous costume and playing the part of Buttons in *Cinderella* (though I've been in *Mother Goose* and *Jack And The Beanstalk* a couple of times too), I know that all the effort's been worthwhile.

I have Bill Kenwright, now a massive theatrical impresario, to thank for giving me my break in panto. It was a late '60s production of *Cinderella* at the Granada, East Ham, and the bill was terrific. I was up there alongside Anne Aston (Bob Monkhouse's glamorous sidekick on *The Golden Shot*), Anna Karen (who looked a lot better in real life than she did playing Olive in *On The Buses*), and Valentine Dyall, alias "The Man In Black" from the popular radio show, *Appointment With Fear*. He was a real old-timer with a soft spot for the gee-gees. Each Saturday, he'd pick up his money, pop his head round the stage door, and say in that big voice of his: "Hello, what's the audience looking like tonight? Right you are! I shall be with you very shortly." Then off he'd trot to the betting-shop where he'd gamble his wage packet away, then come back and say, "Oh well, dear boy, all gone for another week!"

Another great thing about panto is that nothing can ever really go wrong. That was something I'd learned early on, when some scenery started to collapse while I was singing. I spotted it coming down on me in the nick of time, so I sang the rest of the song while holding a large piece of scenery above my head. I got a marvellous round of applause at the end of it, too.

In panto, everything's so last minute, which means that the actors are prepared for just about anything. By some incredible coincidence, my wife Debbie was once in the audience at one of those late '60s East Ham shows.

I was back playing Buttons again during the long, hard winter of '73, this time with my wife Tessa playing the part of Cinderella. As an example of just how disorganised pantomime can be, I can still remember Tessa being stitched into her ball gown seconds before she was due to play the crucial scene.

One of my favourite panto moments ever took place around this time. It was at a matinee show during the love scene between Cinderella and Buttons. I look into Cinders' eyes and asked, "Cinderella, do you love me?" And she replies, crushingly, "Oh, yes I love you, Buttons . . . like a brother!" The audience always erupts into a spontaneous "Aaaah". But on this particular afternoon, one cheeky wag in the stalls called out, "Don't worry, Buttons. You'll be going home with her tonight!"

"I TRIED TO SOLVE THE MINERS' STRIKE – AND FAILED. INSTEAD, THEY TOOK ME OFF THE AIR."

On the face of it, life at *Hollycroft* appeared to be calm and idyllic. But having been knocked off my professional perch, I was getting restless – and a little reckless. There wasn't much peace anywhere else either. During the autumn and winter of '73, the Miners' Strike was bringing the country to a standstill. Every time I turned up for a panto rehearsal, we'd just get started and the electricity would go out. It was bad enough that the three-day week was crippling the nation. But interfering with my attempts to get Cinderella safely to the ball? I wasn't having that!

One morning, I tried to sort it all out and told the miners that they should all get back to work. Bad move. My advice didn't go down too well and the BBC received numerous complaints about it.

I was called up to explain myself to the new Radio One Controller, Douglas Muggeridge, who gave me a severe dressing-down and put me on a two-week suspension. The BBC was not so hot on DJs speaking out back then.

Despite all the fun and flamboyance of glam rock, the early '70s was actually a pretty tough time. National strikes, the Three-Day Week, the oil crisis that sent prices rocketing (and prompted a vinyl shortage), endless debates about the Common Market. The situation became so unstable that two General Elections were called during 1974. The bad times even visited the innocuous world of teenybopper pop that year, and unfortunately, I was on hand to witness it.

David Cassidy's hearthrob status had grown considerably since 1970 when he first starred in the television series, *The Partridge Family*. In 1972, his pop career took off in earnest and he enjoyed a string of massive singles – *Could It Be Forever, How Can I Be Sure, I'm A Clown, Daydreamer* – that sent girls wild. Whenever he flew into Heathrow, he was greeted by thousands of teenage screamers. Everyone was envious, of course, and no one more so than the competition, The Osmonds, The Jackson Five and, waiting in the wings, David Essex.

The whole lot of them no doubt heaved a sigh of relief when, towards the end of his world tour, he announced that he'd soon be retiring from live concerts. By the time Cassidy was ready to perform the penultimate show, at the White City Stadium in West London, the hysteria had reached fever pitch. On May 26, 1974 I found myself standing before 35,000 barely controllable fans attempting to compere the show.

"Hi! You all having a great time?" I called out. Despite the deafening screams and the scarf waving, it was obvious that not everyone inside the stadium was. I'd spotted the crowds pushing against the safety barriers long before the show started, and I remember saying to the organisers, "Do you think it's really safe down there?" I wasn't sure there were enough security staff on hand to control the situation but I was told not to worry, that everything would be fine.

Midway though the concert, there was another great surge from the audience, and it didn't look good at all. Hysteria of a quite different sort began to engulf the crowd, and Cassidy's desperate pleas for everyone to "Move back now!" went largely unheard. More than 500 other fans suffered injuries in the crush. One girl, 14-year-old Bernadette Whelan, fell into a coma and died in hospital a few days later. It was a truly tragic day for pop music.

"KENNY TOLD ME HIS ATTEMPTED SUICIDE WAS THE RESULT OF EATING A STRAWBERRY GATEAU..."

Back at Broadcasting House, I'd settled into my mid-morning slot, and even began to enjoy the handover banter with Noel Edmonds without cursing him under my breath! But my loyalty to the station had been shaken. I even allowed myself to be courted by Capital Radio, one of the new independent radio stations launched in 1973. Six years after killing off the pirates, the government finally saw sense and accepted that commercial radio had an important role to play in British cultural life.

The approach came via Kenny Everett, one of the new station's first recruits, who asked if he could drive over and discuss it with me. I said, "Fine, come for dinner at eight and turn off the M4. Nine o'clock came and still no Kenny. I rang him at home – no reply. It got to 11 o'clock and I said to Tessa, "Kenny's obviously not coming, let's go to bed." Shortly after midnight, there's a knock at the door. It's Kenny. "I think I've just been to Wales and back," he said. "Didn't you notice that anything was wrong?" I asked. "Well, I did see a sign to Bristol but I carried on," he said, straight-faced.

"Then I came to this bridge, and I realised I'd gone too far." About 100 miles too far. But that was Kenny, always in a world of his own.

We made him a coffee, and that's when he said there was a job waiting for me at Capital. I was flattered to be asked, but I can't say I was tempted at all. I'd been listening to the station one day while driving down the M4, but then the signal suddenly disappeared somewhere around the Hungerford area. That was it. There was no way I would consider switching to a radio station that couldn't be heard nationally.

It wasn't long afterwards that Kenny attempted suicide. He later told me he did it was because he'd mistakenly eaten a strawberry gateau that had totally ruined the effect of what had otherwise been a fabulous meal. I'm not even sure he was joking.

I too was about to embark on my own form of self-destruction – at least, in terms of my relationship with Tessa. Though tabloid photographers would turn up at *Hollycroft* and leave with a *Hello!*-style tableau of untroubled domestic delight, cracks were starting to appear behind the scenes.

Once Simon had begun to walk, and grown to trust his nanny, Tessa was ready to get back to work again. I know it sounds terribly old-fashioned now, but I wasn't too happy with the idea. Besides, Tessa was a highly desirable woman. I didn't want her away filming for weeks on end surrounded by men hitting on her all the time. I knew how men behave. And like many men, I too was extremely insecure and insanely possessive. There's only so much of that which a partner can tolerate before things become strained and resentments start to surface.

The things that bind a couple together during the early days of a relationship weren't happening either. While my desire for Tessa was still strong, I didn't feel the same sense of infatuation coming from her, and that upset me. As a consequence, we became less tolerant of each other's tastes and habits. It always surprised me that she wanted to do these heavy dramas, depressing Chekhov plays that even she'd fall asleep in when we watched them on television. My advice was that she try comedy, advice I was to regret a couple of years later . . .

"AS IRRITATING AS I COULD BE, I THOUGHT TESSA WOULD STILL PUT UP WITH ME."

Still wounded from the changes in my professional life, and becoming increasingly anxious about life at home, my reaction was to break out and give my self-esteem a boost. An opportunity presented itself when I found myself in Huddersfield visiting a family of Wombles. It was spring 1974, and with Wombles fever at its height, someone at Radio One hit on the idea of broadcasting a show from the living-room of a real-life Mr & Mrs Womble. Mike Batt, the record producer behind the Wombles, travelled up with me – though it was the night spent with an attractive, slightly older woman named Yvonne that remains the trip's most vivid memory.

My insecure mind and straying ways meant that home was fast becoming a more complicated place to be. The rot really set in after we fell in with a very nice couple, Margo and Roger Webb, who lived down the road. He was a songwriter, she was a well built half English, half Chinese woman and stunning with it. They were an extremely social couple, often hosting showbusiness parties at weekends, attended by everyone from Michael Parkinson to Beryl Reid and Tessie O'Shea. Before we knew it, each weekend would start round at the Webbs for drinks on Fridays, hit its partying peak there on Saturday night and end with a relaxing round of tennis with them on Sunday afternoons. We'd be virtually paralytic the whole time.

On a particularly hot or wild night, the more liberated guests would peel off and swim naked in the outdoor swimming pool.

While all eyes were firmly trained on the poolside activities, I found myself drifting ever closer into the arms of Margo in a more secluded part of the garden. Before long, we were deeply embedded in a steamy affair.

I was a young husband and a father, yet I was already living a double life. I'd look at my young family and I'd feel sad that all the aspirations I had were in tatters. Then I'd fool around with Margo and feel overcome with a sense of relief, as if the act of infidelity would somehow make my doubts and insecurities go away. The truth was that it made everything worse. My relationship with Tessa had drifted into an emotional no-man's-land, but taking the easy way out was no answer. I arranged for a pool to be built at Hollycroft so that Tessa and I might more spend time together at home. But any good that might have done was undermined by the fact that I'd also started renting a room at the Royal Garden Hotel in Kensington so that Margo and I could continue our dangerous liaisons without interruption.

Conveniently, I was appearing on a pop panel game for Radio Two once a week in the evenings, so after I'd finish my show at midday Margo and I would shut ourselves away for a few hours. I knew the manager at the Royal Garden, and he gave me a reduced rate for the room, as well as access to the back entrance of the hotel. It was all very discreet. Even if we wanted coffee, Margo would disappear into the bathroom before room service arrived.

I was living my life on a knife-edge. It was quite uncharacteristic but something kicked in that enabled me to cope with it all. That went out the window the day that Margo let slip that Tessa had been having an affair with her husband. With both of us looking for thrills elsewhere, it was obvious that our marriage was heading for total collapse.

I began to sketch in the full picture. I thought back to all those times I'd called from the set of *Seaside Special*, the BBC television series I began co-hosting with David Hamilton in 1974, when the nanny always seemed to be ready with some excuse why Tessa was unable to come to the phone. Now I knew why.

It was very much our own Home Counties version of *Celebrity Wife Swap* – except that the rules weren't fully explained to one of the couples. I had absolutely no idea that Tessa had either been wanting or having an affair, and I don't think she ever knew about Margo and me, at least not until I went public about it in 1984.

One of the regulars at Margo and Roger's saucy soirées was an ITV television producer. He was developing *Robin's Nest*, a new sitcom spin off from the enormously popular *Man About The House* series. The star of that show, Richard O'Sullivan, was already on board for the title role. But Robin still needed a co-star for his Nest. For a long time, I'd been encouraging Tessa to lighten up when it came to picking her roles, so when she was offered the part opposite Richard, I felt it was the right move for her. What no one had bargained for was Tessa and Richard taking their on-screen chemistry into their private lives.

In the series, Robin Tripp and his girlfriend Vicky ran a bistro. Behind the scenes, Richard and Tessa were falling in love. There was little likelihood of that happening between Margo and me. Our relationship was built purely on lust and mutual desire. She was magnificently attractive, so much so that I even put up with her awful smoking. But while we did eventually share a rented flat while I was divorcing Tessa, neither of us seriously imagined that we'd stay together. Margo was way too wild and off the wall for me. One time, when we were in a restaurant in Kensington, she got the urge to gamble at a nearby casino and simply got up and went. I was left alone at the table with two half-eaten plates of food for company. Margo could be infuriatingly unpredictable.

The inevitable day of reckoning came one Friday in October 1976. Though neither Tessa nor I had been brave enough to properly confront the other with our infidelities, she had nevertheless been openly talking about leaving for several months. As irritating as I knew I could be at times, I still thought she'd stick with it and that the relationship would soon get back on track. I was wrong.

The day Tessa convinced me that she really meant it, I swallowed several Valium, opened myself a bottle of wine and sat down to watch *Fawlty Towers*. The idea was that I'd die laughing, though in truth, I knew I'd not consumed enough of either to cause myself any real harm. Tessa found me slumped on the couch and slurring my words, and when the doctor arrived, he promptly packed me off to bed. Next morning, Tessa came with me to Broadcasting House for what must rate as the strangest radio show I've presented in my life. Kenny Everett would have been proud! But with my head spinning uncontrollably, and my heart heavy with pain, I wasn't proud at all. I was ashamed. I despise failure and it would take me several years before I could come to terms with the destruction of my marriage.

I'd managed to convince Tessa to stay with me for one last weekend. I couldn't bear the idea of her leaving on a Friday and me being alone for two days. She told me that for the past three months, she'd been renting a house in the nearby village of Datchet, and that she and Simon would be leaving on the Monday morning.

For the final supper, on Sunday night, I put on a dinner jacket. "What on earth are you doing?" Tessa asked, looking at me as if I was some kind of idiot. I told her that as I was about to eat the saddest meal of my life, the occasion required a certain formality. It was heartbreaking, especially when I looked at little Simon, not yet four years old, who had no idea whatsoever that his life was about to change dramatically.

On air that following Monday morning, I could barely hold myself together, let alone manage a customary "Terrific!" I had tried and tried and tried, but all in vain. Tessa had fallen out of love with me and nothing I could do or say was ever going to change that. After little more than four years, our marriage was over.

The journey home from Broadcasting House was more awful still, because I knew that the only thing waiting for me at *Hollycroft* was the deafening silence of a failed marriage. I walked in and out of each room, staring at the empty spaces, barely able to think straight. Despite all our problems, I'd wanted us to stay together for Simon's sake. And now all that was left was the lifeless shell of my son's empty bedroom. I broke down and wept like a child. I'm glad I had no idea how long I'd have to wait for the heartbreak to heal. God knows what I might have done if I had.

* * *

TIME FOR (ANOTHER) BLACKBURN
THE SON: SIMON

Being the son of Tony Blackburn obviously marked me out for a bit of ribbing at school, especially when I was around 9 or 10, but it wasn't that bad. There were plenty of other dads that were equally embarrassing! In fact, mine was actually pretty cool. Whereas a lot of the other fathers would turn up at school dressed in corduroys, dad would roll up with a jet-ski towed on the back of his car. His arrival attracted plenty of excitement, so I was glad that one of the other boys was the son of a Bee Gee, which helped deflect some of the attention.

The most embarrassing thing – and this happens if your father's famous or not – is when your dad decides to get involved with a kick-about, bowl a cricket ball or bawl out advice from the sidelines. My dad did all that. But the thing I remember most about him during my schooldays was just how amazingly supportive he was. When I was 17 or 18, and played for the First XI at school, dad travelled hundreds of miles after his Saturday morning show to watch me play. He was my greatest supporter and I really appreciated that.

Thinking back, I'm amazed how he managed to keep awake for me at the weekends, because he'd be up at around 3.30 am for those early morning shows. There were times when he'd collapse on the sofa on Sundays if he'd eaten too many wine gums or something.

When we first used to go out together at weekends, dad was still in his Oasis-style fame days with an audience of millions on Radio One. Probably because I was having so much fun, I'd never notice people pointing and coming up to him like they do now. Both my parents were determined to give me a straightforward and normal life and I'm very grateful to them for that. I don't think I've been adversely affected by their public lives at all.

The only times I'd be forced to take a deep breath and hope for the best was when an article appeared in one of the tabloids. That happened several times during my early teens. Most of the stories revolved around dad's "Ladies man" exploits, or perhaps one of his outrageously politically incorrect outbursts! I found it relatively easy to brush that stuff off. Nobody takes the tabloids seriously.

I was too young to remember dad's 'difficult years', though one day when I was well into my teens, the subject did come up. He was very open about how tough it all was, and I was just at the right age to begin to understand what he went through. It must have been hard having a son that you love very much living with your ex-wife and another man. It is upsetting to hear that sometimes he'd drop me off home then have to break his journey home because he was too upset to drive. But he never showed that side to me. Dad has always been a very upbeat guy, always determined to put a brave face on things.

It's difficult for me to talk about my parents' break-up because I was so young and really it's their stuff. But they did marry quite young . . . I'm just pleased that both of them picked themselves up and got on with their lives. My mother and father don't see much of each other now, but they did throughout my schooldays and beyond, and there was never any animosity. They'd both be there at parents' evenings, and they seemed to get on well together. That's the truth.

In my teens, I went through my own difficult patch though I really wasn't that much trouble. Maybe I rebelled a little more than dad had done as a youth, but still for me it was only surface things such as smoking and wearing an earring. Yeah, I messed around at school, but I didn't get suspended or expelled. And putting an earring in when you're 18 and travelling around Australia is hardly a massive statement!

The low point in our relationship came when I was about 15, and we'd been arguing while sat in his car. I turned to him and said, "You just tell crap gags for a living." Now dad rarely swears, but on this occasion he did and it really shook me up. "Yes, Simon, I do. But it's a fucking good living. And you just remember who you're talking to." I'd never seen him come over like that, before or since.

Dad can be serious in other ways, too. We all used to dread school report time, but he had a very different attitude to it than most parents. He'd skim over the individual subject comments with a cursory, "Don't you enjoy geography?", and go straight to the character references from the headmaster and housemaster. "Frankly, you can get as many A grades as you want," he told me, "but if you're an arse you're not gonna go anywhere." He was serious about that. To him it's the way people conduct themselves that really matters. That's when my perceptions of him started to change. I'm not saying that he's a 100% totally sensible guy off air, but he does have a lot of integrity in the way he lives his life, and I respect that.

Dad was very well behaved when he did his growing up on the South Coast, but I think he's become more rebellious as he's got older. He knows radio inside out and it annoys him when things move so slowly in that field. The people who grant the licences for new stations, for example, average something like 74 years of age. Dad's in his 60s now, though he's still young and dynamic in his outlook, and I'd love to see him achieve his dream of running his own radio station. I'm sure he'd make a fantastic job of it.

Personally, I'd like to see him do something a bit juicier on TV. I know he's critical about his early television experiences in the late 60s, but he always seems to be on something whenever I switch on, and comes across as a natural. And, yes, I do sometimes get that call: "You might just wanna tune in to . . !"

He loves all that, being on the telly and presenting the breakfast show, and in that respect he's a complete extrovert. If he walks into a room, he'll light the place up, and everyone will be in a better mood almost instantly. But at the same time, he's a loner who's quite happy with his own company. Perhaps that's a normal response to having people wanting a bit of you for most of your adult life. He's never enjoyed pubs and isn't big on parties and social gatherings either. His real passion is for his work, his family and the people he loves, and his greatest pleasure in life is to make people happy as much as he can.

I was pleased, and more than a little relieved, when he met and married Debbie. They're absolutely wonderful together and my half-sister Victoria is already developing into a real character. No one likes to see their father on his own for too long, and as I was growing up it was sad to see him go back home to an empty house. Thankfully, he was usually incredibly busy too, and that always keeps his spirits up.

The only time I've really worried about him in recent years was when he decided he was going to do the Jungle programme. My first reaction was, "Oh God, no! Don't". Virtually no one benefits from taking part in those shows, and I was concerned that it might take its toll on him physically, too. More selfishly, I'm a Media Planner and thought, "Hmmm, dad live on the box every day – and I work with people who buy advertising on TV!" But he was brilliant.

I've never told him this, but on a couple of occasions during the series, I got very emotional watching him. After a couple of days, and he became himself, you realised what an amazingly lovely man he is and I was so proud of him. People started coming up to me and saying, "Your dad's a nice chap, isn't he". I suddenly felt very protective towards him, but in all that time, not even the newspapers could find a nasty word to say. I felt as if I'd not appreciated him enough for his qualities as a human being. He was just so good, so patient with the others, and yet I hadn't fully realised that until I saw it for my own eyes on the small screen.

Appearing on *I'm A Celebrity* . . . made him a household name all over again. It was a really smart move. I know dad likes people to think he's the fool but he's actually a very shrewd businessman. How else could he have kept himself in the limelight for all these years? You've got to keep reinventing yourself, and though the papers continue with the old "Popadoodledoo" thing, he's managed to transcend all of that. Most of all, you've got to be incredibly good at what you do in order to survive for so long, and as far as I'm concerned dad's the best in the business.

8

ALONE AGAIN

There is a miserable kind of perfection in the fact that the month I lost Tessa and Simon, the Sex Pistols released their first single, *Anarchy In The UK*. I'm not even sure that I heard it right away, because the group's revolting antics had earned them bans from virtually every avenue of public life. I hated punk rock and everything it represented. Of all the musical styles that have emerged over the past half-century, punk is the only one that struck me as being utterly devoid of any worth or value whatsoever. Quite why anyone would choose to listen to a group of tuneless amateurs shouting abuse at the top of their voices was and still is quite beyond me.

But there's a twist in the tale. Years later, I found myself strangely warming to the punk era's public enemy number one, Johnny Rotten. In 2004, two years after I'd been voted *King Of The Jungle*, it was his turn to be let loose in the Australian rainforest with a handful of strangers. Back in 1977, punk's annus mirabilis, I remember looking at the safety-pinned hordes and thinking, "Oh, do grow up. In 20 years time, you'll all be watching *Coronation Street* with your zip-up slippers on." It might have been worse. Had he not come to his punkish senses and bowed out with one of his trademark expletives, old rotten Johnny was in danger of becoming everything he hated: a national treasure.

As someone who'd already triumphed in the jungle, but had never bothered to sit down and watch just how it happened, I found it fascinating to observe the transformation of someone with such a strong public persona as Johnny Rotten. When he walked in, he was effing and blinding all over the place, and sticking his fingers up at the camera. Yet within days, he'd become this rather sweet, slightly older gentleman who spoke lovingly of the environment in which he found himself, and offered a mature shoulder on which the more vulnerable members of the team could lean on for comfort. I thought, "Hey, this guy's just like me!" He spoke about the richness of the natural colours he saw, and the beautiful skies, and it was obvious that he'd fallen in love with the place. I wouldn't be surprised if he, like me, felt that his life had been significantly changed his jungle experience. But more of that later . . .

Back in '77, though, Rotten was on the rampage and kicking out at everything. And so, in my own way, was I. I didn't go for his ugly brand of rock'n'roll, but I certainly had my fair share of sex and drugs, as well as a few run ins with the authorities. Hooked on prescription drugs to help me through my divorce, numbing my pain with a series of one-night stands, and indulging my petty whims on air, I was behaving like the fifth Sex Pistol: Pretty Vacant.

* * *

"AS THE SAD SONG BEGAN TO FADE, I SAID,
'THIS RECORD IS DEDICATED TO THE PERSON WHO
WILL ALWAYS BE VERY, VERY SPECIAL TO ME.'"

The manner in which the break-up of my marriage was announced irked me for a start. It was one of my colleagues, a latecomer to Radio One and hardly one of the most popular characters at the station, who blew the whistle and told the tabloids. I was extremely upset because I'd explained my situation to him in confidence.

To make matters worse, the reporters got their story wrong, suggesting that Tessa had gone to live with DJ Paul Burnett and his wife. Then they decamped outside her new rented home ruining the privacy that she and Simon deserved. I was so angry that I too went public and named the DJ who'd stitched me up, only to find myself restrained by a gagging order never to discuss him by name in public again. So I won't.

In light of the revelations, on October 15, 1976, I decided to hold a press conference at the BBC, where I broke down having told the assembled throng, "I still love her". I'd started proceedings with a quip that we were "a happily separated couple!", but I just couldn't keep that brave face on. My grief also found its way on air. I introduced a song called *(We've) Throw It All Away*, by R&J Stone (produced by my friend Phil Swern), with the words, "In the unfortunate circumstances I find myself in at this moment, it's pretty appropriate." As the sad song began to fade, I returned to the theme: "This record is dedicated to the person who will always be very, very special to me."

It wasn't the last time I alluded to the breakdown of my marriage on the show either. In a rather cruel twist of fate, the big Number One hit single at the time was a heartbreaker ballad by Chicago called *If You Leave Me Now*. I found it painful to listen to, and sometimes the best way to deal with that was to confide in the listener. Broadcasting came so naturally to me that sometimes the boundaries between public and private life became hopelessly blurred. I like that in a broadcaster. It makes it easier to identify with that person as a human being, rather than a scripted automaton. Even though John Peel was my polar opposite in so many ways, that was definitely something we shared as professionals. And I still do it on air now, often regaling the listeners with stories about the latest film or West End musical I've been to see with my wife and daughter. The mistake I made back in the late '70s was not fully understanding that an audience does not really want to hear bad news. People have got enough problems of their own without suffering a DJ's tragic tales.

It was ironic, really. Just when I needed a strong producer to take me aside and tell me to go easy on the sad stuff, no one did. Things had changed in ten years at Radio One. I was allowed to go on far too often about my marriage breakdown; bored the nation stupid with it, in fact. And no one told me. I mean, the papers did exaggerate it. I certainly didn't harp on about it all the time, but I was extremely emotional during those months and letting it all hang out was, in retrospect, a mistake.

"I WAS TOO BUSY FLOATING THROUGH LIFE DOSED UP ON VALIUM TO TAKE MUCH NOTICE."

The first inkling I had that not all was well with my superiors at Broadcasting House was in autumn 1977, when I was suddenly shifted from the mid-morning slot to the 2-4.30 afternoon shift. It was, I suppose, another mild demotion. But it didn't affect me in the way that the big 1973 shake-up had done. That was because I was too busy floating through life dosed up on Valium to take much notice.

Resentment is not a particularly admirable human trait, but there are times in life when it can get the better of us. I found the split with Tessa, and the subsequent divorce too much to bear, and I ran straight to the medicine cupboard for comfort. I soon discovered that anti-depressants helped blot out the wilder emotional swings, enabling me to function without collapsing in a heap.

One thing that didn't change was that I still visited my parents as often as I could. Now, though, there was an ulterior motive. My doctor father prescribed me the anti-depressant Valium, knowing that it would help me sleep. What he didn't know was that I soon started to take them at any time of the day. I don't think he realised just how addicted to them I became. He certainly had no idea that I was raiding his handsome supply of the strong barbiturate, Tuinol, which he took to ease his incessant back problems. I'd take packets of the stuff back home without him ever noticing.

There are probably some people who might think I've never had much of a grip on reality, that as soon as I walk through the front door I greet my wife with a breathless, "Have you heard the one about . . .?" They're wrong. I am firmly rooted in the here and now, and always have been. I know what my responsibilities are, keep up to date with world affairs, and have a keen nose for news of technological advances. But in the immediate years following the break-up of my marriage, my feet rarely touched the ground. I'd lost the plot. I discovered that by misusing prescription drugs and washing them down with a few glasses of cheap wine, I could blot out my problems. It wasn't right, I knew that. But in my time of need, getting high helped me blot out reality until I was ready, able and willing to deal with it head on again.

In all honesty, I enjoyed the woozy effects of the drink and drug concoction, which was not unlike the sensation of a pre-med in hospital. It put up a protection, gave me a space in which to lose myself in, even if it was a barmy world to be in. After four of those high strength blue Valiums, the room certainly span around quite nicely. Although I made sure not to take them during weekdays, when I was working, the effects stayed with me. I remember almost getting run over outside Broadcasting House one day because I was so relaxed I'd become virtually comatose.

Nobody else had a clue what I was up to. I lived in isolation at *Hollycroft*, a house once such an oasis of love and joy, but now simply a huge, empty reminder of what I'd lost. I'd often spend entire weekends there stumbling around in a drug-induced daze and eating cold food from tins. On a good night, I'd just about stagger up to bed.

The only person who might have had an inkling of what was going on was my mother. I'd ring her up for a chat, doing my best not to slur my words, but sometimes she'd say, "Hey, are you all right?" I'd never tell her the truth. I wanted to grieve alone and saw no benefit in discussing my situation with anyone – either friends or family. I had hit the lowest point in my life.

I had no idea just how dependent I'd become on the heady cocktail of drink and drugs until I had the most terrible shakes while in bed with a lovely Chinese girl I knew. "It's a heart attack!" I said, and immediately phoned my father. "Have you taken your Valium?" he asked. I hadn't. But those words were enough to confirm to me that I was a slave to the stuff. I decided there and then: no more Valium. Checking into a costly rehab centre or seeking out any other complicated methods of withdrawal didn't occur to me. But the simple exercising of one's willpower was by no means easy. "One tonight won't hurt," I'd tell myself, "just to help me sleep. No more tomorrow." My father suggested that I take it slowly, so I did. After a few weeks, I'd weaned myself off the habit and have never, ever been troubled by the blotto urge since.

* * *

"'I SHALL NEVER AGAIN MARRY ANYONE IN SHOWBUSINESS,' I LOUDLY DECLARED. I MEANT IT, TOO."

During that period, I found myself saying and doing some pretty crazy things, but I experienced a few moments of real clarity, too. In the summer of '77, while the Sex Pistols were poking fun at the Queen's Silver Jubilee, I was more concerned with overthrowing another old institution – the antiquated divorce laws, which seemed to be unfairly weighted in favour of the woman. "A man can lose his children, his house, in fact everything he has worked for, simply because his wife walks out," I told one newspaper – carefully omitting any mention of magnificent Margo. In fact, I'd been telling the newspapers that neither of us had strayed – a double lie.

On November 7, 1977, I was granted a quickie postal divorce from Tessa on account of her adultery with Richard O'Sullivan. I was now free to be seen with Margo in public, but financially, the settlement hit me hard. I had no problem paying around £5,000 per year for Simon's schooling, nanny and general upkeep. It was alimony to Tessa that irked me most, although as soon as she and Richard moved in together, I was no longer obliged to pay it – and I didn't. "I shall never again marry anyone in showbusiness," I loudly declared. I meant it, too.

Two things kept me going throughout this personal nightmare. One was my radio show, which proved that an invisible audience won't ever let you down even if the real people in your life do. The other was my son, Simon. Throughout the divorce negotiations, I'd made it very clear that I didn't want any other man being referred to as my son's "daddy". I was Simon's father, as I probably reminded my listeners a little too often during those difficult days.

Now, when I turn the pages of an old photo album and see Simon's smiling face staring out between those of his proud parents, it makes me sad to think that Tessa and I messed it up for him. Then I think of how he's turned out, a magnificent young man who's making a success of his career in the advertising world and who is always kind and considerate to other people, and I stop beating myself up about it. After all that happened between his parents, Simon has grown up to become everything I'd hoped he would be.

Apart from the very worst moments of my descent into a private hell, I made sure that I was always there for my son. It was difficult to accept that I was just a weekend father, but then I'd already compromised my ideals back at *Hollycroft*, when I agreed to the idea of putting him in the care of a nanny. I didn't want him to go away to school either, but that happened, too. But what no one could take away from me were those times when I'd pick him up after doing my Saturday morning show and spend the rest of the weekend with him. As he grew up, he developed a passion for football, which meant that I had to travel around the country to cheer him on – and in all temperatures! – despite having no interest in the game whatsoever. But I wanted to be there for him as much as I could, and I soon got used to freezing to death on the touchline alongside a few other fathers.

Despite the obvious difficulties that came from separation, I think I had a great relationship with Simon while he was growing up. When you're a weekend father, there's a tendency to over-compensate and shower the child with armfuls of gifts, no doubt turning them into ungrateful so-and-so's in later life. Before we'd go off and see a film, I'd often take him to Bill Wyman's Sticky Fingers restaurant just off Kensington High Street, which was very close to where I was living at that time. Simon knew there was a toyshop round the corner, and we'd always make our way there afterwards, and I'd buy him something. One day, I explained to him that he probably had enough cars and that no one should expect presents every week. From that time he's never asked me for anything!

In the early days of the divorce, I struggled with the arrangement. After several lovely hours together, I'd drive Simon back to Tessa's place, have a strained but always polite conversation with his mother, then I'd say goodbye and walk back to my car alone. On many occasions, I'd pull the car over to the side of the road and cry my eyes out. Dropping him off brought everything into sharp focus. I was estranged from the son I adored, and that was as heartbreaking as it was just plain wrong.

I know that Simon will be embarrassed to read that I regard him as an exemplary young man today, successful in his career and with a lovely girlfriend too, but there was a time when our relationship became strained. Happily, his spell as a rebellious teenager didn't last long, and that earring and smoking habit only turned out to be a student-era phase. But I did find it frustrating when this once sweet and considerate boy suddenly transformed into an uncommunicative refusenik. He'd pick holes in everything I said and did. Almost overnight, young Simon Blackburn seemed to know it all.

"Oh, so you've become a teenager at last," I told him, trying to make light of it. I didn't get much of a response, so I laid the boot in a bit. "You're going through that awkward stage. You've become annoying." He looked sheepish and remorseful, quickly apologised, and he's never been any trouble since!

I know it sounds far-fetched but Tessa and I have never really had a moment's worry from him. Everybody loves him and nobody more than I do. Despite being born into a showbusiness family, Simon never really picked up Tessa's acting bug, and he's far too private a person to get involved in what I do. Media planning is his thing, and I'm very happy for him, and proud too.

* * *

"MY BOSSES WERE TELLING THE PRESS, 'TONY IS JUST NOT HIMSELF AT THE MOMENT', BUT I WAS SO SPACED OUT THAT I HAVE NO RECOLLECTION OF IT."

While my son generally conducted his teenage years with remarkable dignity, I must confess that his father was still in many ways floundering aimlessly. In a rather unfortunate bit of timing, my agent and protector Harold Davison had upped sticks and moved to California bang in the middle of my divorce. I lost my PR man Les Perrin, too, when he died suddenly of a heart attack in 1979. With my decade-long support system collapsing all around me, I decided to take the initiative myself and blow the lid on my whiter-than-white public image. "Believe it or not, I do drink," I told one tabloid reporter shortly after my split with Tessa. "And I actually did have sex with girlfriends before I married." I might as well have added "during the marriage" too.

Even my patience with the BBC was wearing thin. During the winter of '77, I'd thrown myself back into panto, partly to give me something else to think about. But doing three shows a day at weekends in addition to my weekday afternoon show proved too much on top of everything else, and by March 1978, I'd made myself desperately ill with it all. Charles McLennan, Controller of Radio One at the time, advised me to take a short break, though as a measure of just how out of sorts I was at the time, I have barely any recollection of this episode in my life at all. But the dog-eared black-and-white newspaper cuttings in front of me don't lie. Here's Derek Chinnery in one report, insisting that "Tony is just not himself at the moment". Here's another, this time that ubiquitous "spokesman for the BBC", saying that I "clearly wasn't well" during my late February broadcasts. It appears that I took a one-week rest on the advice of a throat specialist in Windsor, so my voice was in shreds, just like the rest of me. A year later, I admitted in the press that I'd been taking tranquillisers to help me through what was turning out to be rather a long rough patch.

It wasn't wholly, unremittingly bleak. It was the era of *Saturday Night Fever* and *Grease*, and I loved the new disco music almost as much as I hated punk rock. At the time, everyone in the music industry seemed to be knocking disco. Some even wore "Disco Sucks!" badges, no doubt those very same people who today claim they loved ABBA and The Bee Gees all along. Disco was fun, feelgood music aimed directly at the dancefloor – and it worked. The nightlife came alive again during this period, and in my best moments, so did I. I particularly loved KC & The Sunshine Band and Sister Sledge, though the song that sums up everything that's wonderful about the disco era has to be Village People's *YMCA*. I just adored that song. I defy anyone not to clap and sing along to it while it's playing.

Disco music also upped the fun quota at all those Radio One Roadshows. Although Johnny Beerling disputes this, I believe I came up with the original idea for the Roadshow. Whatever the truth, from the early '70s on the Roadshow was a key event in the Radio One calendar, and one that most of us looked forward to each summer. Several of us would be packed off for a week or so at a time, broadcasting from various town and city centres or beaches dressed in our regulation 275 T-shirts and jackets.

The Radio One Roadshow also provided the more demonstrative among us with the perfect excuse to excel in a spot of DJ buffoonery. Dave Lee Travis (DLT), the gigantic hairy cornflake of the airwaves, was especially good in front of a live audience. Later on, Peter Powell, Mike Read and Andy Peebles in particular also came into their own on the Roadshow.

Because I was usually portrayed as Mr Goody-Goody in the press, I'd sometimes receive a bit of ribbing from the more drunken elements in the crowd. It wasn't particularly pleasant to hear the occasional chorus of "Tony Blackburn's a wanker!" from a few blokes at the back, but one of the first rules you learn about partying and having fun is that there'll always be someone wanting to spoil it. It's annoying, but it's also a fact of life.

Funnily enough, even though I'm famous for making people laugh (or, perhaps, cringe) at my gags, I don't enjoy practical jokes. Unfortunately, an enormous amount of practical jokery went on behind the scenes, mostly involving Noel Edmonds and Mike Read. I remember Mike once placing a dead fish behind my radiator, and waking up the next morning wanting to wretch because of this most awful smell. The apple pie bed, which I'd not experienced since school days, was a particular favourite too. That's where some clown double-folds your bedsheet so that when you pull it back to climb in, you find that you can't, which means that you have to remake the bed from scratch. Exceedingly tiresome. The only practical joke that I've ever found in any way amusing is the fart machine. I still have one upstairs, though regrettably, I've not had much use out of it recently.

The best laughs were spontaneous and unplanned – such as the day when Rosko and I were hosting the Roadshow in Weston-Super-Mare and the tide came in so quickly that by the time the show finished we were up to our knees in water. We were the lucky ones – most of the crowd, and their belongings, were floating in front of the stage! That, together with the increasing numbers of yobs who'd come out of the pub and start throwing bottles and cans at the stage, forced the organisers to move the Roadshow to a late morning slot.

There was not much we could do about the occasional rogue who would charm his way up to the microphone. Once, Rosko was doing his usual, "It's so nice to be here with all you mummios and daddios" bit, when he thrust his microphone under someone's nose and asked, "What's your name?" The lad didn't even bother to introduce himself. "Is Dusty Springfield a lesbian?" he said. "Er, well," the Emperor cringed, "she's a wonderful singer, the greatest white soul singer of 'em all .. !"

John Peel was hardly first out of the tracks when it came to these audience participation radio fun functions. But he had an extraordinarily memorable experience the day he made it up to Mallory Park, a motor racing track in Leicestershire, for what was billed, "BBC Radio 1 Race Day". It was July 30, 1978 and, though punk was still all the rage, Radio One played it safe and booked The Bay City Rollers as the day's star attraction. By then a good two or three years past their peak, the Rollers' arrival by helicopter still brought out the screamers, many of whom were dressed in the band's trademark tartan.

However, the moment John Peel later described as the most remarkable in all his years at Radio One had nothing whatsoever to do with The Bay City Rollers. Or the DJs "Popstacle Race". Or the mediaeval tent that had been specially erected for the event. At some point in the afternoon, John gazed out across the lake just in time to see me waving wildly from a speedboat that was being driven by a Womble. He'd often recount the memory of this spectacular vision in his later years, always insisting that he'd never again see anything comparable to that in his lifetime. I'm glad I finally did something to make Grumpy Old John happy after all those years!

It's a pity Peel wasn't travelling on the train from Liverpool to London the day Mike Batt and I were making our way back from a Radio One personal appearance. As we left, I said to Mike, "Do you know what? I fancy having a bit of a Womble". He knew exactly what I meant. "Well, go on then, pop it on," he urged. And for the entire journey, I sat in a First Class compartment dressed head to toe in a Wombles outfit. It felt great! And we had the carriage to ourselves all the way back home.

* * *

Poptastic

"I SET MYSELF UP AS A SEX THERAPIST ON AIR... MY ADVICE WAS SIMPLE AND TO THE POINT. 'WHY NOT SPLIT UP AND FIND YOURSELF ANOTHER GIRLFRIEND?'"

Wombling antics aside, I found myself becoming a little more belligerent as the end of the decade approached. One day, when I was guesting on a regional talk show with the agony aunt Anna Raeburn, she suddenly laid into me and implied that I was a woman hater. I was furious and gave as good as I got. I remember saying to her, "How can anyone trust all this advice from someone who got married after a three-week whirlwind romance?" We got into a stand-up fight, which became so animated that the producer extended the programme by half an hour. Anna and I didn't let it stop there, and continued our battle back at the hotel afterwards. Oddly, whenever we've met since, we get on fine as if the incident never happened.

I've always been suspicious of these self appointed agony aunts, though. I don't think that sorting out other people's problems is half as difficult as they like to make it seem. To prove the point, on my sex'n'soul show for Radio London in the '80s I set myself up as a sex therapist, a "self-ordained priest repairing shoes while you wait!". Someone would ring into the show and say, "I'm not getting on well with my girlfriend. We argue the whole time." My advice was usually along the lines of, "Why not split up and find yourself another girlfriend?" You just can't argue with the plain-speaking commonsense view. It's so simple that it's almost a thing of beauty. An agony aunt would be the last person I'd ever turn to for advice. They've almost all got worse track records than the people they're purporting to sort out.

Another commentator that got me hot under the collar was *The Telegraph*'s radio critic Gillian Reynolds. In a piece that ran in the May 30, 1979 edition of the paper, she complained of the "saccharine jollities" of daytime DJs such as myself, Peter Powell and Kid Jensen. I couldn't let that go. I called her "a frustrated broadcaster" and worse on my afternoon show, and Derek Chinnery called me into his office to explain myself.

I wasn't unduly concerned. It didn't seem to be the worst crime anyone had ever committed on air, and after all, the main drift of my argument was to defend my profession against opinion-formers who didn't know what they were talking about. In the days that followed, I led a charm offensive in the press, stating that far from saccharine, "My jokes are there to irritate people as much as to make them laugh". I even reeled off a few as if to prove that I'd not lost my ability to elicit a mass groan from a good portion of my six million-plus afternoon audience (up from four and a half when I first took over in 1977):

"Have you heard the one about the Eskimo who's wife left him in the cold?"

"Isn't it wonderful to be a doctor. In what other job could you see a woman take off her clothes and then send her husband the bill?"

Imagine my surprise, then, when Derek Chinnery called me back into his office that summer and announced that my on-air indiscretion was in breach of my £20,000 a year contract and that, once again, I would be on the move. I would broadcast my final afternoon show on August 28, 1979, a show that would then pass into the capable hands of Andy Peebles. From the start of September, I would present the two-hour Sunday chart rundown – the successor to Alan Freeman's *Pick Of The Pops* – and from November, I would also get *Junior Choice*, the three-hour Saturday morning slot aimed at young children. I was not particularly happy.

Neither, it seems, was the public. As soon as those "Tony Gets The Axe" headlines hit the news-stands, the BBC was inundated with sacks of mail, mostly from housewives who enjoyed the show as an enjoyable treat after all that housework. I bowed out of the final show with a characteristically groan-worthy joke – "Hey fellas, the best way to keep a stiff upper lip is to starch your moustache" – and told the press that it was time for a change. But, in truth, I hated the idea of no longer being a weekday fixture on radio. A year later, I admitted as much, saying that the demotion had "made me suicidal". I had really taken those "Bye Bye Blackburn" headlines to heart.

Help was at hand in the shape of Phil Swern, a wonderful friend whom I'd known since he was a record plugger back in the early days of Radio One. You'd only have to look at Phil and your mood would instantly lift. His clothes were always two sizes too big, and he'd invariably have a plastic carrier bag full of records under his arm.

Although I generally shied away from help during those darkest moments after losing Tessa, Phil Swern was the one person I found myself able to confide in. In fact, he'd been so good to me that I gave him a namecheck on my very last weekday afternoon show, for "his help through the toughest times". Now, with my professional life thrown into turmoil, he was there for me again.

Shortly after I began presenting the *Top 40* show on late Sunday afternoons, I'd got into the habit of visiting Phil and his parents for Sunday lunch at their place near Wembley. It was a lot of fun, especially when the similarly lost and lonely Alan Freeman joined us, dressed in of his weird and wonderfully ridiculous kaftans. When, soon afterwards, I decided it was time to sell up *Hollycroft* and find myself a base in Central London, the Swerns took me in while I was between houses.

By 1980, I was settled into a new house in Logan Mews, just off Kensington High Street, and eager to get back into the swing of life as a single man. Rather stupidly, and without the ever-vigilant Les Perrin around to stop me, I blabbed a little too much to the newspapers, who were always eager to find out how I was coping with life after Tessa. Well, "Very nicely, thanks!" was my stock answer to that one, before explaining my seduction technique in intimate detail. It was the year I became over-confessional and both the *Sunday Mirror* and *The Daily Express* plastered details of my lurid exploits under their sensationalised headlines.

"*Girls Galore – But None Like Tessa,*" screamed one. Perhaps it wasn't such a good idea, especially now I'd started presenting *Junior Choice* on Saturday mornings, but neither was it too far from the truth. I discovered the news that Tessa, now living in Sunninghill, Berkshire, was pregnant with Richard O'Sullivan's child the previous winter. Their son James was born in May 1980. Though some wondered if his arrival might drive a wedge between Simon and me, those fears were completely unfounded, because Richard was a nice man who read the situation extremely well.

Four different partners each week was my way of staving off the sadness. "Like shuffling through a pack of cards," was the way I described my bachelor ways to the press at the time. I'd got into the habit of going to this particular wine bar in Kensington with Phil Swern, which had a bit of a reputation as a pick-up joint. It might sound shallow, but at the time I wasn't looking for a full-blown relationship, just a bit of fun. Not every partner was a one-night stand. I mean, occasionally the relationship went on for at least a couple of days, which might also have included an evening out at my favourite Notting Hill restaurant. That was the place that did the best tomato omelette, and whether alone or accompanied, I'd go there every day. The waiters were excellent, dutifully observing the "lights dimmed for pudding" mating ritual.

Until I wrote my first autobiography in 1984, I hadn't given much thought to any of this. It certainly wasn't an obsession, though today I'm sure some sexpert would class it as a "compulsive sexual disorder" and pack me off to some expensive corrective facility. What a load of nonsense! Why can't people accept that making love is simply one of life's most pleasurable pursuits? I certainly enjoyed every moment of it. And, when you tot it up, having 250 or 300 lovers over the course of 20 years only works out at something like a different partner every couple of months. My friend Peter Stringfellow would surely regard that as a complete disgrace!

Now that I've been happily married for over 15 years, that 'Get it while you can' mindset seems a lifetime away, though I can't see that I've been damaged in any way by the experience. In fact, I have absolutely no regrets about it at all. This country is still very uptight about sex. I mean, all the papers do is gossip about it, whereas I just got on with it.

"ALCOHOL MADE ME AGGRESSIVE. I FOUND MYSELF GETTING INTO ARGUMENTS WITH PEOPLE OVER THE MOST TRIVIAL THINGS."

I know it would have been far more damaging, both physically and mentally, had I chosen to hit the bottle instead. There were times during these wayward years when I used to drink a little over the odds, but I soon realised that I didn't like the effect it had on my personality. Alcohol made me aggressive. I found myself getting into arguments with people over the most trivial things. Whether this was because I was seething with anger inside is impossible to say. All I knew was that, in excess, alcohol was bad news.

Though I've never hit anyone in my life, I could feel how the effects of booze could make someone flip if they were more inclined to get physical. It's abundantly clear – and all the statistics back this up – that alcohol's a terribly destructive drug and I've never understood society's glib acceptance of booze and mass demonisation of pot. If you can do without any artificial stimulant at all, that's obviously the best option, but why alcohol – when drunks fill our hospitals every Friday and Saturday night – has emerged as the accepted drug of choice in our culture beggars belief.

Though I have been obsessive in other ways – with girls, gadgets and arriving on time, for example – I could always take or leave alcohol. I'm lucky in that respect, for in many ways, booze oils the wheels of the entertainment industry. I shared a wonderful bottle of champagne last night with my wife Debbie and I thoroughly enjoyed it. I don't even get hangovers. In this sphere of life, moderation comes naturally to me, though I have had my moments. One night, while out with Doreen Davies, one of Radio One's executive producers, I remember downing more than 20 double Scotches. And I mean, remember. The next day, I was up right as rain to host another glitch-free Radio One roadshow.

At the risk of sounding like those poptastic presenters, Smashie and Nicey, I genuinely believe that the essential thing to overdose on in life is fun. If you start relying on stimulants to kickstart yourself into action, chances are you might end up in a spot of bother further down the line. I've seen it happen so often in the music business and regrettably, to some of the most likeable characters.

"'THE CHILDREN'S SHOW IS IDEAL FOR ME,' I SAID'. BUT I WAS LYING THROUGH MY FULL SET OF EVER SMILING TEETH."

After 15 years at the top of my profession presenting various daytime radio shows, at the end of 1979 I found myself spinning *Nellie The Elephant* and *Puff The Magic Dragon* on Radio One's Saturday morning children's show, *Junior's Choice*. Ed Stewart had made the programme his during the '70s, and Derek Chinnery was hoping that I'd take to the 8am-10am slot just as effortlessly. "It's ideal for me," I told reporters at the time. "I'm really a big kid at heart." But I was lying through my full set of ever smiling teeth. Broadcasting to children just wasn't right for 'Uncle Tony'.

To make matters worse, the BBC decided to link the programme – renamed *Tony Blackburn's Saturday Show* in 1982 – with Keith Chegwin and Maggie Philbin's Saturday morning children's television slot. I enjoyed working with them tremendously, but because their profile was so much higher with youngsters than mine was, I often felt like a spare part on my own programme. That was difficult to take.

But Keith and Maggie were a lovely couple, and I was delighted to be with them at their wedding, on September 4, 1982. It was joyous and fun-packed occasion, and one of the first modern-day celebrity knot-tying events to receive blanket media coverage. There was a galaxy of stars from the entertainment world, a live radio broadcast, a fly-past from the Royal Air Force and a subsequent television documentary. Unfortunately for the happy couple, it all took place before the days of the *Hello!*-style wedding, so everything was done for glory not hard cash.

The evening before the big day, I met this very attractive lady in the hotel bar and we had a long, night-time liaison. She was there on business, making sure the condom machines were kept filled, of all things. In the morning, there was a knock at the door and it was my good friend Doreen Davis, who was Executive Producer of the outside broadcast. I panicked, and made this girl jump out of the bed and scurry behind the curtains. It was like a scene from a Carry On film. I let Doreen in, and she immediately noted that the sheets were all over the place. "Oh, Tony, you've not slept very well, have you." "No," I replied, "I was thrashing around all night. Couldn't sleep a wink!" All the while, this shivering woman from the condom business was desperately trying not to wriggle or giggle from behind the curtains.

The Cheggers' wedding aside, the laughter that had been an essential ingredient to my work at Radio One was now being

Driving away from our
wedding reception in 1972.
Tessa and I spent our
wedding night at the Savoy
Hotel in London

With Tessa and Simon at
Hollycroft, our lovely country
home, in the mid-'70s.

Perry Como enjoying yet another magic moment with one of his keenest fans.

With Diana Ross around the same time that I convinced Motown to release *I'm Still Waiting* as a single. It became her first solo Number 1.

Backstage at Wembley with the great music legend Stevie Wonder. I've known him since the '60s and watched him transform into a superstar.

With disgraced pop entrepreneur Jonathan King and Kenny Everett at a function promoting Hawaii – hence the garland around Kenny's neck.

Backstage at *Top Of The Pops* with Noel Edmonds and the programme's executive producer Robin Nash, for once not exposing his nipples.

Celebrating the 500th edition of *Top Of The Pops* in 1973 with Noel Edmonds, Kenny Everett, Pan's People and Roxy Music.

Back on the steps of All Souls Church in 1977 to celebrate 10 years of Radio One. Finally a woman joins our ranks – Anne Nightingale, front and centre.

At a reception with Mud singer Les Gray, Cliff Richard and *Tiswas* presenter Sally James. Another favourite shirt with a typically '70s outsize collar.

One of my pin-up shots. Well, it did it for me . . .

Andy Peebles impersonates Jimmy Savile, together with other Radio One colleagues including Mike Read and Dave Lee Travis. The rest are so well disguised I can hardly recognize them.

The Radio One football team, none of whom could really play the game at all. My old adversary John Peel is in the back row, second right, wearing the bobble hat.

For some reason, me, Keith Chegwin and Maggie Philbin, my colleagues on my Radio One Saturday morning children's show in the early '80s, are all wearing rubber wet suits – though what we do in our spare time is our own business.

Long before we began courting, Debbie appeared with me in panto. Here she is, second right, in the red dress dancing in the chorus line. Had she known what lay ahead, she might have done better to have hopped up those stairs and made her escape!

The luckiest woman in the world! With Debbie on our wedding day, 13 June, 1992.

At our wedding reception on the terrace at the House Of Commons. That's actress Anita Dobson (second left) and my best man David Hamilton (second right).

"DJ Tony Blackburn, at home with his charming wife Debbie, proudly celebrate the arrival of their beautiful new daughter, Victoria." Yes, it's the celebrity magazine photo-shoot!

Mid-'70s: A proud father with son and Charlie Drake lookalike, Simon!

Holding the famous red book at the end of *This Is Your Life*. Note that Cheggers, ever the pro, has nudged aside the relatives to get into the shot!

Kid Jensen and I both proudly show off our Sony Music Awards. I have a suspicion that mine was more important than his!

Even before *I'm a Celebrity...*, I found myself back on all manner of TV shows, none more fun than never *Mind The Buzzcocks*. Here I am with Phil Jupitus and Guns 'N' Roses guitarist Slash.

Kicking out at Heathrow with fellow *I'm a Celebrity...* jungle mates Uri Geller and Nell McAndrew.

Happy and victorious after my jungle success. I'd lost one and a half stone out there in just two weeks – another good reason for doing the show!

Together with mum, Jackie and Victoria, at a family get-together.

Back again! Front row:
Pete Murray, Ed Stewart,
Mike Raven, Mike Ahern,
John Peel. Middle row:
Bob Holness, Terry Wogan,
Chris Denning, Johnny
Moran, Pete Myers. Front
row: Me, Jimmy Young,
Robin Scott, Duncan
Johnson, Pete Brady,
David Symonds.

My son Simon, and my
daughter Victoria, both
doing the infamous
"DJ point".

30 July 2006: *Top Of The Pops* bows out with a special edition that mixed presenters new and old. I don't like closing programmes down, but this was probably my favourite ever moment on the show.

Still at the controls and loving every minute of it!

noticeably undermined by my relegation to weekend broadcasting. I enjoyed presenting the Top 40 show, particularly when revolting punk music began to fade and a new era of fabulous dancefloor acts such as Shalamar, Odyssey and Spandau Ballet revealed themselves. Thank God for the '80s, I say.

Times had moved on, but there were still one or two of the eccentric old-timers on the BBC payroll. One of those was the producer of my *Top 40* show, Bernie Andrews.

Bernie had been around the block by that time. He was the man behind John Peel's *Top Gear* show in the early days of Radio One, and was responsible for booking up-and-coming names such as Jimi Hendrix for the programme. By the early '80s, though, he seemed far more interested in his own peculiar pursuits than in discovering new acts that would alter the face of popular music. He had a place in the country by then, though he'd pop in to Broadcasting House once a week to feed his fish. That aside, the only other communication we had was when I'd ring him up with timings for the show. I don't know why but whatever time of day I called, he'd always be sawing through something. "Oh, is that the running order?" Zzzzzzz.... zzzzzzzz. "Good work!" Zzzzzzz....zzzzzzzz. He was the perfect producer because I hardly saw anything of him.

Bernie and I did have one thing in common. Like him, I too knew that my best days at Radio One were well and truly over. In January 1982, I lost the Top 40 countdown, though I continued hosting the Saturday morning children's programme for another couple of years. The station was changing. It had to. Radio One, the musical heartbeat of the nation, couldn't afford to carry a generation of long-in-the-tooth DJs who were approaching middle age when its audience was young and bushy-tailed. A credibility gap had opened up. Unfortunately, I was one of those destined to fall into it.

I wasn't young any more. But I did know I was still more than capable of hosting a dynamic weekday show, so when one came along, I jumped at it. Within months, it had developed into the best radio programme I would ever present. What soon became known as *The Sex'n'Soul Show* lasted for four very happy years. I'd never had so much fun on air in my life. And, so they still insist more than 20 years later, neither had the listeners.

9

SEX 'N' SOUL

It might be stretching the point to describe the previous six or seven years of my life as an extended equivalent of John Lennon's infamous *Lost Weekend*, when he left Yoko, moved to Los Angeles and made a complete fool of himself. But I had spent much of that time drifting aimlessly, and sometimes behaving a little recklessly. My once serene private life had become a rollercoaster ride of instant highs and lonely lows. Professionally, I'd gone from being the best known DJ on radio to a marginalised figure stuck presenting programmes that didn't suit my style at all.

Even the olive branch offered in 1982 by BBC Radio London – which had no connection whatsoever with the similarly named pirate station – snapped in half almost as soon as the ink on the contract ran dry. Yes, it was great to be hosting a weekday radio show again for the first time in three years, not least because having nothing much to do in the week had been driving me quietly mad. But, as its name suggests, Radio London was a local station. Though it served millions of listeners in the Greater London area and beyond, it was the first time since 1967 that my keynote show was no longer aimed at a national audience. (I continued presenting my Saturday morning children's programme on Radio One until 1984, but that was hardly an essential aspect of my work.) The London show was in the afternoon slot, too, never my preferred option. Worse still, the programme was bloody awful! Try as I did, I just couldn't get into the format, which was so sluggish and clogged up with guests plugging their books or giving gardening tips. There was only thing to do: rip it up and start again.

"I WANT THE SHOW TO BE TERRIBLY RUDE... I WANT THE SHOW TO GO PLACES THAT NO OTHER RADIO SHOW IN THIS COUNTRY HAS EVER BEEN."

Derek Amory had been Executive Producer on the *Nationwide* television current affairs programme, before a little internal scandal sent him on a sideways "promotion" to take charge of Radio London. One day, he took me out to an Italian restaurant in Marylebone High Street, and I told him what I thought of the afternoon show. His solution was to offer me a show called *BBC* – Blackburn, Barnes and Company – which I would co-present with a woman called Suzie Barnes. I said, "I'm sorry, Derek, that sounds dreadful. I'm going to have to resign." "Oh, no, no, no, let's rethink this. You can't resign," he answered. "All right, I won't," I said, waiting for his next move. Because Derek was quite a drinker and was famous for his rebellious streak – I'd heard he once fired a water pistol at a Board Of Governors meeting – I expected anything from spaghetti on the walls to an instant walkout. But not this.

"First you resigned. And now you're back with us. So I'm sacking you."

"You can't do that. I just resigned."

"You did, but then you said you hadn't resigned."

"So I did. OK, don't sack me. Let's do the programme."

"Fair enough."

"So, you haven't sacked me?"

"No, Tony, you're still with us."

"You still want me to do that programme?"

"Yes, please."

"Well, in that case I resign."

I felt as if I was caught up in one of those mid-20th century absurdist dramas.

"Oh, I dunno," said Derek, who by this stage was at least as confused as I was. "Have I sacked you or have you resigned?" I said, "I've got absolutely no idea." He was becoming exasperated by his own game. "For God's sake, Tony, what do you want to do?" And so, at last, I had the opportunity to sketch out my ideal radio show. And the man who had the power to make it happen was all ears.

I told Derek that I'd been spending a lot of time listening to several of the new pirate stations that had been springing up, particularly Kiss and Jackie, both of which had been providing a much needed outlet for soul music. I said, "They're all on to it, Derek, but there's no legal station picking up on it." I added that I was fed up playing the same old rubbish that everyone else was. He shot me a look that suggested he was interested.

"There's something else," I said, resisting a temptation to smile. "I want the show to be terribly rude. I want listeners to phone in and me to flirt with them. I want the show to go places that no other radio show in this country has ever been." Derek raised his eyebrows. "Give it a chance. You can trust me. I know how far I can go with it."

"I think that's a great idea," he said. "When do you want to start?" "Whenever you want," I told him, my pulse racing. "How about

Monday morning at 9am?" he suggested. "It'll be a bit over the top," I warned him. "That's all right," he said. "I want you to do it." I also think Derek secretly desired to niggle the stuffed-shirts at Broadcasting House and test the limits of what was acceptable within the constraints of the BBC charter.

And that's how we came up with my sex'n'soul show, which ran for four fabulous years, from 1984 until 1988. No interminable meetings or focus groups. Just a hunch, and a receptive, creatively minded boss willing to take a risk.

Derek hastily rustled up a producer. Cheryl Garnsey had been working on Robbie Vincent's phone-in show, which she adored, and it was immediately obvious to me that she didn't want to be involved in my programme at all. I confronted her that very first Monday morning. "You really don't want to do this, do you?" "No," she said, with clinical predictability. I was grossly offended. "I think you should be honoured to work on the show," I barked, trying to temper my annoyance. Cheryl hit back hard.

"Well," she said, "as I've been lumbered with you, I'm going to bring you back." I wasn't sure if I'd heard correctly. "What do you mean, bring me back?" I sniffed. She looked me in the eye and said, "You don't get it, do you. You just don't realise how far you've tumbled. Take a look at yourself. You used to be on Radio One. You used to be the top DJ in the country." I felt as if I was listening to Norma Desmond's keynote speech in *Sunset Boulevard*. "I'll bring you back!", she announced. "Together we'll make a success of this!"

It was the beginning of a quite wonderful working relationship, one of the best I've had in over 40 years of broadcasting. And Cheryl did exactly what she promised. My young new producer had a headful of great ideas and put a fabulous team together. Between us we created a magnificent monster of a show. I love working with talented, dedicated people who know what they're doing, and with whom I can share a vision.

Once we'd cleared the air that first Monday morning, Cheryl turned out to be an absolute treasure to work with.

I began the show as I meant to go on. The '80s was the era of the 12-inch single, and I had them coming out of my ears, many direct from the States via the soul music specialists Bluebird Records. The format gave me the perfect vehicle for the kind of innuendo-laden style I'd intended for the programme. Barely a quarter of an hour went by without my mentioning "whipping out my 12-incher". After the first show, Derek Amory came in and said, "Great, but I thought it was going to be a bit more rude than that." That was all the encouragement I needed. The audience, too, soon played its part to perfection.

The role of a lascivious shock jock came naturally to me. "Oh, you do sound lovely . . . I'd like to nibble your neck . . . Are you wearing any clothes? . . . You are? . . . Well, I'd like you completely naked and then I'll work my way down to those areas that we're not allowed to talk about." It was incredibly risqué, but we just about got away with it.

Instead of a conventional weather bulletin, I'd do what I called "The Nipple Test". If my nipples were soft, that meant it was going to be a nice day. If they were hard and erect, then of course we'd be in for a bit of a chiller. I'd encourage the listeners to take the test too. "And if there is someone close by, you might like to feel theirs too." God, I enjoyed that show!

It made no difference to me if my saucy chat-up lines were being directed at a man or a woman; they'd get exactly the same treatment. "Hi, big boy . . . Oooh, what a lovely voice you've got! . . . Do you enjoy dressing up in women's clothes?" We billed the programme as an X-rated show, so if anyone rang up and complained, we'd simply tell them, "If you don't like it, please switch off. This is a specialist programme." It was probably more mock-jock than shock-jock, but because it went out in the mornings, we'd always be careful to tone it down during the school holidays.

"'WHERE WOULD YOU LIKE TO GO ON YOUR FIRST DATE?' I ASKED. 'I'D LIKE TO TAKE HIM BACK TO MY PLACE AND GIVE HIM A GOOD FUCK!' SHE SAID."

Despite the potential for the unexpected profanity, we never employed a delay system. Incredibly, in the four years that the show ran, just one person ever uttered the F-word. It happened in this section of the show called Dial-a-Date, where listeners could ring in and ask someone out on air. One young woman rang from her office and said that she'd been eyeing up this guy in the hairdressers' opposite all day long. She desperately wanted to ask him out. "Where would you like to go on your first date?" I asked. "I'd like to take him back to my place and give him a good fuck!" she said.

We all sat in the pub afterwards and people kept coming up saying how hilarious they thought it was. When I took a cab home, the first thing the driver said was, "I enjoyed that girl . . ." And that was one of the real joys of the programme. Polite society might have baulked at the naughty nature of the show, but it appealed to the widest possible audience. That's what I'd always aimed for, of course, but the beauty about this show was that for the first time I was playing music that I genuinely loved. It was especially satisfying when records I'd been playing to death for weeks ended up on the Radio One playlist and in the Top 30. Phyllis Nelson's *Move Closer* was one of the show's biggest successes, though Five Star, Alexander O'Neill, David Grant, Jackie Graham and Galaxy, who had a great record called *Dancing Tight*, all benefited greatly from our exposure.

Now I began to understand how John Peel must have felt blasting out all those obscure records he loved. The *Sex 'n' Soul Show* at last gave me a real opportunity to fight the corner for music I truly believed in. Chris Hill and Robbie Vincent who had his own once-a-week soul show on Radio London, were soul enthusiasts too. The difference between them and me was that they kept it a little too elitist for my liking. I wasn't interested in 'ghetto' broadcasting, presenting a soul show that preached only to the converted. In the words of the immortal Diana Ross, I wanted to reach out and touch . . . everybody's hand!

You didn't have to be clever to enjoy soul music. It was just great, emotionally charged music that deserved the widest possible audience. If that meant dressing it up in suspenders and stockings, racy knickers and posing pouches, and "12-inch" car stickers that we sold by the truckload via the show, then I was more than delighted to oblige. By the time I left Radio London, in 1988, Marylebone High Street looked like one long Ann Summers sex shop. As we used to say on the programme, "We love 'r' soul music!" and we didn't mind how we got our message across. And who could complain about the rude bits? Soul was, after all, the sexiest music around.

Despite the success of the show, the station as a whole wasn't doing particularly well, especially in the face of competition from the commercial sector. Capital Radio (which I liked to refer to as "Crapital") and LBC were competing hard for a share of the London audience. That's what inspired me to come up with the idea of the Radio London Soul Night Out. We needed to extend our audience as much as possible. But first I had to convince Derek Amory to make me an Executive Producer for a department at the station that didn't exist.

Ever since my first day at the BBC, I'd been quietly obsessed by that vast rump of middle management that wandered round the place with inflated self-importance without appearing to do anything to justify it. I mean, Executive Producer? He's the one puffing out all that hot air with a briefcase jammed under his arm. In a way, I grew to admire these people for getting away with it for so long – all at the expense of the taxpayer, of course.

As a way of cementing my relationship with Derek Amory and Radio London, I asked him if I could become the station's Executive

Producer Of Light Entertainment. "Why do you want to do that?" he asked. But because Derek, like most of the people who've worked in the BBC's Marylebone High Street building, is just a little bit barmy, he soon corrected himself. "Why, of course! Would you like a clipboard? Do you want blue or black?" I was a soul man. I went for the black. Derek took it all quite seriously. He had an official metal badge made up for me that I'd carry around just in case anyone asked who I was. And I'd show them: "Tony Blackburn – Head Of Light Entertainment".

The brilliance of it was that if "the department" failed, nobody would ever know about it and I'd always get to keep my job! In some ways, though, I wished the department had existed because my one big initiative turned out to be a tremendous success.

"I'M SURE THAT ONE OF THE BIG REGRETS IN STEVIE WONDER'S LIFE IS THAT WE DIDN'T SIT DOWN IN A STUDIO TOGETHER AND RECORD OUR DUET."

The Radio London Soul Night Out probably did more for bringing Londoners together than anything that ever appeared on the statute book during that period. Apart from one ugly night, when we took over this club in Leicester Square and the evening ended in murder, the Soul Night Out was a joy-filled weekly event where everyone, black, white and all shades between, united around a shared love for the music.

On the inaugural night, held at the National Club in Kilburn, an incredible 5,000 people turned up. The police set up a roadblock and I had trouble getting into the venue myself. The place was so packed that it was virtually impossible to dance, which defeated the object to some extent. But when Stevie Wonder put in a surprise appearance to thank everyone for supporting the music, the crowd erupted. He very kindly thanked me too, acknowledging the part I'd played in helping Motown establish a foothold in this country. We even sang a duet together. I'm sure that one of the big regrets in his life is that we didn't sit down in a studio together and record it. Stevie's unannounced arrival set a precedent, and over the next few years, we welcomed a revolving door of top class soul acts to the podium. Everyone from Bobby Womack to Five Star joined in on 'r' soul night.

My role for these evenings was to MC and come up with ever more outlandish stage antics. The man who spun the records was Steve Walsh. He was brilliant, a big, loveable rogue, and my best friend throughout this exhilarating period in my life. Like me, he loved audience involvement, rather than cosy elitism for the music that he lived and breathed for. Steve was always up for anything. One night, he sang his own '80s groove record, a cover of The Fatback Band's *I Found Lovin'*, while I hovered above the audience on a wire dressed in a Superman costume. He saw no shame, either, in my infamous Erotic Balloon Dance. I'd come onstage dressed only in a pair of outsize underpants and strategically arranged balloons. Then I'd invite members of the audience to come up and pop them while I continued to gyrate in an erotic fashion. Well, sort of erotic. . .

I was shocked and horrified when, in July 1988, Steve was hospitalised after a car accident in Ibiza, then flown back to England where he died of a heart attack a few days later. His loss remains painful because we had such a lot of fun together.

The Soul Night Out, which we'd take around the region, even venturing out to places like Southend, ran so beautifully well. Perhaps it was too good to be true. It seems that we were too successful, because the powers that be came down on us for making too big a profit. That, they said, had not been part of the remit and they closed us down. But I'd already proved my point. By the late '80s, soul music had become an accepted part of the pop music mainstream.

"IT'S NOT TONY TALKING ABOUT SUSPENDERS AND STOCKINGS THAT BOTHERS ME. I JUST WISH HE'D STOP WEARING THE THINGS!"

Someone else who hadn't been best pleased with 'r' soul show antics was Radio One Controller, Derek Chinnery. When the show first started, in 1984, I was still presenting the children's programme on Saturday mornings. There didn't seem to be a conflict of interests in the beginning, but when the ratings started to filter through, Chinnery noted that the sex'n'soul show was eating into Radio One's daytime figures. He put in an angry call to Radio London boss Derek Amory.

"Can't you stop Tony Blackburn going on about stockings and suspenders?," he said. "But Derek, you can buy stockings and suspenders in Marks & Spencer." Amory told him. "Anyway, it's not Tony talking about them that bothers me. I just wish he'd stop wearing the things!"

That conversation virtually sealed the end of my career at Radio One. Seventeen years had passed since I'd opened up the station with such concentrated enthusiasm and the nation's full attention. But by autumn 1984, I could hardly have cared less. I was having such a ball at Radio London that the loss of a two-hour Saturday morning children's slot was not going to break my heart.

On September 23, 1984, I uttered my last "Morning, gang!", gave an ironic "Thanks" to the BBC management, and closed the show by playing The Move's *Flowers in The Rain*, the song with which I'd opened up the station. When the time came for me to say farewell, "Thank you very much for listening, look after yourselves, and I love you all," I did get choked up. But it soon passed. What really hurt, though, was losing my beloved *Sex 'n' Soul* show four years later.

It was Matthew Bannister, the man who carved up Radio One so dramatically in the early '90s, who played the executioner's role. His timing was immaculately senseless. A short while earlier, I'd been discussing the idea of a non-stop FM station that played nothing but soul and jazz-funk music with Arnold Miller, who supervised the BBC's local radio stations. It was very much a prototype for what Kiss 100 or Smooth FM would become, though Arnold couldn't quite see it. He was more interested in selling me the idea of a show called Grey Londoners aimed at the 70-plus market.

When you've been in radio for as long as I have, you get used to new management coming in and stamping their mark all over the station. I'd heard that Bannister was about to make sweeping changes – he'd already given the station a new name, Greater London Radio, which everyone was immediately ordered to refer to as the more finger-poppingly swinging GLR. I knew my days were numbered, and so with the heaviest of hearts, I found myself new employers at Capital Radio and tendered my resignation. I'd just spent the most marvellous six years of my broadcasting career at Radio London, so it was a difficult decision to make. But sometimes, you just have to be practical about these things and do what's best for your long-term career.

There's nothing that people in authority hate more than having power snatched away from them. That probably explains why, in June 1988 and with three weeks of my notice still to serve, Bannister pulled the plug on the show immediately, ordering me out of the building by four in the afternoon. It was the American way of doing things, all butch and bully, and I didn't like that at all. In fact, it prompted me to launch into one of those, "Listen young man, if it wasn't for people like me you wouldn't have a job . . ." speeches, which I'd always sworn I'd never make.

The young gunslinger had the dignity to offer me the GLR breakfast show as compensation, but the mix of music and politics wasn't for me. Besides, I was already signed up to present a show for Sky TV, as well as the Capital job. I was on my way . . .

It was a disappointingly shabby end to what had been a fabulous, six-year association with the station. After leaving Bannister's office, I remember going across the road with Cheryl for lunch and bursting into tears. We'd both put so much into the show and for it to end in such a mean-spirited fashion broke my heart.

"I'D TURNED INTO SOMETHING OF A CARICATURE LADIES MAN NOT DISSIMILAR TO THAT LOUCHE TELEVISION SLEUTH JASON KING."

Although my musical preferences had hardly changed at all, my taste in women had moved on since the days when I only seemed to go for the petite blonde type.

Throughout the '80s, I spent much of my private time 'home alone' in my house in Logan Mews, with little hint that one special person might enter into my life. Professionally, I might have been having a wonderful time. But on a personal level, I continued to drift, usually from one short-lived relationship to the next.

Photographs from the time suggest that I'd turned into something of a caricature ladies man not dissimilar to that louche television sleuth Jason King.

I seemed to have a permanent tan, though contrary to rumour, I've never used a sunbed in my life. My skin was just made that way. I hung on desperately to the same mid-length hair style I'd sported, with little variation, since the mid-'60s. My shirt – usually silk – was invariably unbuttoned down to the waist revealing a luxuriant carpet of chest hair. I didn't skimp on the jewellery, either, with an outsize medallion dangling from my neck, a heavy bracelet rattling on my wrist and one of those oh so classy sovereign rings on my finger. I was now well into my 40s and seemingly bent on growing old disgracefully.

There were some beautiful women around to help me on my way. For some strange reason, several of them were Oriental. *Nancy Kwan And The World Of Suzie Wong* had always been one of my favourite films so perhaps that had something to do with it. I've always found Oriental women to be gentle, polite and very pleasant to be with, though I never clicked with one long enough for it to develop into something more serious.

When I dated a beautiful woman from Barbados, I noticed that it didn't go down too well with some of the black guys at the soul concerts and that saddened me. My attitude was quite the opposite. When I was doing the *Sex 'n' Soul* show, I'd proposed that we initiated a National Banging Day, where everyone slept with someone of a different nationality. If only we'd all taken that seriously. It would hasten the day when, as the song put it, the world would be one big melting pot, and as a consequence, racism would be consigned to the yellowing pages of history.

Of course that's a naïve and utterly simplistic hope. But whenever I visit the Dutch-Caribbean island of Aruba, off the coast of Venezuela, I am always knocked out by the wonderful people there, who have Chinese features and black skin alongside all other combinations, really beautiful. And, best of all, no racism. Even the vehicle number plates carry the message: "One Happy Island". If anyone wants to know, that's where The Blackburn Revolution begins.

"UNTIL I ATE THAT HASH COOKIE, I'D NEVER REALISED THAT THE CHANGING OF THE TRAFFIC LIGHTS COULD BE SO SPECTACULARLY HILARIOUS."

My growing worldliness and desire to bring the whole world together received an unexpected boost the time I mistook an e for an Aspirin. People don't believe me when I tell them I was 40 or so before I was offered an illegal drug, but it's absolutely true.

I was out with Steve Walsh and his girlfriend one night in London when this awful headache came on. "Here, have this," he said. I blithely assumed it was an Aspirin tablet. It wasn't long before I felt uncomfortably hot and sweaty. "Christ, I feel awful," I told them. "Oh dear," said Steve. "That was actually a tab of ecstasy." I was not happy. The pair of them tried to persuade me to go on to a club, but I couldn't bear the idea of being out in public with no control over my senses. Steve instructed the taxi driver to drop me off at home, and when I got there, I sat in front of the television totally transfixed by the *Nine O'Clock News*. I'd never seen it looking so lovely before!

I was too anxious to properly enjoy the experience. With Valium, you know that it's been manufactured under strict medical conditions. But when you're messing with illegal drugs, anything from chalk to Strychnine could be lurking about in there. I knew this wasn't for me.

The best time I ever had in the subterranean world of illegal drug-taking was eating a hash cookie while visiting a soul radio station in New York during the early '80s. I loved it, had a totally terrific time! I'd never realised that something as simple as the changing of the traffic lights could be so spectacularly hilarious. Better still, it was July 4th, American Independence Day, and every firework in the country seemed to be transforming the sky into a Jackson Pollock painting.

Unsurprisingly, we were completely incapable of finding our way back to the hotel, so we did what we'd always been taught to do: ask a policeman. I can clearly remember him saying, "Can you recall anything about the area it was in?" "Yes," I said, "I think it was near a tall building". Try keeping a straight face to that one when you're stoned out of your mind! This stuff was amazing. The streets were like a moving escalator, and the memory of it all is as clear as yesterday. But I was adamant that my two-hour hash cookie trip would be a one-off experience I'd not need to repeat. I found the bizarre realities of life interesting enough.

10

SMASHIE, NICEY AND LOVE AT LAST

Some time in the early '90s: I was watching television one night, as I so often do. This particular evening, though, I took a keener interest than usual. That's because the two characters I'd chanced upon seemed so strangely familiar. They were Mike Smash and Dave Nicey, played by comedians Paul Whitehouse and Harry Enfield respectively. This chronically funny couple, who purported to work for the fictitious Radio Fab FM, quickly became the most high profile DJs in Britain. And, thanks to them, I became a hot property again in the 'Icon of popular culture' market.

Smashie and Nicey, as they were more popularly known, were based on a hybrid of classic era Radio One DJs, most specifically myself (Mike Smash) and Alan Freeman. I thought they were absolutely hilarious. When I saw them on Harry Enfield's show for the first time, my initial tingle of recognition soon grew into a, God, that's me! roar and I collapsed in a heap laughing. I said to Debbie, "Look at this, it's so funny – and so accurate." Obviously, the pair of them were taking the piss, but I'd been sending myself up for

30 years so that really didn't bother me. I think it's very flattering when people take the mick out of you like that.

I soon realised the implications for my career, and quickly built in elements of their wonderful characterisations into my act, all that Popadoodledoo stuff. Sometimes, I find myself spontaneously breaking into it, as if I'm some caricature of a caricature. Someone called up on air the other day, on my Classic Gold show, and as soon as he said, "Hi, Tony", I was straight into, "Popadoodledoo, mate! And how are you? Isn't it a lovely Thursday, and Friday? I can't wait for Friday, it's only a few hours away. And wasn't Wednesday great? And, Saturday, hey, let's talk about weekends! What am I gonna do at the weekend? I'm gonna go to the supermarket. Isn't the supermarket great, mate?" And I did the whole thing in that daft Dave Smashie voice. Oh, it's such great fun being a DJ, you know!

Soon, the nation's living-rooms, pubs and offices were full of impromptu comedians doing Smashie and Nicey impersonations. It certainly raised my profile, but being the butt of someone else's joke demanded that a delicate balance be struck. Some time later, Alan Freeman and I were invited to join Paul Whitehouse and Harry Enfield on *Noel Edmonds' House Party*. It was hilarious. They were mimicking us, we were mimicking them, and the entire show collapsed in a heap of DJ banter over! id.

While I was there, I said to P. a Whitehouse, "Who are you meant to be, mate?" He said, "Well, actually, you mate!" Dave Lee Travis always thought Smashie was based on him. Others could see a little bit of Noel Edmonds in there, too. But according to the creators, Alan Freeman and myself were the main inspirations.

The obvious problem with the sketch, which ran for a couple of series, was that it made us out to be complete dinosaurs – which, of course, we weren't by any stretch of the imagination! It portrayed the Class of '67-'77 as cheesy and way past its sell by date, and that didn't help any of us when it came to negotiating deals with

Programme Controllers, most of whom seem to have endured a humour bypass as a necessary requirement before landing the job. Many industry insiders reckoned that the sweeping changes made by Matthew Bannister at Radio One in 1993 was partly inspired by the desire to purge the station of its so called 'Smashie And Nicey' image.

The immense popularity of this "Poptastic" pairing inspired me to make a spectacular return to the clubs and discos and play up my Smashie credentials to the hilt. It quickly spilled over into my broadcasts, too. I'd often find myself saying, "Good morning, thanks for tuning in! It's eight minutes past eight o'clock and those eight minutes, ooh, aren't they great?! I do love that particular time check, don't you?"

I agreed to take part in a 1994 one-off farewell special, *Smashie and Nicey: The End Of An Era*, where I was booted out of a disco before being packed off to Radio Quiet in the middle of nowhere. But there was also a particular strand of the storyline that they hadn't told me about, where Mike Smash was shown falling to pieces at the break-up of his marriage.

Some time later, Paul Whitehouse apologised to me for that. He admitted that he'd felt very guilty about doing that sketch, and I told him that had I known they were going to include the sketch, I probably wouldn't have taken part in the show. I still think it was a bit underhand the way they did it, but what could I say except, "It's all right, forget it, it's done now".

"CHRIS TARRANT WAS GIVING AWAY £10,000 EVERY MORNING, WHILE I'M ON THE SISTER STATION GIVING AWAY KEYRINGS."

Since 1988, I had been at Capital Gold, Capital Radio's oldies station, where I presented the breakfast show. I stayed there for 14 years, until late 2002, and while I enjoyed my early years at the station, relations certainly become more strained when new management came in. Eventually, it all became too corporate, too methodical, and that important fun factor, which I'd had in abundance at Radio London, was noticeably lacking.

Happily, it's all change again at the station these days. Back in the '90s, though, with Capital FM the flagship, the management didn't seem to give a damn about Capital Gold, which was quite clearly treated as the poor relation. It gets very frustrating where you've got Chris Tarrant giving away £10,000 every morning, and his Capital FM show being plugged on television commercials, and I'm on the sister station giving away keyrings.

The Managing Director for much of my time there was Richard Park, now much better known as the Headmaster on television's *Fame Academy*. As regular viewers of that programme will no doubt appreciate, Richard was an extremely difficult man to work for, though in many ways he was quite brilliant too. Particularly when it comes to bluffing. I went to his office one day to complain that while my show was virtually running neck and neck with Chris Tarrant's, I was hampered by the fact that I was doing it all on a shoestring. He looked at me and said, "But, Tony, you're giving away something listeners can't buy. To them, your keyring is worth more than a £10,000 cash giveaway, because it's what you're doing on the show that matters to them." I didn't believe him for a second.

Richard had a habit of using sporting metaphors. "At the moment you're on the reserve team, but you could be up front," that kind of thing. I've never been a big fan of football, and when he said after one of my early shows that I'd "scored a few own goals", I thought he was being complimentary and smiled back at him. It was some time before the penny dropped and I realised that I wasn't doing as well in his eyes as I'd imagined.

Football-speak was at the heart of one of the most infamous stories involving Richard. Having taken DJ Pat Sharp out for a delightful lunch, Richard concluded it in his own inimitable way. "Well, it's been lovely," he said, "but I'm going to have to show you the red card, I'm afraid." He then pulled a referee's red card from his top pocket. That was his special way of saying, "Bye, bye Pat." When it was my turn to receive one of his dreaded lunchtime invitations, I fully expected him to whip his card out once again. But I got off relatively lightly: instead, he took the breakfast show away from me, and moved me to weekends.

Another time, he was taking a meeting that was dragging on a bit. "Apologies, everyone, but I'd better leave," said Mike Read. "I'm on air in a few minutes." "Oh, don't worry, there's no rush," replied Richard, knowing full well that someone else was already installed in Mike's hot seat and about to go on air.

Although Richard was – and still is – a tough cookie, I've got a terrific amount of respect for him because he does know his job. As well as becoming a television anti-hero, he's also the Programme Controller at Magic, which he's turned around very successfully. In fact, he does he seem to make a success of anything he turns his hand to, and you just have to respect that.

But I'll never quite be able to forgive him for what he did during his time at Capital, which has established the tone for commercial radio ever since, and in my opinion ruined it. That's because, overnight, he decided to change the format to 'Three in a row and a time check'. He'd been to America, heard how they were doing it there – more music, no personality – and introduced it into this country. It certainly saved on the wage bill because broadcasting talent was no longer required. Instead, he could bring in what I impolitely call the monkey brigade to replace all the skilled professionals that were costing him too much money.

I found the change maddeningly annoying, and it made me quite sad, too. Listeners began to ring up and ask, "Are you all right? Where are you? There's nothing happening in your show any more." After a few days, Richard asked me up to his office and he said, "Well, what do you think?" I told him. "It's just awful." He asked me to explain myself. I said, "You've got Kenny Everett, myself, all these personality jocks presenting personality-free programmes. The station sounds so slow, so boring." He wasn't at all happy with what I'd just told him. "You can fuck off then," he said, "and by the way, what's your agent's number again?"

I was far from happy myself. "Hang on, ask me again," I said. Richard seemed confused by my request, but he then obliged. "OK, I asked you what you thought of the station." And I said, "I think it's great, I think it's fabulous, I've never heard anything so good." "Now you don't mean that, do you?' he said. Of course I didn't. "I'm just telling you what you wanted to hear. And if you don't want to hear what I think, then don't ask me!" And I walked out. It was the first time I'd ever done anything remotely like that, and Richard knew I was riled. He even took the trouble to ring me at home later that evening. "I'm looking forward to your show tomorrow morning, Tony," he said in a conciliatory tone. I said, "Really?" He knew he'd gone too far on that particular occasion.

Despite the fact that he introduced the change that helped make commercial radio a toothless shadow of its former itself, I'd say that Richard generally does know what he's doing. I think we have a mutual respect for one another. He's a difficult person but he's a perfectionist and has an ability to get audiences; a skill which I admire.

When I watch Richard Park on *Fame Academy* now, there's a part of me that actually likes him very much. He's quite unintentionally hilarious; he makes everything a drama, including himself. He's now this magnificent caricature, as if he's done a Smashie And Nicey job on himself. If he ever offered me a job again, I'd probably say yes, because he is still one of the most talented people working in British radio right now.

"ON THE WALL BEHIND HER THESE DEER'S ANTLERS WERE POSITIONED IN SUCH A WAY THAT THEY LOOKED LIKE THEY WERE COMING OUT OF DEBBIE'S HEAD."

The tables had begun to turn once again in my see-saw life. Just as I was being forced to grin and bear my new professional situation at Capital, my personal life was taking several giant leaps forward. Early in 1990, I met Debbie, a wonderful girl some 17 years my junior though of course considerably more mature than me in most other ways.

We'd first met about a decade earlier while I was doing a pantomime in Palmer's Green. I was Buttons, she was one of the chorus girls, and probably still in her late teens. I was still seeing Margo at the time, who was dabbling in a bit of publicity for the show. I remember doing a dance routine with Debbie, but that's about it. I would have been in my mid 30s by then and more interested in women my own age.

The next time we met, Debbie was playing Frigid Bridget in a '60s styled musical show called *A Slice Of Saturday Night*, at the Arts Theatre in Leicester Square. It was all a bit awkward, actually. She'd been instructed to invite me up on the stage in the second half of the show to do some kind of duet with Binky Baker, who was Anne Nightingale's husband at the time. I'd met him a year or two earlier and he'd poured a port and brandy over my head after I dared to tell him not to interrupt Anne and I while we were having a conversation. As some kind of mad revenge, he made a record about me and called it *Toe Knee Black Burn*. I don't even think it sold as well as mine had! I politely declined Debbie's offer, and stayed put in my seat.

There was a little drinks party afterwards, and we had a brief chat, though it wasn't particularly easy because I had another female companion with me. My solution to that was simple. A day or two later, after my breakfast show, I picked up some Capital Radio headed notepaper and dropped her a line care of the theatre. Dated November 15, 1990, it read:

"*Dear Debbie,*

I just thought I'd drop you a line to say how good I thought the show was. I really did enjoy it. I felt very guilty not coming up on stage with you but I am a dreadful dancer as you can probably remember.

I looked round for you after the show to have a chat but only saw you when I was about to go, and as I get up at four o'clock each day to do the Capital Gold breakfast show, it was getting late. I also do a chat show each day on Sky TV, so I try not to look too shattered whenever possible, and as the years go by, it gets very difficult!!

I thought that you were excellent in your part, and judging by the programme, you have done well since the panto days. Anyhow, I'm sorry that we didn't have a longer chat. I wanted to tell you in person how good you were, something I forgot to do at the end of the evening.

If you feel like having lunch some time, give me a ring. It would be nice to get together, and believe it or not, you're the first person I've come across who I've worked with in panto.

This is my number (the answerphone is always on if I'm not in).

Just let me know the best way to get in touch as I don't like to ring the theatre.

> *Hope to hear from you, but even if you don't call, all the*
> *very best for the future.*
> *Yours,*
>
> *Tony (Blackburn)"*

That was the letter I sent, and it's since cost me a fortune! Oh, I jest. The reality is that about a week later, I received a reply from Debbie agreeing to my idea of having lunch together. That's where it all started, and we've been together ever since.

Debbie was so easy to like, so easy to fall in love with. I mean, she looks like me for a start – round face, plenty of teeth! Well, just slightly . . . I found her very upbeat, lovely to look at, and there was obviously a good deal of chemistry there right from the start.

I took her to an Italian restaurant near Euston and we sat down for lunch. It was a slightly *Fawlty Towers* moment, because on the wall behind her were these deer's antlers which were positioned in such a way that they looked like they were coming out of her head. As it was the first time I'd been out with her, I didn't like to say, "You wouldn't mind moving, would you?" because I keep wanting to laugh. Instead, I kept quiet about it, which lent a mild air of lunacy to the date. I've never thought of not being with her since. She was someone I was genuinely able to feel totally relaxed with.

The only time we've really been apart, aside from my Jungle escapade, was when she went on tour with a show fairly soon after we'd met. I felt very alone without her and one night, after going out drinking with a friend, I came back home fairly drunk and called her up. She could tell I was a little out of sorts, not least because I happened to mention that I'd fallen over a couple of times, in typical pub-bore fashion!

That wasn't typical of me at all. Neither is the fact that in nearly 17 years together, I've not been unfaithful to Debbie once. Not even thought about it, either, and that's a wonderful feeling. I have such a great life with her, and with our daughter Victoria too, that I've simply got no inclination to do anything that might mess that up. Believe it or not, I think I've acquired a little wisdom in that department as I've grown older.

Despite my insistence that I'd never start up a relationship with someone else in showbusiness, Debbie's very different to most of them. She's a lot more genuine and down to earth, has no interest in being in the limelight, and besides, her kind of showbiz is more the song and dance stuff I like anyway. Perhaps it's something to do with being brought up in London's East End, the home of all those old music-hall venues. She's also very into family life, and though I never dared to suggest it, she chose to give up acting so she could spend more time at home. The fact that she was genuinely interested in marriage, and in doing everything she could to make it work, filled me with tremendous confidence. Given my track record as a bit of a secret self-loather, that's been really important to the love and stability I've felt these past two decades.

Debbie and I married on June 13, 1992. It was a gorgeous, hot day and after signing the paperwork at Chelsea Registry Office, with David Hamilton as my best man, we had a blessing ceremony at St Margaret's in Westminster. We then took the short walk across to the House Of Commons, where the reception was held on the terrace in the shadow of Big Ben. Halfway through, a little guy ran up to us and said there'd been a bomb scare, and that no one should leave the building. Debbie assumed it was a hoax. My first thought was, "Oh, God, the bar bill!" But it was a delightful day, and every time I tune in to *News At Ten* and hear the chimes of Big Ben booming out at the top of the programme, I am reminded of the happiest day of Debbie's life and the most expensive day in mine!

We honeymooned on Marco Island in Florida and things couldn't have been more different than back in 1972. Being together is effortless and so blissfully enjoyable. There is nothing that comes in the way of our love, respect and trust for each other. Oh, and what a relief that is! I've never once doubted her – but then, perhaps she's being terribly unfaithful to me down the years!

Finding true love with Debbie, then sealing it with the arrival of Victoria a few years later, brought a perfect end to all the sadness that blighted my life during the late '70s and early '80s.

"KENNY ONCE TOLD ME THERE WAS THIS MACHINE AT ONE OF FREDDIE MERCURY'S PARTIES THAT SHOT COCAINE RIGHT UP YOUR NOSE."

When I met Debbie in 1990, I was still living at Logan Mews, just off Kensington High Street, my home for much of the previous decade. It was an exclusive residential area, but that didn't stop me putting up a huge satellite dish – and at 1.9 meters wide, I do mean huge – on my flat roof in full view of the neighbours. My interest in technology, massaged into action by my father at a young age, was always more important to me than matters of aesthetics. In fact, I was rather proud that I'd turned my residence into West London's version of Cape Canaveral. It used to rotate, too, though the reality of its capabilities was shamefully limited by today's standards. All I could pick up to begin with was Sky and the American news channel CNN. Most people's eyes glaze over when I start to talk about technological things, but I can get quite nostalgic thinking about the excitement I felt at owning one of the first satellite dishes in the country.

The only other neighbour in the area to get planning permission to put one up was Andrew Neil, then editor of *The Times*. I certainly didn't see any trace of one on the roof of the most famous Logan Mews resident, Freddie Mercury. He had one of the cottages in Logan Mews as well as the big house at the end of Logan Place, which was protected by a high brick wall. I rarely saw him, though I know that Kenny Everett was a fairly regular visitor, and Dave Clark (of The Dave Clark Five and 'The Tottenham Sound' fame) used to park his Rolls-Royce in the Mews, too. According to Kenny, the parties round at Freddie's could get pretty raunchy. I won't forget his description of this machine that used to shoot cocaine directly up your nose in a hurry!

As rumours of Freddie's illness spread during the early months of 1990, the press began to decamp outside the high walls of his house hoping to catch sight of a man that we'd heard was fast becoming a pale and skeletal shadow of his former self. I'd met him once, many years earlier on the set of *Top Of The Pops*, though we exchanged little more than a quick "Hello". Come to think of it, that's really the sum of most celebrity conversations.

Sometimes I'd sunbathe on my roof, and I can remember catching him once sitting in his garden looking desperately unwell. It was the middle of the summer and he was just sitting still with a coat wrapped around him.

When I left each morning to drive to Euston for my early morning show on Capital Gold, there was always a light on in Freddie's bedroom. Then one day, on November 24, 1991, I looked up to his room and there was no light. On my drive in to work, an announcement came on air: Freddie Mercury was dead.

His death was unfortunate for two reasons. We had lost one of the greatest showmen in pop. And it was also goodbye to the tranquility of the area around Logan Mews, which soon began attracting coachloads of fans who'd scrawl messages all over his old wall and transform the place into the thriving epicentre of National Freddie Mercury Day.

Though I thought Freddie was a great stage performer, I can't say I was particularly impressed by Queen's music. Several years later, I met the band's guitarist Brian May, whose wife Anita Dobson is a good friend of Debbie's, at a birthday celebration at The Ivy, one of London's top eateries. I found myself sitting next to Brian, and I just had to tell him: "That record of yours, *Bohemian Rhapsody*. God, it's long!" "Don't you like it?" he asked. I told him I'd never really sat all the way through it. "It's a very useful record, though, because it gives you enough time to get to the loo and back while you're on air." Brian probably thought I was joking, but it really is one of my least favourite records, yet I don't know anyone else who doesn't like it. I think Brian May's a lovely guy, and I know that Queen were such a hugely successful group, but they just don't do it for me.

"SOME IDIOTS ACCUSED ME OF BEING CRUEL TO RUNNER BEANS BECAUSE, IF YOU LISTENED HARD, YOU COULD HEAR THEM SCREAM AS THEY WAS BEING COOKED."

Luckily, given the reasonably promiscuous decade I'd had since my divorce, I managed to survive all the new and increasingly dangerous hazards associated with the pleasures of the flesh. In fact, while everyone around me would often fall foul of all the bugs and flu that spreads so quickly in the metropolis, I rarely suffered from ill health of any kind. I put that down to the special Blackburn diet.

Food fads really started to come into their own during the '80s. As I'd been a vegetarian since the days of rationing, I was probably among the first to turn my nose up at a good old-fashioned British roast or fry-up. I lost count of the number of times I'd have to send a meal back because the waiter refused to accept that I simply wanted a plate of mashed potatoes with vegetables.

I must say I was rather disappointed when vegetarianism started to become popular in the '70s with the hippies, then even the punks adopting it as a statement against the rest of the world. If something's in fashion, I tend to stay clear of it, so I wasn't happy when all the trendy bandwagon jumpers started to join in. They came over all righteous about it, whereas I accepted that while the idea of killing anything in order to eat it revolted me, I was prepared to let others do it if they were happy with the idea. What I hated most were those twits who tried to defend their position by accusing me of being cruel to carrots and runner beans because carrots have feelings and if you listened hard, you could hear a runner bean scream as it was being cooked. Oh, come on! Vegetables don't have a nervous system, so I'm prepared to accept that they feel nothing when we eat them.

A new generation of food advisers started to emerge to police our eating habits further. To me, their advice was about as barmy as that doled out by those mistresses of misery, the agony aunts. For 17 and a half years, from the time of my divorce to well into the '90s, I survived on a daily diet of tinned lentil soup and processed peas. Occasionally as a treat, I'd put a potato in! Of course, I enjoyed dining out and did so regularly at my favourite Italian restaurants. But in my kitchen, you'd not find a piece of fruit or a fresh vegetable anywhere from one year to the next.

Staying healthy probably has as much to do with having a positive outlook. I'm sure there are advantages to eating sensibly, too, but I certainly wasn't bothered by that and it didn't seem to do me any harm. Every day, we're bombarded with stories telling us that things we've always taken for granted are actually killing us. I don't let it worry me. People worry too much and give too much credence to all these buffoons who tell them, "You should eat this or drink that". What you've got to remember is that these experts are making a good living out of their priceless advice – which seems to change from one year to the next anyway.

Today, I've become more sophisticated in my eating habits. When I'm out, I always start with minestrone soup – piping hot. Then I'll follow it with either spaghetti Napolitana or a simple pizza. It's most important that the soup is hot, though. Valentino's in

Hendon Way does a wonderfully hot soup, though I'd say that Paparazzi in Potters Bar serves the hottest soup in the country. I think they see me coming and now fall over themselves in a bid to make it untouchably hot!

"NOEL EDMONDS SLAMMED THE DOOR IN MY FACE AND SAID, 'I'VE BEEN WANTING TO DO THAT FOR YEARS.'"

One of the most memorable meals I've ever had was with Noel Edmonds. Since quitting the Radio One breakfast show in 1978, he'd made even more of a name for himself on television, first hosting the children's Saturday morning show, *Multi-Coloured Swap Shop*, then switching to prime-time Saturday night viewing with *The Late, Late Breakfast Show*, then *The Noel Edmonds Saturday Roadshow*. By 1991, the latter had developed into *Noel's House Party*, which reigned supreme on the small screen throughout the '90s. I had a regular part on the show, playing the village idiot, which suited my sense of humour perfectly.

Noel and I grew friendlier than ever. He would invite Debbie and I to his massive estate in Devon, set in some 500 acres of land. When you stayed with Noel and his wife Helen, you'd have an entire house to yourself, which was the beautiful thatched cottage next door. He was, as you might imagine, the perfect host: champagne, long walks across the nearby fields, plenty of laughs.

One Sunday morning, I suggested that we all go out for lunch. Within minutes, the blades on Noel's personal helicopter were whirring wildly, and we were on our way via aerial views of the Devon and Cornwall coastline.

When we arrived at Noel's recommended destination, it quickly became obvious to all that our waitress was far more interested in me than in the host of one of the most popular programmes on British television. It turned out I'd sold her a dehumidifier on the QVC shopping channel a week or two earlier.

I appeared on *Noel's House Party* virtually every week for three or four years alongside Frank Thornton (Captain Peacock in *Are You Being Served?*) and that wonderful character actress Pat Coombes. There was no contract. Each of us would wait impatiently for the weekly call-up. We'd ring each other up and say, "Have you had the call yet?" It was the highlight of the week. We all loved doing the show.

Noel once played up to the apparent rivalry between us during the '70s by slamming the door in my face in one early episode. "I've been wanting to do that for years," he told the audience. "You really meant that, didn't you, Noel?" I said. "Yes, I did," he replied. And from that moment on, we've been the best of friends.

I don't get to see Noel as much as I'd like to, but he did put in a memorable appearance at my 60th birthday party, and said some kind words that really made the evening.

"THE GOD SQUAD ARE ALWAYS SO TERRIBLY DOUR AND SERIOUS."

The best move for my health had nothing to do with food and everything to do with geography. In 1994, nearly two years after Debbie and I married, we decided to quit Central London for the green belt of Hertfordshire on the northern perimeter of the capital. I don't like living in the city. It's a concrete jungle with a strong sense that everyone feels trapped.

We've been here for 13 years now and, as much as I love the coastal area where I did my growing up, I don't anticipate moving away from here for some time yet. With horses grazing in the near distance, it feels like countryside, and yet just the other side of a small copse of trees there's the motorway that connects you with the rest of the country. It feels like Devon and yet it is just 20 minutes to London's West End.

The closer I am to natural beauty, the better I feel. I have no interest in architecture, for example. It's man-made, and really, there's nothing particularly extraordinary about that. But a fish, or a flower or a flock of migrating birds – now that's fascinating to me.

My wife loves churches, but I can't see any beauty in them at all. All those stained glass windows with images of Jesus Christ being crucified on a cross. That just gives me the horrors, ugh, sends shivers down my spine. I can't understand the way God is represented in church. He's not exactly a barrel of laughs, is he. I thought the whole idea is that religion is meant to give you comfort and happiness, and yet the God Squad are always so terribly dour and serious.

I can't see that religion gives much pleasure to people at all. If someone genuinely believes that they're going to end up in heaven, surely they should be spending their entire lives with a huge smile on their face. I don't go along with any of it. It seems so patently obvious to me that the whole thing is one big con, one giant delusion of wishful thinking, and all it does is pit people against each other and creates at least as much damage and bad feeling as politicians do. The world would be a much safer, happier place if people embraced the idea that death just might be the end, so why not try and do good while they're here on earth, not get away with hatred and murder in the expectation that they'll be forgiven in the next life. It's as selfish as it is stupid.

* * *

TIME FOR (ANOTHER) BLACKBURN
THE WIFE: DEBBIE

When I started to date Tony, I had no real preconceptions. I knew who he was and I'd appeared with him in my first panto when I was 17, so I had a vague idea of what he was like. He was going through his divorce at the time and us dancers were running around with the stage hands, so there was no one close to him at that stage. I knew all about him being the *King Of Corn*, though. That's not particularly my humour, but when we met again when I was about 30, I didn't let that affect my judgement.

I was doing a '60s musical in the West End and at one point in the show, it was my duty to go into the crowd and collect the person that had been unsuspectingly selected backstage. And this night, it happened to be Tony Blackburn. As soon as I made a beeline for him he made it quite clear that he didn't want to join in. I was thinking, "Please, come on!" but he said, "I can't dance" and refused to budge. I had to swallow my pride, move along the line and pick out someone else.

He came backstage at the party and I apologised for pestering him. I reminded him that we'd been in a panto together many years earlier, and he pretended that he remembered me, but of course he didn't! And that was that. A few days later, a letter arrived at the theatre saying how nice it was to meet me and would I like to go out for a drink. The idea was that we'd reminisce about the old panto but nothing of the sort happened.

I'd half expected him to come on a bit strong but he turned out to be very gallant and gentlemanly, opening doors and holding my coat for me. He was absolutely charming if you want me to be totally honest. I knew he was considerably older than me and, while that didn't bother me, I wasn't entirely sure about going out with him again. But my friends said, "Go on, it'll be a laugh! See where he takes you!" I think the girls in the theatre were more interested than I was at the start. I asked around and I found out that he'd been out with loads of women, so many that he could have been perceived as a bit of a lecher. He didn't come across that way at all. It worried me more that I didn't find him so!

Neither his past flings or the age difference bothered me at the time. It was only when things became serious, with thoughts of marriage and possibly even children, that I considered the age gap. That couldn't have been further from our minds on our first lunch date when, apropos of nothing, Tony suddenly announced, "You know of course that I'm never going to get married again". I remember thinking, "What are you talking about? I've only come out for lunch . . ."

Things moved pretty quickly after that. We felt so good, so at ease together that it wasn't long before I'd moved in with him. I also remember him saying on that first date, "You're very straight-talking, aren't you", and I think that appealed to him.

There was never any game-playing and when we went out neither of us was eyeing up anyone else. He knew that, if it occurred, I'd have just walked out because that wasn't what I was looking for, and neither was he.

He wasn't necessarily lonely when I met him, more like a man reasonably content with his own company. I probably thought there'd be a lot more happening in his life, but I quite liked the fact that he was happy at home and kept things relatively simple.

A good example of that came in January 2003, when I arranged a surprise get-together for him at the Chesterfield Hotel in Mayfair to celebrate his 60th birthday. While the rest of us sat down and tucked into a delicious, five-course dinner, the chef made a special fuss of Tony, bringing his meal on a silver platter, and ceremonially lifting the lid to reveal . . . his favourite dish of egg and chips. He was absolutely thrilled!

Bearing in mind what had gone before, I was surprised when he asked me to marry him, and he was probably surprised when I turned him down! We were living in Kensington at the time and he was a bit drunk so I said, "No, you can do it when you're sober and when you really mean it. Otherwise I'm not interested. A drunken 'Well, shall we go and get married then?' just won't do!"

When he picked his moment the second time it wasn't that romantic but he did wrap an elastic band round my finger in the absence of a ring.

He's always had a very young and vibrant attitude towards life and when Victoria came along, I soon realised that my destiny was to be a single mother of two children! She'll come in traipsing her muddy feet all round the house and I'll say, "Come on, you're getting older, you have to be a bit responsible now", and she and Tony will go off muttering in a corner. And I'll find myself having to tell them both off, and thinking, "No, this isn't right". I look towards him to back me up and he laughs at me trying my best to be a grown-up.

His work keeps him young, too. He loves it. He often says, "When I grow up I'm out of a job", and there's probably some truth in that. Being a DJ is not on the same level as being a surgeon, for example. But that's his excuse and he's gonna stick to it!

I was worried about him going into the jungle. It was all about survival, and he's such a home-loving man that I worried that keeping up with all these fit people such as Nigel Benn and Nell McAndrew would kill him. I knew that he'd do his best to keep up with them because that's the way he is. When he chooses to do something he'll give it 110% and I really wasn't sure he should expend all that energy just for a television show.

On the night before it all kicked off he phoned me to say that if he was out first, he'd be able to call me in a week's time. He also said that everybody was arguing madly, even before the cameras started rolling, and that he didn't like it. I said, "Come home now, don't put yourself through it". But, and this is typical Tony, he said, "Look, I'm here now, I've got to do it". Thankfully he did and the show turned out brilliantly.

I was a nervous wreck as each episode unfolded. My friends said they'd come round and sit with me, but I couldn't bear the thought of that. I had to watch it alone. It wasn't a pleasurable experience, that's for sure. It was bizarre watching the way the press picked up on the show and started warming to him. He had absolutely no idea that "The man with the tan, the toothy grin and the corny jokes" soon transformed into the one everyone was backing to win. I sat there thinking, "How the hell did that happen? I wish I'd put a bet on him!"

Because I was so wrapped up in the programme I didn't vote until the last day. And when I did, I hit that 'redial' button a few times. On that last night, my mum was with me and she genuinely thought I was having a heart attack when they announced that he'd won, because I screamed at the top of my voice, went a deep shade of red and jumped up and down. I was truly uncontrollable.

It had been two weeks since Tony and I had spoken, and his first words to me after the obligatory "I can't believe it" were "I can't stay on for long because Granada TV are paying for the call". I told him not to be stupid, and we said we loved each other hundreds of times and that was it.

I really admire his energy to do something like that and give it his all. What impresses me rather less is his enthusiasm for service station tat. He swears that he'll never find a more satisfying egg and tomato sandwich than the one he picks up on the way back from work. And very often I'll come home from work in the afternoon and find a wind-up lantern stuck on the kitchen table. "Isn't it wonderful?" he'll say. I'll tell him, "It'll look great under the shrubs where no one will see it." It's plastic! It's horrible! But he doesn't see that at all. He's gone and paid £10 for it and thinks he's got a bargain. I'd pay someone a tenner to take it away.

11

KING OF THE JUNGLE

A couple of years ago, I was asked by an interviewer, "What's the most interesting thing you've ever done?". I didn't think twice about my reply. "Making *I'm A Celebrity, Get Me Out Of Here*", I said. "You said what?" my wife exclaimed when I told her. "That jungle programme? More important than the opening of Radio One?" Sure, Radio One was hugely important to me from a career standpoint, but from a personal point of view, it was *I'm A Celebrity* . . . Doing that show had more of an impact on me, my life and the way I felt than I'd ever experienced before. I'm not a spiritual person by any means, but spending two weeks in the Australian jungle brought me the closest I've ever come to it.

It was my agent who put me up for the show when he heard they were looking for celebrities to appear in the launch series. That was Michael Cohen, from MPC Entertainment, who have transformed my career again after almost two decades of associations with other agents. Like Harold Davison, Michael's more than an agent; he's a friend. He'll never miss my birthday, or Victoria's for that matter.

Agents are so important. They make or break you, and the best ones can protect you from the more unsavoury aspects of showbusiness.

Michael suggested me for the show as a joke, I'm sure, but the team at Granada Television, which was making the series, seemed to take him seriously. "How would you like to be dropped in the middle of the Australian jungle and attempt to survive with a handful of strangers for two weeks?" he asked. "Terrific," I said, and thought no more about it. About a week later, he said, "Granada would like to see you." Now I really thought he was joking.

I went along to see the programme makers and they explained how the programme might pan out. I remember being pretty impressed when they told me that 400 people were going to be working on it. "But why do you want somebody like me?" I said, "I'm a vegetarian, for a start. I wouldn't kill an animal under any circumstances." Then they asked me if I enjoyed camping and outdoor life. I was honest and said that I didn't particularly. Neither did I take any I exercise. And when I answered that question, I thought, "Ah, now I am beginning to understand what kind of show this might be."

Another three weeks or so passed before I received the call from Michael who said, "They want you!" Almost everyone close to me, especially those I loved such as Debbie and my mother, tried to talk me out of it. They thought I was too old for such a gruelling survivalist adventure and that I wouldn't be able to stomach the other contestants. Maybe they might irritate me, I thought. But I wouldn't have taken on anything I didn't think I could handle.

I said to Debbie, "I've gotta to do this. This kind of opportunity only comes around once and I'm not one for dithering, only to see someone else make a success of it". She wasn't convinced. But I hated the thought of watching the show in a few months' time and kicking myself for my indecision. I had to do it. I also wanted to go to Australia, a country I'd never visit. As it turned out, for the entire two weeks of my stay there, all I saw of the place was the inside of a rainforest.

Even my agent and his wife began to have second thoughts. The programme makers took Debbie and I out for dinner one night because they wanted to be sure that I'd made the right decision. I assured them I could handle it.

"I DIDN'T KNOW THAT I WOULD END UP BECOMING THE HENRY KISSINGER OF THE JUNGLE RESPONSIBLE FOR KEEPING THE WARRING FACTIONS APART."

I had no clue who I was going to be up against in the jungle. Apart from that, the organisers at Granada TV were upfront about virtually everything else. They said, "You're going to have cameras on you 24 hours a day, so if there's any character trait or private habit that you wouldn't want the public to see, we advise you not to do the show." I couldn't immediately think of any appalling habits I might have had. So in late August 2002, I found myself on a long-haul flight to Australia, seated next to another contestant, the posh and sometimes problematic It Girl Tara Palmer-Tomkinson.

I missed out on the first photo session for the programme because I'd been holidaying in Corfu with Debbie and my daughter Victoria in a bid to get myself into shape. I did a fair bit of swimming in an effort to build my stamina up, but I must confess that I detest exercising. There's only one thing more boring than working out and that's people who are obsessed with it. When I see joggers pass me in the street, they always seem so pale and unfit. They're invariably attached to a water bottle, too. Someone should tell them that if they drink too much water they might turn into a puddle.

I have no idea why I ended up on a plane with all the women. When we landed and were driven off to a hotel in Cairns, in the northern part of Australia close to the jungle location, all the other fellas were already there. Perhaps that explains why I bonded better with the women on the programme. I do enjoy the company of women, as this book has made unblushingly clear. In the hotel some of the contestants were arguing before the show had even started. I had no inkling at that stage that I would eventually become the Henry Kissinger of the Jungle, the peacemaker responsible for keeping the warring factions apart.

On the first day we were given a course on how to survive in the rainforest. The whole thing's a mental game, really, between the producers of the show and the contestants, and it was important that we had some idea of what we might face in the weeks ahead. An expert was on hand to show us the different varieties of snakes we might encounter. He'd say, "Don't go anywhere near one like this because it will kill you." It puts the fear of God into you even before you've started, and I suppose that's the whole idea.

One of the aspects of the show that quickly became clear to me was that when things start to get a bit cosy, the producers would put another spanner in the works to get everybody at each other again. I think that's what threw boxer Nigel Benn. He seemed to think it was going to be a physical game, which would have been a bit daft, as he would have beaten us all hands down because he was obviously so much tougher than the rest of us.

"CHRISTINE HAMILTON WAS AS NUTTY
AS A FRUITCAKE, COMPLETELY BONKERS.
I THOUGHT SHE WAS WONDERFUL."

When the time came for the challenge to begin, we were dropped in to the jungle by helicopter and were met by an Aussie bush-whacker who led us to the camp. It was about a 40-minute hike, and for the entire duration he kept warning us, saying things such as "Don't brush against that tree because it's home to life-threatening insects". They really messed with your mind and I was exhausted before we'd even got there.

It might sound incredibly short-sighted of me, but I'd not even thought about the natural dangers that lurked in the jungle at all. The truth was, of course, that these things are usually more scared of human beings than we are of them. I never actually saw a snake the whole time I was on site. I'd heard that they cleared the area before we went in, but even so, one apparently did manage to find its way in.

Ostensibly, we were being led towards the camp. In truth, we were actually being walked around in circles, which was another tactic in disorientation. When we finally arrived at our makeshift camp, none of the beds were made up, which is where Christine Hamilton, wife of the disgraced Conservative politician Neil Hamilton, first made an impact. She was like a Scout leader, very well organised, and knew every knot going! She was as nutty as a fruitcake, completely bonkers, and I thought she was wonderful.

It was a strangely serene environment, quite beautiful with a stream running through it. I found myself drawn to the water, and would sit there for hours with Nell McAndrew, the young model, who I thought was utterly charming.

I found the first week very difficult because nobody seemed to get on at all. Everyone was swearing at each other, and I kept thinking, "Don't you realise that this is a television show?" I never once lost sight of that, It wasn't that I was putting on a pretence but I was always aware that at some stage I was going to have to come out and face the real world again. I didn't want my mother or my five-year old daughter to feel embarrassed by me effing and blinding – not that I really do much of that anyway.

One evening, I had a go at the comedian Rhona Cameron, who was being particularly irritating and trying to wind me up. I said, "Look, if you don't stop, I'm going". Then I realised that simply wasn't true. I was going nowhere – at least not until the public voted me off the show.

"URI GELLER BENT ALL THE CUTLERY AND TRIED TO SEE THE DEEPER SIGNIFICANCE IN ABSOLUTELY EVERYTHING WE DID."

None of us was particularly happy that Uri Geller kept using the spoons for his 'bend it' party piece, either. It was all very clever watching him bend them out of shape, but there were only a limited number of spoons on camp.

He was a very nice guy, though he did try to find meaning in absolutely every single thing you did. He'd say, "Tony, does that mean something to you?' I said, "What, the fact that I'm having a cup of tea?" And he'd say, "But doesn't it mean anything more to you?' I'd say, "No, not really!" It got to the stage where you were frightened to pick something up for fear of being grilled about its deeper significance. No, Uri, I'm picking up a spoon because I want to eat something!

Rhona Cameron and Nigel Benn were constantly at each other's throats, probably because she was a lesbian, and he seemed to find that tantamount to provocation. On the other hand, she was deliberately winding people up. Tara had this running problem with the singer Darren Day. They'd obviously crossed paths at some earlier stage in their lives and there was still some tension between them – though I couldn't quite work out what the problem was. The odd thing about being thrown into that environment was not seeing everything that was going on, which means you don't know what people are saying behind your back either.

As the guys gradually got voted out, I entered the final week with only girls for company. It was very peaceful, a bit like having a harem in the middle of the forest! Everyone was much happier without all that testosterone flying around the place. It was interesting because I thought to myself, "Actually, this is exactly how it works in the world outside, too."

I suppose I was regarded as something of a kindly uncle figure. I don't think I posed a sexual threat to them. I certainly didn't get propositioned while I was there! During that second week, I developed a close bond with Nell. Perhaps the fact she was a tall, beautiful, slim, gorgeous, fabulous blonde might have helped a bit! Actually, I'm joking. She was very sweet, and when she put the jungle hat on, she reminded me of my first love, Doris Day.

Before we put our heads down for bed each night, I'd said to Nell, "Would you mind putting the hat on for me?" And she would! I had to tell her that she looked a bit like Doris Day – wholesome, lovely looking, beautiful teeth. I don't think Doris ever got into nude modelling, though.

Nell wouldn't ever say much on camera. In fact, she usually refused to do the interviews outright. "But Nell," I'd say, "we're doing a TV show. You're not gonna be on television much if you don't do it." She said, "Oh it's so lovely here, I don't want to be interrupted!" Another reason she didn't do the interviews was that she didn't really have a lot to say. She was very quiet, not an extrovert at all.

Christine Hamilton was the flamboyant reverse. "Come on, everybody, let's do this now!" A lot of people were bothered by the bugs, which come out in droves when it rains, a situation made worse by the fact that the bedding wasn't waterproof. The only unpleasant visitor from the animal kingdom to affect me was when a leech attached itself to me and blood started pouring down my arm. "Oh, don't worry about that," said Christine, who then yanked it off me with one tough tug.

I had absolutely no inkling, or even any desire, to win the programme. But in the hours before it all started, when we were sitting around with the producers and the cameramen, one of the production team told me they'd all had a bet and that I was the favourite to win. "You must be joking!" I said. "The cameras – and everyone at home – will fall in love with all these young people. You've wasted your money there."

"THOSE LOGS WERE LIKE OLD FRIENDS. I TALKED TO THEM. 'OH, I REMEMBER YOU. YOU'RE A VERY, VERY NICE LOG. YOU'RE ONE OF MY FAVOURITES.'"

Another asked me what my tactics would be. I asked, "Have people really worked out game plans?" My only thought had been to go in there and enjoy it – and I stuck to that. Obviously I knew that if I said something funny, it was probable that they'd use it. I think that's how I ended up talking to the log! By the end of the fortnight, I was quite fond of that log. Logs were crucial to our survival out there. If the fire went out, you couldn't cook anything, so I was always off down the river to collect more logs. It was good exercise too. Because I always get by with something like four hours sleep a night, I'd go off and collect more logs simply for something to do. The producers told me at the end of the show that I'd collected enough to keep the fire going for several weeks. No wonder some of the contestant started singing, "It's raining logs . . . Hallelujah!" I'd collected so many that the view of one of the cameras was almost being obscured, so I was told not to collect anymore.

As the show reached its inevitable climax, with I think just three of us still in there, some bright spark in production had the brilliant idea of removing all the logs while we were away from camp. It absolutely broke my heart when I returned and saw what they'd done. I'd put all that work into collecting them, and now I had to start all over again.

It was obvious they were trying to get me riled. I was really upset about it but all I could think to do was start collecting all over again. And when I went back to the place where I used to find the logs, I noticed that one or two of them looked remarkably familiar. That's when I started talking to the logs. When I recognised one by its shape or any particularly strange markings it was like being reunited with an old friend. "Oh, I remember you. You're a very, very nice log. You're one of my favourites." I genuinely hadn't realised there would be a camera on me in that obscure spot. I can still picture one particular log as I write.

Despite the doubts of my friends and family, I'd taken to the jungle setting very well. I did wonder whether my years adrift on the pirate ships had steeled me for the experience. When we were down to three, one of the broadsheets noted that all of us – Tara Palmer-Tomkinson, Christine Hamilton and myself – had all been public school boarders. I wouldn't suggest for a minute that anyone who goes to public school is any better than someone who hasn't, but I suppose being trapped somewhere and surrounded by annoying people when you're young must have helped.

There was a psychiatrist on hand, both before and during the show, to check that we were coping with the strain of being cooped up in a dangerous environment with a bunch of celebrity strangers. But as soon as she started talking, I realised I was almost certainly more sane than she was!

I was fine. The only thing I suffered from in there was mild dehydration, which meant that I'd wake up in the mornings feeling a bit dizzy. They gave us pills for that.

* * *

"I'M NOT RELIGIOUS AT ALL, BUT FOR THAT MOMENT,
I WAS GRIPPED BY SUCH A POWERFUL AND PEACEFUL
FORCE IN A WAY THAT I'D NEVER EXPERIENCED BEFORE."

I never forget that *I'm A Celebrity, Get Me Out Of Here* was a television show. But under the full glare of the cameras I underwent a strange, life-changing experience. It happened while I was sitting beside that beautiful stream, with no mobile phones to interrupt my thoughts and nobody around. And sitting there, gazing up at the beauty of the trees, listening to the trickling sound of the stream, observing the subtle shades of nature's colours; the moment just got to me. I'm not religious at all, but for that moment, I was gripped by such a powerful and peaceful force in a way I'd never experienced before. Nell was with me, and both of us felt the same. I thought, I don't think I've ever experienced more inner peace and serenity than I do at this precise moment. I also wondered how fleeting that thought might be. But, I'm happy to report, it's never left me. I have the makers of a popular television show to thank for that.

It was the closest I'd ever come to having a spiritual experience. Of course I still get riled sometimes but there is more at the core of me now. The experience of living for a fortnight with a group of strangers, some of who could be grossly irritating, definitely had its part to play in this revelation. I seemed to handle it so well that I even began to annoy myself!

I've really no idea why people voted for me. Perhaps it's linked to how you're perceived as a public figure and then revealing a surprising dimension. I'm sure people thought that I'd act the clown, first thing in the morning launching right in there with, "Have you heard the one about the . . .?" And I'm not really like that at all.

The only time I tried to win the show was on the last day. By that time it was down to just Tara and me, and I thought she was really sweet and very candid. I remember having a long chat with her about her problems with drugs and so forth and I couldn't help but offer some fatherly advice. I wasn't aware that I was doing it and it was only when I watched the programme later that I noticed it. In fact, the final episode was the only one I ever bothered to watch after I returned home.

On that last day, Tara and I had all these tasks we were asked to perform, picking up snakes and all that stuff. I thought, "Well, I really don't enjoy doing this kind of thing but I put myself here so . . ." I really went for it. Whatever the challenge, I wouldn't eat the bugs though. I think that's where Uri Geller came unstuck. He's a vegetarian, and then he started eating all these creatures. I had a spat with him about that. I told him, "I don't admire for you for doing that." He said 'Why not?' He tried to make out it was for his charity, and that if he said no, he'd be letting the charity down. I said, "No, you're letting all the world's vegetarians down."

"THE PRODUCER SAID, 'LET'S PUT IT THIS WAY. 'I'M A CELEBRITY, GET ME OUT OF HERE' IS GOING TO CHANGE YOUR LIFE.'"

When it was announced that I'd won, and I was crowned King Of The Jungle, I was obviously surprised and of course extremely flattered. For decades I'd been under the impression that the public didn't like me that much, that I was more of a British irritant than a national treasure, which is what the press started calling me! I thought Tara had been a marvellous jungle partner, so when I accepted my victory, I added, "And this is my queen." She was a lovely person with whom to spend those final hours in the rainforest.

As I walked across that bridge, back to life, back to reality, I was greeted with cries of, "All hail, the King!" All I could think of in that moment was to turn to the producer and ask, "Did anybody watch it?" He said, "Let's put it this way. *I'm A Celebrity, Get Me Out Of Here* is going to change your life. And I, as its producer, have got a job for ever."

At Sydney Airport, we were met by a group of people who'd flown out there for a holiday. These people were nothing to do with the show, just interested well wishers. "Have they really been watching this back in Britain?" I asked. "The entire country has been transfixed by it," came the reply.

When I arrived back home, I remember filling up my car at a petrol station, and this dear old man got out of his car and hobbled over towards me on a pair of sticks. He must have at least 80. He tapped me on the shoulder, and said, "Well done, old boy. You've done our age group a world of good." I was actually around 20 years his junior yet his words really affected me. I returned to my car and cried a few tears. It was a strange sensation to have touched so many people. I thought that, despite all the bad press this country gets, British people really don't like the bullying types.

Home life, too, changed quite a bit afterwards. Victoria's friends at school all began to greet me with a chorus of, "He's the *King Of The Jungle*". Even my wife started talking to me again! Despite their deep reservations before my departure, my entire family seemed to be as proud as they were relieved.

"I WAS SURPRISED TO COME HOME TO THE NEWS
THAT *I'M A CELEBRITY* HAD 'RESCUED MY CAREER'.
I THOUGHT I'D BEEN DOING REMARKABLY WELL!"

It had been an amazing experience. I'd been to Australia, where I'd never been before. I had something akin to a personal revelation. And I'd won something. The only downside was when I returned home to discover just how badly I'd apparently been doing before

I'm A Celebrity . . . "rescued my career". I thought I'd been doing remarkably well! At the time I agreed to do the show, I was working six days a week on radio at Capital Gold, and I was doing all sorts of bits for television.

> DEBBIE BLACKBURN: *Mindful of all that Smashie And Nicey banter about "doing it all for charidee", Tony's been rather shy in coming forward to say that his appearance on the show raised over £200,000 for the National Autistic Society. A cousin of mine is autistic, and Tony has a friend whose son has autism, so that's why he nominated the N.A.S. as his chosen charity. He was typically self-deprecating when he first approached them, too. He said, "Don't expect much. It's a survival programme, so I don't think I'll be around long."*

I'm A Celebrity . . . has been perceived as the show that gives a bunch of Z-list celebrities the opportunity to rescue – or destroy – their careers. I didn't see it like that at all. I'd simply been asked to take part in a television programme that sounded rather appealing to me. That said, it certainly did my career no harm. Shortly afterwards, I felt confident enough to switch radio stations, from Capital Gold where I wasn't really happy, to Classic Gold, which has proved to be an infinitely more pleasurable place to work. I also started to broadcast for Jazz FM where I was given the chance to play more soul music. And GMTV began calling up too, putting me together with Cheggers for some early morning on-screen madness.

The first spin-off, though, was co-presenting *Animals Do The Funniest Things* with Tara Palmer-Tomkinson. She's a lovely person but she can also be a little bit demanding and the series didn't last that long. Had I been partnered with Christine Hamilton the show might have gone down a lot better. If Tara and I were an obvious double act, it was only because I was the winner and she the runner-up. I never thought it quite worked when it came to presenting a show together.

Tara wasn't the most professionally motivated person I've ever worked with either. One night, despite the fact that we were contracted to stay on set until 10.30pm, she announced that we'd all have to finish up by nine because her father was taking her out to dinner. I thought that was a bit ambitious but she insisted. "If you're awkward with them," I cautioned, "you know we'll never work for ITV again." She stared at me and said, "Well, fuck ITV!". Her family's loaded so she can probably afford to lose jobs left, right and centre. But it wasn't a great attitude, I must say. Maybe that gets people places these days, but it's not the way I like to conduct my life – either professionally or at home.

* * *

TIME FOR (ANOTHER) BLACKBURN
THE DAUGHTER: VICTORIA

He's not like the usual dad; he's more like a three year old! I know he's done a lot in his life, and has all these awards up in his room, but to me he's as much a friend as anything else. He's older than most of my friend's dads, but while they're more up to date with the newest fashions, my dad play fights with me and we always have a good laugh.

Sometimes I think of dad as a brother because I can tell him anything, even if I'm worrying about something. In fact, I think he's kinder than a brother. He'll sit down and play a board game with me even though he hates it. I don't think a brother would do that. I can see it's important to him that I'm having fun.

At the same time, he can be serious, too. He always cheers me up if I'm feeling down. If there's a problem with someone at school, he'll listen, and then he'll do something about it. He's not the sort of person who pretends to take an interest. He really does, and I think that's lovely.

He's not that strict when it comes to school. He's never told me off for getting a bad grade. I think that's good because it would be sad to take grades so seriously. They are important, though as dad's always told me, they're not the end of the world.

I was only about two or three years old when I first saw him on television. Mum said, "Daddy's on TV, do you wanna have a look?" I was amazed that my dad was sitting next to me and yet he was on the TV at the same time. I couldn't understand that at all. I thought he'd managed to pop himself into the box without me looking. It was actually quite scary.

When he appeared on I'm A Celebrity, I was old enough by then to understand that it was one of the biggest moments in his career. I wasn't allowed to watch all of it. It was on late and it also included naughty bits. But mum had video them so I was allowed to see the best bits. It was lovely to see him getting on with everyone, play with his logs and generally be himself. We knew he'd gone in it for a laugh, and none of us expected him to win. That was an amazing surprise. I know this probably sounds really horrible but we were so proud.

The moment it first really hit home that dad was such a public person was when he took me and my best friend to Planet Hollywood for my birthday. We were trying to eat and all these people kept coming over and asking dad for his autograph. I didn't think they'd ever stop. I'd been out with him before when he's been asked for autographs, but never like that. I didn't mind. It's nice to think that some people really, really like him and the things he does.

"HE'S NOT LIKE PARIS HILTON OR SOMEBODY LIKE THAT. COMPLETELY THE OPPOSITE, REALLY."

Some of my friends have been a bit scared to meet my dad, but when they do, they find out that he's really fun to be with and they can't wait to come back. He's not like Paris Hilton or somebody like that. Completely the opposite, really. He doesn't think he's better than everyone else. He can talk to anybody and I much prefer him to be that way. The thing about dad is that what you see is what you get. Whether he's at home, out at a party, or on television messing around with Keith Chegwin, he's exactly the same.

I know some people really do think he sits around cracking jokes all day. Well he doesn't, but he is still really, really funny to be with. He can also be serious when he wants to be. I've begun to notice that when he gets a new job, he goes up into his little room and starts fiddling with all his tapes and things. Sometimes, he'll ask me, "Should I play this one or that one?" He makes a laugh out of it but I can tell he's taking it seriously.

It's funny. A lot of people think that celebrities do what they do for the fame, the glory and the money, but he's not. He's doing it because he has the most fantastic time behind that microphone! I hear him up there sometimes. He has this little microphone that doesn't really work, and I can see him with his headphones on practising for the next show. You know, "Hello, this is Tony Blackburn here!" I like to spy on him while he's listening to his old tunes, bopping up and down, and having a great laugh. He can be quite embarrassing up there, but I don't mind because we've all got used to that by now. And it's funny!

It's lovely that he enjoys his job. I hope he carries on doing it until his dying day. Quite often I hear him say, "Well, I'm getting too old now", but we all think he's got a good few years left in him yet.

Sometimes he gets to go on cruises as part of his work, and mum and I always say, "What a hard job you have, having fun and relaxing the whole time!" But if you think about it, he still has to put on a happy face even if he doesn't really feel like it. Most of the time he can, because that's just the way he is, but there must be times when you just want to close the door and hide.

He really doesn't care what people think of his image. He cares what they think of him as a person. He doesn't like being horrible to people. I know he had a bit of trouble with the pool man earlier today, but I bet you anything he'll ring them up and say, "I'm so sorry, I didn't mean to say it like that." He's a really forgiving man. He always apologises right away, even if he's not really in the wrong.

I'm like my dad in quite a lot of ways. I think that we're both quite forgiving. If a friend has done something really bad, then I might hold a grudge, but if it's something stupid like a fight over a lunch tray, then I'll always make it up with them as quickly as I can. Right now, most of my friends are trying to be teenagers before they really are. I don't try to be like that. I prefer to be playful and climb trees rather than try and act all cool. I'm also like him because I enjoy talking to people, to open up to them. I can meet someone and within five minutes, we'll be chatting away like best friends.

He's a bit crafty sometimes, because even though he puts on that jokey, "I'm very dumb" kind of thing, he is – even though I'm horrified to admit it – actually quite bright, especially when it comes to general knowledge and electrical things. He went on Supermarket Sweep and he knew lots of the answers. He's actually a lot smarter than he lets on.

I know that my relationship with dad will change as I become a teenager. He's already realising that I'm growing up and that we'll not be play fighting for much longer. Recently I've put the phone bill up by 28 million per cent because I'm on it to my friends practically all the time. He doesn't seem to mind. He knows that my friends are important to me and that it's important for me to talk to them. But, really, he's my biggest friend of all.

12

LIFE GOES ON

For the past five years I've been getting up at three in the morning, earlier than I've ever done before, to present my breakfast show. That's partly because my current job at Classic Gold is based a 40-minute drive away, in Dunstable. And it's partly through choice as my desire to make the most of each and every day has intensified these past few years.

Surviving amongst all that personal rancour in the alien beauty of the rainforest taught me a wonderful lesson about myself. Meaanwhile, life at home with my wife and daughter has shown me the true meaning of love and happiness. I just wish I were young enough to still have a lifetime ahead of me to enjoy it!

In every year that ends with a 7 – and in 2002 for the 25th anniversary – Radio One's Class Of '67 reunites to celebrate yet another milestone. Inevitably, we all end up back on the steps of All Souls Church beside Broadcasting House and recreate the original photograph that introduced the first intake of DJs to the world. It never quite works. For a start, we're all a lot more wrinkly and wider around the girth than we used to be. More worrying still, every time we reconvene there are always one or two more empty spaces in our Radio One rogues' gallery.

It will feel very strange this September without three of the men most closely associated with the station – John Peel, Alan Freeman and Tommy Vance. I am acutely aware that one day, they'll be doing it and in the place where I should be standing – back row, far left – there will be just thin air.

It's rather the same feeling at the annual the lunch for *The Oldie* magazine, which I've been invited along to ever since they made me Oldie Of The Year after my appearance on *I'm A Celebrity . . .*. I walk in and the conversation is always the same: "Oh well, made it through another year!" It's a lovely event, though I never understand why they hold it at Simpsons in the Strand. While it's a classy, old-fashioned venue, there's no lift and the stairs are just too steep. I spend half my time helping people make their way up to the top where, inexplicably, the function is always held.

Having a blissful home life with a wife I love and an adorable young daughter is a stark reminder that I've not quite as long left as I'd like in the scheme of things. I enjoy life immensely though I'd be lying if I said that I didn't think about dying. It's not an all-consuming passion by any means, but with the day I pick up my pension book fast approaching, I can't exactly bury the subject in the sand. It's when you hear about the death of, say, *The New Avengers* star Gareth Hunt, someone who not too long ago was a young and vibrant household name, that really brings it home.

Though it does concern me, not least because I'm looking forward to seeing what Victoria does with her life, I can't help but see the funny side of death too. Reincarnation? I must believe in it because I've altered my will and left everything to myself!

Actually, I don't. Though I would dearly love to believe there's this magical afterlife that we all float off to, where everything is wonderful and my mum and dad are there waiting for me, I just can't see it. That's why I don't get too fixated on death or the religious mumbo-jumbo that surrounds it. My attitude is, enjoy it while you can. Why worry about life after death when in all likelihood there isn't one? It must be such a bummer to die and suddenly be hit by the realisation that there isn't anything afterwards and that was all you had!

My philosophy is to be nice to people, so if by chance you do end up at the gates of heaven you'll be in poll position. If there is a God, he's hardly going to turn you away, is he?

"EVEN IF I DO FIND MYSELF USHERED THROUGH THE PEARLY GATES, HOW THE HELL AM I GOING TO FIND MY LOVED ONES? I DON'T IMAGINE I'D SEE A SIGNPOST SAYING, 'THE BLACKBURNS – WALK THIS WAY'."

The death of my mother in October 2006 hit me hard. Despite common sense saying that death is so final, such a permanent thing, I do find myself talking aloud to her when I'm driving alone. I say, "I do hope you're all right", that kind of thing. Perhaps I'm hedging my bets. I love the very idea that one day I might be reunited with my parents, and my uncle Nick who I adored, but even if I do find myself being ushered through the pearly gates, how the hell am I going to find them? I just don't see there being a signpost saying, "The Blackburns – third on the left". That's why losing her has affected me so badly. I always like to face the reality of a situation head-on, but without the easy comfort of life after death to cling on to, that does make dealing with it all the more difficult.

I lost my father while I was working at Radio London. He'd always had a wonderful sense of humour, but as he'd grown older, the back problem that had plagued him through life got much worse. He'd endured a couple of operations, and took handfuls of pills to numb the pain. I sometimes think he washed them down with just a little too much gin which is hardly a mirth-inspiring drink at the best of times, let alone when your head is buried in a serious newspaper or you are watching the latest news report on famine or warfare.

We'd spent quite a lot of time chatting in his later years, about life in general as much as anything else, but I can't help but think that he made himself tired of life far sooner than he needed to. It's a mistake I have no intention of repeating.

Nevertheless, I found the news of his death difficult to fathom. My mother was in London, visiting her brother but I still made my daily call home. "How's everything?", I said to Jackie. "Dad's dead," she said. I thought it was a crank call so I said, "Let me ring you back". Second time round, I knew it was no mistake. A police officer came to the phone to tell me that my father had suffered a massive heart attack in the back garden.

After dad died, I knew that my mother and Jackie at least had each other for support. That's why I was particularly dreading the news about my mother. I realised that when she was gone Jackie would be alone and I worried about the effect on her, especially given that they'd spent the best part of sixty years together in the family home.

I'd always promised my parents that when the time came I would look after Jackie. By that, I had simply assumed that she would move in with us up here. It hasn't happened.

Apart from losing a little of her confidence in driving, Jackie whizzes around the place in her electric wheelchair, and has managed to fill her time with an amazing social life that would put most of us celebrities to shame. Since my mother's death she and I have become a lot closer, too. Unfortunately, none of that really helps numb the pain of losing a mother.

My mother had always been extremely healthy. She was slim and attractive in her young days, and as she got older, she was still very agile, walked everywhere and never gave the impression that she was an older woman. At the age of 82, she'd still walk all the way into Bournemouth, while my sister travelled alongside her in her chair. I don't think she ever suffered a day's illness in her life. Mum was one of those enormously fit-and-healthy characters and that made it virtually impossible to comprehend that one day she wouldn't be around any more.

That perception began to change one morning in 2005. As usual, I rang home after coming off air, only to hear my sister telling me that our mother was in a bed in Poole General Hospital. She'd had unbearable stomach pains through her night, and had been rushed there a few hours earlier. I drove down immediately, thought, "What a dreadful place", and had her transferred to the far more hospitable Harbour Hospital.

The problem was that doctors didn't know what was wrong with her. When they operated, a bit of metal was found in her stomach which they removed. We'd hoped that would be the end of it. Unfortunately, it wasn't. Shortly afterwards, the stomach pains returned and during a second stay in hospital, she was diagnosed with cancer.

The news was a dreadful shock but the specialist assured us that after a course of chemotherapy, the cancer could well go into remission. I wouldn't take his word for it, though. I simply needed to know more. I did some research on the internet and quickly discovered that she had the most aggressive type of cancer, the one that was the most difficult of all to treat.

After a second course of chemo, the specialist said there was very little more he could do. Mum went home and Jackie and I had to steel ourselves for the worst. About two weeks before she died, she went downhill very quickly and wanted to go into a hospice.

Jackie and I persuaded her not to because we wanted her to be at home, in the place that was filled with so much love and so many magnificent memories.

Mum had these wonderful Macmillan Cancer Support nurses caring for her while the doctor did the best he could by fitting her to this machine that pumped morphine into her system on demand to help relieve the pain. I remember watching all this going on, and holding back the tears as my mother was trying to make light of the situation. "Oh, just another adventure!" she said. But, mercifully, it was short-lived because a couple of days later she died.

The last time I spoke to my mother was on a Friday and she was still conscious. By the time I drove down after my show on the Saturday afternoon, she had lost consciousness and was breathing very heavily. After trying to get some sleep later that night, Jackie and I were both up again at four in the morning and we sat with her, unable to do anything but listen helplessly as those loud breaths signalled that the end was desperately close. We went outside for some air and, when we came back, she was gone. With a nurse quietly watching over her, mum just drifted peacefully away. As Jackie and I sat with her, holding her hand, the room filled with this huge massive silence – and quiet sense of loss.

My mother had requested that there be no funeral ceremony. Like the rest of us, she had little truck with the ritualised pomp and circumstance of organised religion. Instead, she made sure that everything was done with the minimum of fuss, making it terribly easy for Jackie and me.

There was no one there for the cremation, which took place in nearby Bournemouth – Jackie and I simply took the ashes home. One lovely sunny morning, after I'd finished my Classic Gold breakfast show, I drove back down to the family home in Lilliput. Jackie and I took the ashes to the top of the garden, and gently sprinkled them around the base of one of her favourite trees. I absolutely adored the simplicity of that. There's nothing worse than standing around at a funeral ceremony feeling obliged to make small talk when all you really want to do is grieve and contemplate in private.

"MAKING A CHILD FEEL WANTED AND RESPECTED SIMPLY SOUNDS LIKE COMMON SENSE TO ME."

Thinking about my mother now, as I put the finishing touches to this book, brings home once again the enormity of the loss. Earlier on, when I played those jingles from my days on the pirate ships, my eyes were filled with tears of nostalgia. But writing about my mother, Pauline, the nearest thing to a best friend a person could possibly wish for, is still so painfully raw for me. I have dusted myself down and got on with my life, and my broadcasting since her death in October 2006. But as soon as I allow the memory of her to fill my thoughts, I still find it very difficult to hold my emotions together.

Watching Victoria bring such wonderful life and fun and creativity to the household helps enormously. I've only ever wanted one thing for my son and daughter and that's for them to be happy. Bringing up children doesn't have to be as complicated as some people make out. Neither of my parents was strict or gave me a hard time and I never gave them a hard time back. That seems like a reasonable exchange to me.

I remember hearing someone on the radio saying that so many parents don't take time to talk to their children, or praise them when they've done something good. Making a child feel wanted and respected simply sounds like common sense to me.

Victoria is an absolute delight. Debbie and I regard her as the third and equal part of a tight-knit trio rather than a lower status member of the family as some children are made to feel. She comes with us on holiday, she goes out with us to shows and social events, and why not? She's always such great company. I don't see the point of having a child if you're going to lock them up with a nanny, send them away to school for months on end, or simply tell them to shut up all the time.

DEBBIE BLACKBURN: *Although Tony and are very different in many ways, we are both dedicated to the idea of what we call our 'Special Sundays'. That's when we simply lock the doors on the world, and do simple, family things. We've been doing it ever since we first met. For the rest of the week, we might accept invitations out, or take Victoria to a show, but on Sundays, we'll get a board game out, potter around in the garden, go for a country walk and then sit down and watch a film. Neither of us would have it any other way.*

The only time Victoria's really given me cause for concern is when she was a year or so old. I went up to her and made a funny noise with my mouth hoping to elicit some kind of humourous response. She didn't react at all. The thought crossed my mind: My God, I've got a child who's got no sense of humour whatsoever. Happily, as she's grown up, she's learned how to talk rubbish and laugh a lot, so it's obvious that I would find her tremendous fun.

"CONTEMPORARY COMMERCIAL RADIO HAS BECOME AS STAID AND AS FORMATTED AS THOSE STUFFY OLD PERFORMERS FROM THE DANCE BAND ERA."

I wish I could say the same for domestic commercial radio, but I'm afraid I can't. Don't get me wrong. I have been at Classic Gold for four years now, presenting the weekday breakfast show, and I love it.

I have a wonderful team around me and sound off in a section I call "This Show Thinks: The Frank And Fearless Comedy Column On Air". And of course I get in those all-important time checks. I might even play the odd record, too. But that, I hasten to add, is where the problem of British radio now lies.

I remember back in the Capital Gold days, during the early '90s, a listener came up to me at one of those outdoor promotional events and said, "Why do you always play The Beatles' *Help!* at 8.15 every morning. I said, "Do I?" And, essentially, he was right. Other listeners would write in saying basically the same thing – too few records on endless rotation. It was as if I'd suddenly become a latter day Jan Ralfini playing *Wheels Cha Cha* at 8.45 every evening.

The notion is depressing but contemporary commercial radio – once the sound of a new and thrilling future – has become as staid and as formatted as those stuffy old performers from the dance band era. The audience had noticed, and yet no one in radio with the power to reverse the rot was willing to listen.

Tune into any commercial station and you'll not have to listen too hard before you'll get the picture – Fleetwood Mac's *Go Your Own Way*, The Police's *Every Breath You Take*, ABBA's *Dancing Queen*, Tina Turner's *Simply The Best*. None of them are bad songs by any stretch of the imagination, but to hear them on rotation several times a day each and every day is surely enough to drive even the most casual listener away – or mad! The irony is that in purporting to offer more choice, commercial radio – driven by financial constraints and play-it-safe executives – is today no less regimented and predictable as Radio Moscow was back in Stalin's heyday! One station, and I won't mention which one, only plays 90 different records in any given week. In a culture as potentially exciting and diverse as ours, that statistic is a damning indictment.

Sometimes, drastic situations deserve drastic measures, which is why in June 2004, I defied my bosses on Classic Gold and played Cliff

Richard's records on air. In some ways, my decision was inspired by the big hoo-hah about Radio One DJs receiving an order from on high insisting that they no longer played Status Quo records. I'd also read interviews with Cliff in which he complained that his music had virtually slipped off radio playlists. I thought it was ludicrous that stations weren't playing his records simply because some idiot's declared that he's out of fashion. Who says so? Cliff Richard is a national institution who has been making great records for 50 years. Why not help bring him back – and while we're at it, let's help ourselves to a ratings boost at the same time.

I said to my Managing Director John Baish, "I can't understand why we aren't playing Cliff Richard records. I think his music would bring in listeners, so I'm going to start playing them." He wasn't really sure how to respond. But I kept my promise and the next day, and for several days afterwards, I made sure there was a Cliff Richard record in my show. It worked. Listeners called and wrote in applauding the move. I was serious about righting a wrong.

John was not pleased. He sent me an email that said he'd rather I didn't add records that were not programmed on the playlist, and gave me an official warning. I tore the email up on air. The next thing I knew, John had suspended me.

Being fired for playing Cliff Richard records quickly became a massive story in the press. I even ended up discussing the episode on Radio 4's Today programme. One or two newspapers suggested that the entire thing had been a stunt. How cynical people can be!

Fortunately I was soon re-instated. Cliff sent me a bottle of champagne, which I've still got somewhere, although I was a bit miffed when he went on Michael Parkinson's show to discuss it and he didn't give the programme any credit whatsoever. After all, his records have been a staple of goldies radio ever since.

* * *

"I NOW FIND MYSELF ONCE AGAIN IN A POSITION WHERE I MAY LOSE MY SHOW. IT'S VERY UPSETTING."

The history of my career always seems to follow the same pattern. I settle into a show, make it mine and pull the listeners in. Then some extraneous force comes along and whips it away from me. At the time of writing, and just a month after signing a new contract, I now find myself once again in a position where I may lose my show. It's very upsetting, not just for me but for the entire team at Classic Gold, who have made the show such a pleasure to be on these past four years.

We'd known that something had been afoot for several months, and that a buy-out was imminent. As it turned out, G-Cap, the company that owns the Capital stations has bought us out and that means there will be a merger of the two Gold stations.

Of course, I am hoping that I'll hang on to my treasured morning slot. I also have a programme on BBC Radio London on Saturday mornings. That's great fun, and I get to play more of my kind of music on it. But I'm afraid it's no substitute for the king of the broadcasting slot, the breakfast show. After 43 years, my enthusiasm for waking people up with a cheery "Good morning!", then keeping them amused with a load of old nonsense for two or three hours, interspersed by a few bright and breezy pop records, is as strong as ever.

I love the fact that my audience is entertained when I tell them about picking up some new fangled gadget that's tickled me. And I will over-enthuse about it because exaggeration is funny. And the fact that my wife will not take any pleasure whatsoever in me bringing this new gadget – such as the wind-up clock I found the other day for a tenner – makes the tale even more fun. It's this stuff to which my audience can relate.

I also make sure I get out some evenings, because I know that I broadcast better if I'm slightly tired. It's living on the edge in broadcasting terms and I like that! You've got to experience a bit of a life too because that gives you something to talk about. Audiences like to hear that "I met old so and so last night, and by God, they're looking a bit rough!" If you don't do that, you'll simply become bland and inconsequential.

I know I was once the clean-cut, ever-smiling Mr Nice of Radio One all those years ago. But with my jokes, political broadsides and lovelorn exhortations, added to my undying sense that radio should be fun, fast and entertaining to the point of absurdity, the one thing I hope I've never been in my career is bland.

There have been two famous insomniacs in British culture over the past half century – ex-Prime Minister Margaret Thatcher and Rolling Stones guitarist and all round bad boy Keith Richards. At first, I thought that insomnia was probably the only thing I'd got in common with either of these wildly contrasting figures. But in their time, both have courted controversy, often dividing opinion right down the middle. These days, like them or loathe them, both have been given credit for doing what they've always believed in. Not that I'd compare myself with either, or even would want to, but I hope that my belief in the enervating and above all the entertaining power of popular, good quality radio broadcasting has come across during the course of this book.

Back in autumn 1967, in one of the many interviews I did as part of the promotional drive for the recently-launched Radio One, I explained that, "The secret is to talk to your public not at them". There's a subtle but crucial difference. Perhaps having ploughed through this relatively joke-free zone for the past 258 pages, you too might better understand exactly what I meant by that, and a little more about why that approach has best suited my broadcasting career.

Oh, and thanks very much for listening.

APPENDIX I
THE TERRIFIC TWENTY!

Like everyone else's, my Top 20 varies from day to day, though there are always a handful of evergreens that I always go back to.

Some people are surprised when I tell them that music now is at least as good as it was during the days of the pirates and the launch of Radio One. But, it's true: I genuinely believe it. While I'm often saddled with the "60s" tag, I also regard the '80s decade as another musical high point, with soul and jazz-funk making huge inroads into popular consciousness.

In fact, while people always go on about how great the '60s were, there was a lot of rubbish around that they conveniently forget. Some of the singers look so laughably old-fashioned from today's vantage point. Even The Beatles do. I would never describe them as great performers. Nowadays, bands such as Take That are much more dynamic. Of course I still enjoy hearing songs such as Del Shannon's Runaway, but I get much more of a thrill when something by Destiny's Child or Alicia Keys comes on. Of course, nothing quite compares to the king of soul himself, the late, great Marvin Gaye . . .

1. *WHAT'S GOING ON*
Marvin Gaye (Motown, 1971)

This, the title track from what I regard as the best album ever made, is pure genius. Though the song flopped in Britain on its release, both single and album are now rightly regarded as masterpieces. For me, '*What's Going On*' epitomises everything that's wonderful about soul music – heartfelt, human and, despite all that pain and trouble, ultimately redemptive and uplifting – while Marvin Gaye is soul music's finest exponent. '*What's Going On*' might have fared better had Radio One not stopped me from playing it. I was told the song was "too depressing".

One of my biggest regrets is never having seen Marvin Gaye perform live. I've seen and met most of the Motown acts over the years but Marvin's performing days were cruelly ended on April 1, 1984 when he was shot dead by his Minister father, Marvin Snr. I was in Los Angeles when the news came through on the radio and it remains far more shocking in my memory than the similarly awful deaths of President Kennedy and John Lennon.

2. *REET PETITE*
Jackie Wilson (Cora, 1957)

This was one of my father's favourites and probably the song that first turned me on to the sound of young black America. Jackie Wilson was another singer I never managed to see in concert though thanks to the internet's wonderful retro pop resource, YouTube, I can now watch him perform this in glorious black-and-white. Another of Jackie Wilson's songs, '*Lonely Teardrops*', runs this a close second.

3. *LOVE IS THE ANSWER*
England Dan & John Ford Coley (Big Tree, 1979)

Beautiful song and sweet, peace-filled message. I know very little about the singers except that, although they're not black, they do manage to turn in a particularly soulful performance on this late '70s single. Whenever I bow out from a radio show, I tend to play this as my parting record. I don't know why. It just has a kind of healing quality to it, I suppose. Even now, when I'm driving to work before dawn, I'll call up Keith Butler who's on air for Capital Gold at that ungodly hour and he'll play it for me as I hare along the motorway.

4. *I'M STILL WAITING*
Diana Ross (Tamla Motown, 1971)

As I've explained in the main body of the book, I first heard this as an album track and was responsible for getting it released as a single. It became Diana Ross's first big solo hit and, thanks to me, she's not looked back since! I saw a bit of her during the early '70s and compered some of her shows. The enormous fame she's enjoyed since has left its mark on her – the more legendary she becomes, the bigger the sunglasses she wears! I last saw her at The Prince's Trust Picnic In The Park in 2002, where I got the sense that she seemed somewhat detached from our world. Nevertheless, she still knows how to put on a great show.

5. *REACH OUT I'LL BE THERE*
The Four Tops (Tamla Motown, 1966)

I've been a Tamla enthusiast since the label's early days but I think we'd be hard pushed to find a more thrilling Motown 45 than this. More than 40 years on since its original release and it's still a big hit in the clubs. I was DJ-ing on a cruise a few weeks back and as soon as I put in on, everyone was up and loving it.

The Four Tops have had so many incredible hits over the years – and I particularly rate their 1965 ballad, *'Ask The Lonely'*, too. They performed many of them at the Hilton Hotel a while back, at a fundraiser for the Variety Club. There was only one original member left, Abdul 'Duke' Fakir, while the rest of the band was made up of distant relatives. But I swear they sounded even better than when I saw them two generations ago.

6. *SMOKE GETS IN YOUR EYES*
The Platters (Mercury, 1958)

The Platters sang beautiful close harmonies in the '50s and this song take me right back to my days at Millfield School, when I'd tune in illicitly to Radio Luxembourg to hear the latest releases. As soon as I heard this extraordinary song I dashed out on my bike in the pouring rain to nearby Glastonbury, but by the time I got there the record shop was shut. All I got was a bad cold – and had to wait another week before I could buy the disc.

This song is such an evergreen. When I played it a couple of weeks back, I received an avalanche of emails from people who said how nice it was to hear it on air again. Groups such as The Platters mean little to most radio programmers today, who are invariably in their mid-30s and try desperately hard to appear youthful.

7. *COOL WATER*
Frankie Laine (Philips, 1955)

This is the song that inspired me to leap up in front of the mirror at home and perfect my would-be pop star moves. *'Cool Water'* sounds very dated now but at the time it was a total thrill. As soon as the stylus dropped down onto my fast-spinning 78rpm record I was instantly lost in the magnificent drama of the song, which I'd accentuate by thrusting my arms out to an audience of invisible admirers.

I'm glad to see that my daughter Victoria is following in her father's footsteps. I'll often catch her prancing about in her bedroom to an audience of precisely one – herself. But, then, that's how so many legends start . . .

8. *RAG DOLL*
Four Seasons (Philips, 1964)

I adore harmony groups so it was appropriate that the first record I ever played on air – on Radio Caroline South on July 25, 1964 – was this; two and a half minutes of instant pop joy. That's what's great about '60s music. None of the songs ever outstayed their welcome – at least not until late in the decade with The Beatles' *'Hey Jude'* and Richard Harris's epic *'MacArthur Park'* – and that's great for radio programming because it keeps things fast-paced and exciting. Little did I know back in '64 just how many years I'd spend in a studio sharing music like this with so many people . . .

9. *FLOWERS IN THE RAIN*
The Move (Regal Zonophone, 1967)

Unlike *'I'm Still Waiting'*, which I helped make a hit, *'Flowers In The Rain'* was already in the charts when I decided it would be the perfect record with which to launch Radio One. For that reason, the song will be forever associated with me, though it's not a particular favourite of mine. However, I do admire the songwriter, Roy Wood. He hasn't changed at all over the years. He still looks the same with all that straggly hair. And every December, you'll find him somewhere belting out his 1973 hit, *'I Wish It Could Be Xmas Everyday'*.

I caught him in concert in Hammersmith some time back. When he started, he had just four or five people up on stage with him. By the time he finished, there were a couple of dozen or more. Even Roy seemed bewildered! I love him for his shambolic, celebrity-shunning, laid-back attitude. The whole thing ended up like some massive party and that was all that mattered. I met him afterwards and said, "Roy, just how many people are there in your group?" He admitted that he had no idea. Unlike those people who describe themselves as eccentrics, displaying a self awareness that rather undermines their case, Roy Wood is the real thing – a genuine British oddball.

10. *UNCHAINED MELODY*
The Righteous Brothers (London, 1965)

Two wonderful white soul singers – whose other classic, *'You've Lost That Lovin' Feelin''*, has the distinction of being among the most requested songs on radio. At least it was in the days when we asked the listeners what they wanted to hear. This particular song also reminds me of Debbie, because it features in the film *Ghost*, which I took her to see at the Odeon, Leicester Square, on our first date together.

11. *TIE A YELLOW RIBBON ROUND THE OLD OAK TREE*
Dawn (Bell, 1973)

This infectious early '70s novelty hit became a staple of my pantomime routines, no doubt because it was a doddle to sing. Long before we started dating, I sang it with my future wife Debbie when I was playing Buttons in Cinderella and she was one of the chorus girls. I remember her and another dancer standing in front of me as we sang, no doubt protecting the audience from the hideous spectacle of my awkward dance moves. On another memorable panto occasion, the scenery collapsed on me while I was halfway through the song and I was forced to sing the final verses while holding up a fake kitchen wall!

12. *WE'VE ONLY JUST BEGUN*
The Carpenters (A&M, 1971)

While I was holidaying in LA in the early '70s with my friend Phil Swern, Richard and Karen Carpenter invited me to lunch in a place along Sunset Strip. I'd previously got to know them when I presented a Carpenters documentary for Radio One and we all hit it off and kept in contact. After the meal, they asked me to join them in the A&M studio where they were putting the finishes touches to this song.

I was devastated when I heard about her death in 1983. I had no inkling that she suffered from any illness, let alone the eating disorder that killed her. Like millions of people during the '70s, I was seduced by her pure and haunting voice. And, unlike so many major stars, The Carpenters could recreate their studio sound in concert.

13. *RUN TO HIM*
Bobby Vee (London, 1961)

Though it's nowhere near as well known as *'Rubber Ball'* and *'The Night Has A Thousand Eyes'*, *'Run To Him'* has to be my favourite Bobby Vee song. It has more drama. I'd seen Bobby perform back in Bournemouth during the early '60s, so when I caught up with him again at the Café de Paris a few years back, I wasn't expecting him to be half as good. How wrong could I be? He was absolutely tremendous, singing better than ever, and with a terrific sense of humour. I also had the pleasure of meeting him afterwards – a lovely, friendly man. But I didn't have the nerve to tell him that several years earlier, Richard Park took away my daytime programming responsibilities on Capital Gold all because I included *'Rubber Ball'*, which he reckoned was too old and staid.

14. *TWENTY FOUR HOURS FROM TULSA*
Gene Pitney (United Artists, 1963)

Gene was a fabulous person and a friend and we'd always meet for breakfast or lunch whenever he was in the country. That happened pretty regularly, too, because he had a loyal audience here and he loved touring. I once asked him what was so special about Tulsa and he said he hadn't a clue because he'd never been there! So many people had told him it wasn't up to much so he spent most of his life desperately trying to avoid the place.

I couldn't believe it when I heard that he'd died, in April 2006. He seemed to be as fit as a fiddle and a cheerful, delightful person who deserved to live longer than he did.

15. *UPTIGHT*
Stevie Wonder (Tamla Motown, 1966)

I've known Stevie since the mid-'60s and there's no doubt that he's one of the 20th century's genuine music legends. '*Uptight*', his first hit here, is such an energising song although he's written many other classics too. Even that 1963 single, '*Fingertips Pt 2*', with that memorable harmonica sound, showed just what a prodigy he was. I don't take my son Simon along to many concerts but he was particularly delighted when I took him to see Stevie at Wembley and introduced him to the great man backstage afterwards.

16. *SECRET LOVE*
Doris Day (Philips, 1954)

My passion for Doris Day will be no secret to anyone who's already read this book from cover to cover. I've had a huge crush on her ever since I was a boy, have seen all her films, and I admit that she's the only woman I would ever leave home for. (My wife says the same about Donny Osmond.) Obviously, she's well into her 80s now but I'd still welcome the opportunity to meet her and tell her how much pleasure she's given me over the decades. To me, she is the epitome of womanhood, her films and voice are amazing, and she's an animal lover too – a perfect 'secret love'! I'm no hero worshipper. In fact, there's only one other person I yearn to meet and that's David Letterman. I think he's one of the chat show host greats.

17. *THE SOUND OF MUSIC*
Julie Andrews (RCA, 1965)

Though she doesn't have that Doris Day effect on me, Julie Andrews is nevertheless a wonderful English rose with a lovely voice. Just as so many people did in the mid '60s, my family and I went to the cinema to see *The Sound Of Music* on numerous occasions and I'm still watching it today. Unlike, say, *South Pacific*, it just doesn't seem to date at all.

18. *TELL ME WHY*
Bobby Womack (Motown, 1984)

I don't think Bobby would mind if I described him as a loveable rogue! But he's also one of the most underrated singers (and songwriters) of our time who sings from the heart and gives everything in concert. At least, he does when he chooses to turn up! In my experience, Bobby can be unreliable, but then, great artists aren't renowned for being the most organised of people.

19. *WALK ON BY*
Dionne Warwick (Pye International, 1964)

This song is so evocative of the mid-'60s. It's probably the best of a brilliant bunch of collaborations between songwriter Burt Bacharach and his muse Dionne – whose surname is pronounced 'War-wick', by the way. I know that because she once told me so. I saw the pair of them together on stage at the Festival Hall and it was wonderful. They were trading memories between performances of the songs, which she then sang beautifully and he played impeccably on piano. The last time I saw Dionne, though, she was hosting infomercials for The Pyschic Friends Network on American TV dressed in a dodgy jumper! Perhaps she should stick to singing . . .

20. *AND I AM TELLING YOU I'M NOT GOING*
Jennifer Holliday (Geffen, 1982)

This is just fabulous, right up there with the best of them in terms of its heart-wrenchingly soulful delivery. When I watch Jennifer sing this song, originally written for the Broadway stage show *Dreamgirls*, it's immediately apparent that she's oblivious to everything else around her. She's able to get inside the song and live it. The version sung by Jennifer Hudson in the film version of *Dreamgirls* gives Holliday's a good run for its money, though. It's a wonderfully written song and you've got to be spectacularly good to be able to handle it properly.

APPENDIX II

A DATE WITH BLACKBURN

29 January 1943 One big moment for me, one giant leap for mankind! Born in Guildford, Surrey. I couldn't help but notice there was a helluva racket going on.

1946 Having done my bit for the war effort (screaming down the enemy planes, etc), I was whisked off by my family to the considerably more temperate climes of the Dorset coastline in Lilliput, Poole.

1948 Mrs Mudge's Play School was meant to be fun, but I took an instant dislike to it. Screamed the walls down on the first day, but still my mum made me go each morning.

1949 It didn't get any better at Prep School, Castle Court, where I regularly got slippered. That made me despise the school regime even more. I tried to make the best of my time there by captaining the cricket team.

1956 Despite me failing my entrance exam for Repton in spectacular style, my father nevertheless found a home for me at Millfield, where I spent the best part of the next three years grazing on a field. Once in a while, I'd kick or throw a ball, but I certainly didn't learn anything. One day, I simply walked out, took a train home and stayed there.

1960 Having passed ten O-levels thanks to some last minute private tuition, I entered Bournemouth College Of Further Education where I took an HND in Business Studies. I studied economics, British Constitution and accounting, all of which of course proved indispensable in my work as a DJ! More fruitfully, I was gainfully employed in the evenings as a singer/guitarist in the Jan Ralfini Orchestra.

25 July 1964 The day I first broadcast to an unsuspecting public. I'll always be grateful to the pirate ship Radio Caroline for giving me my first big break. "Hey, there could be a career in this!" I thought.

1966 Jumped ship to Big L, Radio London, the best radio station ever and the future of British broadcasting – or so I thought.

30 September 1967 After a successful trial on The Light Programme's Midday Spin, I opened up the BBC's new, all-pop station, Radio One. I managed to get through my first day without saying anything controversial, so they kept me there, on the breakfast show, for the next six years.

June 1973 Moved to the mid-morning slot. I wasn't too happy about that, but did my best to readjust.

Autumn 1977 Another move, this time to afternoons. Got the feeling that things were slipping a bit.

September 1979 Shunted off to weekends. On Sundays, I hosted the afternoon Top 40 chart rundown, while I spent my Saturday mornings playing songs such as *Puff, The Magic Dragon* and *Sparky's Magic Piano* to under-eights. Really thought things were going down the pan...

1982 Help was at hand thanks to BBC Radio London where, after a dodgy start on an afternoon show, I came up with a morning sex'n'soul format. Without a doubt, it was the best show I've ever done. We came up with a lucrative club spin-off, too, the Radio London Soul Night Out.

1988 New Programme Controller, new broom, new station. This time, Capital Gold, where I started out doing the breakfast programme and ended up seeing people home safely with the drive-time show.

August 2002 After receiving strange sounds inviting me out to the jungle, I was off to the wilds of North Australia for the launch series of *I'm A Celebrity, Get Me Out Of Here!* Two weeks later, I emerged as the winner and returned home to a hero's welcome with a new epithet, King Of The Jungle! Shortly afterwards, I quit Capital to host a new soul show on Jazz FM and a breakfast show on Classic Gold. I'm still doing the latter, which is probably the happiest show I've done in my life, as well as a Saturday afternoon slot on BBC Radio London, which I also love doing.

INDEX

278

Index

Index

Acknowledgements

GHOSTWRITER'S BIOGRAPHY

Born in 1959, Mark Paytress grew up in Bournemouth acutely aware that Tony Blackburn was one of the locality's most famous sons. His father Norman regularly served Tony's dad "Dr Blackburn" at the local TV and record-playing equipment shop, Bourne Radio, during the '50s. An avid schoolboy Radio One listener, Mark has since written several rock biographies, including the definitive book on Marc Bolan, *Bolan: The Rise & Fall Of A 20th Century Superstar* (Omnibus Press), is a regular contributor to *MOJO* magazine, and is a part-time university lecturer in Popular Music.

ACKNOWLEDGMENTS

Mark Paytress would like to thank Tony Blackburn for his no-holds-barred approach to the project. A wonderful professional, always entertaining – and a generous provider of family-sized boxes of chocolate biscuits and service station egg-and-tomato sandwiches! Also, Sara Morrison, for superlative keyboard assistance and Andy Neill for digging out that classic archive interview. And, of course, Mediaeval Melpomeni, for love, support and all-round Baebeness.

PHOTOGRAPHY ACKNOWLEDGMENTS.

Photos supplied courtesy of Tony Blackburn; additional images and credits follow.
Colour plate section one: 6 top Mirrorpix; 8-9 BBC Photo Library; 10 top Getty Images; 10 bottom BBC Photo Library; 11 top Mirrorpix; 12 Mirrorpix; 13 top & bottom London Express; 15 top Roy Keirby; 15 bottom Acton Gazette & West London Post; 16 top Leslie Bryce; 16 bottom Getty Images/William Vanderson.
Colour plate section two: 2 top Doug McKenzie; 3 Steve Rapport; 5 top Rex Features/Robert Taylor; 5 bottom BBC Photo Library; 6 bottom Daily Express /Steve Wood; 10 bottom Mirrorpix; 12 top BBC Photo Library/Brian Ritchie; 12 bottom Camera Press/David Dyson; 13 Rex Features /Brian Cassey; 15 top, 16 top BBC Photo Library; 16 bottom Topfoto/Topham/PA.

ACKNOWLEDGMENTS

In loving memory of Ken and Pauline, my wonderful parents, and my uncle, Nick. My sister, Jackie, who has influenced my life more than she will ever know. My wife, Debbie, whom I adore. My son, Simon, who I'm so proud of, and my lovely daughter, Victoria, who fills our home with singing and makes me laugh every day. My agents, Michael Cohen and Nick Canham (not just my agents but my friends) and the team at MPC Entertainment. Mark Paytress, who helped me write this book and had to listen to me for hours talking about myself. Harold Davison, whose guidance made all this possible (my second father). Jo Gurnett, who looked after me for so many years. Jackie and John – see you at The Ivy! Phil Swern, for being such a good friend. Steve Walsh for so many great memories. Radio Caroline, where it all began, all the other TV and radio stations I've worked for, and my wonderful listeners, for putting up with me for so many years. Finally, to all those people I have worked and had fun with over the years. You know who you are. Many thanks!